NUCLEAR DAWN

THE ATOMIC BOMB
FROM THE MANHATTAN PROJECT TO THE COLD WAR

OSPREY
PUBLISHING

NUCLEAR DAWN

THE ATOMIC BOMB
FROM THE MANHATTAN PROJECT TO THE COLD WAR

JAMES P. DELGADO

First published in Great Britain in 2009 by Osprey Publishing, Midland House,
West Way, Botley, Oxford OX2 0PH, United Kingdom.
443 Park Avenue South, New York, NY 10016, USA.
Email: info@ospreypublishing.com

Every attempt has been made by the Publishers to secure the appropriate permissions for materials
reproduced in this book. If there has been any oversight we will be happy to rectify the situation and
a written submission should be made to the Publishers.

A CIP catalog record for this book is available from the British Library.

ISBN: 978 1 84603 396 4

Cover and page layout by Myriam Bell Design, France
Index by Alan Thatcher
Cartography and line drawings by Peter Bull
Typeset in Bank Gothic and Adobe Caslon Pro
Originated by PPS Grasmere Ltd, Leeds, UK
Printed in China through Worldprint Ltd

09 10 11 12 13   10 9 8 7 6 5 4 3 2 1

Front cover: A fiery mushroom cloud rises into the sky following the test detonation of an
11-megaton nuclear device codenamed "Romeo" over Bikini Atoll on March 26, 1954.
(© Corbis IH109113)
Previous page: The second atomic test, Baker, detonated a submerged Fat Man bomb from a suspended
container 90ft below the surface of the lagoon. While some viewed the Able test as a disappointment,
the blast and radiation effects of Baker were far more spectacular. (US National Archives)

For a catalog of all books published by Osprey please contact:

NORTH AMERICA
Osprey Direct, c/o Random House Distribution Center
400 Hahn Road, Westminster, MD 21157, USA
E-mail: uscustomerservice@ospreypublishing.com

ALL OTHER REGIONS
Osprey Direct, The Book Service Ltd., Distribution Centre, Colchester Road,
Frating Green, Colchester, Essex, CO7 7DW
E-mail: customerservice@ospreypublishing.com

Osprey Publishing is supporting the Woodland Trust, the UK's leading woodland
conservation charity, by funding the dedication of trees.

www.ospreypublishing.com

CONTENTS

PREFACE AND ACKNOWLEDGMENTS

The concept of a super-weapon has dominated military thought and development since the beginning of warfare. From spear to bow, ballista to cannon, Greek fire to gunpowder, and from black powder to dynamite, human beings have sought increasingly deadly ways to achieve victory in war. The rapid discovery of the secrets of the atom, beginning in the late 19th century and intensifying in the first four decades of the 20th century, resulted in a crash program – a veritable race – to develop and deliver the world's first atomic bombs during World War II. The success of that effort saw an initial test followed by the first military use of the new bomb in 1945.

The atomic attacks on Hiroshima and Nagasaki, Japan, in early August 1945 forever changed warfare in a way that no other weapon in history had done. For the first time, humans had created a weapon that could, in its ultimate form, devastate the planet and quite probably destroy all life on earth. The military, political, and social implications of a weapon known simple as "The Bomb" have profoundly affected civilization ever since. This is the story of the beginning of that new era in human history and of the weapon that changed not only warfare, but also global society and international politics.

A number of colleagues and institutions provided information, advice, reviews, and support through the years. I would like to thank Roger Meade of Los Alamos National Laboratory, Lloyd Graybar, Jonathan Weisgall, Gregg Herken, Norman Polmar, Hugh Gusterson, Betty Perkins, Jack Niedenthal, and Ed Linenthal on matters of the bomb, defense, and Bikini. I would also like to acknowledge the support of those veterans of the Manhattan Project, the 509th, and Operation *Crossroads*, especially the late Woodrow Swancutt, Leon Smith, Bob Henderson, Ernest Peterkin, Dick Laning, Enders Huey, Hank Arnold, Lewis Talley, Alvin Brommer, Edward Clevenger, George Culley, Harold Demarest, and W. R. Dill.

I thank my National Park Service colleagues in the Submerged Resources Center, the History Division, and the National Historic Landmark Program for their support when I was working with them on the Bikini Atoll project – Ed Bearss, Rowland Bowers, Jerry Rogers, Dan Lenihan, Larry Murphy, Larry Nordby, Jerry Livingston, John Brooks, Candace Clifford, Kevin Foster, Harry Butowsky, Jim Charleton, Robbyn Jackson, and Steve Haller. Thanks also go to those who made the initial and later trips to Bikini informative and adventurous: Fabio Amaral, Len Blix, John Brooks, Werner Zehnder, Ken Hiner, Eric Hiner, Catherine "Kitty" Courtney, Lee McEachern, George Lang, Edward Maddison, Kane Janer, Al Giddings, Roger Joel, Wilma Revlon, John Lajuan, Dave Campbell, Mike Messick, Harry Nashon, Stephen Notarianni, Bill Livingston, Jeanne Rawlings and Bill Robison.

The following organizations and institutions were also a great help: Los Alamos National Laboratory, Los Alamos, New Mexico; Lawrence Livermore National Laboratory, Livermore, California; US Department of Energy Archives, Las Vegas, Nevada; US National Archives, Military Branch and Still Pictures Branch, Washington, DC; US Naval Historical Center, Washington, DC; the Library of Congress, Washington, DC; the National Air & Space Museum, Washington, DC; the US Naval Institute, Annapolis, Maryland; White Sands Missile Range, Alamogordo, New Mexico; the Los Alamos Historical Society, Los Alamos, New Mexico.

The review and editing of my assistant, Kathy Smith, once again made the task of writing easier. I owe her my usual debt of gratitude. I also wish to thank the Osprey team, especially Jaqueline Mitchell and Ruth Sheppard. Last, but not least, I thank my wife Ann for her constant support and love.

James P. Delgado
August 2008

CHRONOLOGY

1915   Einstein publishes the general theory of relativity.

1919   Rutherford creates the first artificially induced nuclear reaction when he bombards nitrogen gas with alpha particles and transmutes it into an oxygen isotope.

1929   Ernest O. Lawrence of the United States develops the concept of the cyclotron to increase the speed of protons hurled at atomic nuclei. John Crockcroft and E. T. S. Walton develop the first linear accelerator for accelerating protons to study atomic transmutation.

1931   Ernest O. Lawrence builds his first cyclotron.

1932   James Chadwick of Britain discovers the neutron.

1933   Physicist Leó Szilárd is the first to realize that "a chain reaction might be set up if an element could be found that would emit two neutrons when it swallowed one neutron." Frédéric and Irène Joliot-Curie of France discover artificial radioactivity.

1934   Enrico Fermi of Italy is the first to achieve nuclear fission in an experiment, but he does not realize his achievement.

1938   Otto Hahn of Germany conducts experiments that result in nuclear fission.

1939   Publication of Hahn's results excites physicists around the world, who begin to conduct experiments in fission. Alarmed by the possibility of a uranium bomb, Albert Einstein writes to colleagues, who forward the letter to US President Franklin D. Roosevelt. Roosevelt responds by creating a committee to look into the military applications of atomic research. World War II begins.

1940   Scientists in the United Kingdom secretly encourage a British atomic bomb project. Using the cyclotron, scientists Philip Abelson and Edwin McMillan at the University of California, Berkeley, bombard uranium-238 to create "elements 93 and 94."

1941   The United States enters the war. Scientist Glen Seaborg discovers that element 94 is plutonium. American scientists determine that it can be used to make an atomic bomb. The British "MAUD" Project determines that it is possible to make an atomic bomb with uranium-235.

1942   The United States creates the top-secret Manhattan Project to develop an atomic bomb. An experimental reactor "pile" at the University of Chicago generates the first self-sustaining nuclear reaction.

1943	The Manhattan Project establishes a top-secret city and laboratory at Los Alamos, New Mexico, to design and build the atomic bomb. Other secret facilities are built to create weapons-grade plutonium.
1944	As the US effort intensifies, German attempts to create an atomic bomb begin to lag. The race to develop the first atomic weapon is effectively over.
1945	The first atomic bomb is successfully tested at Trinity Site, New Mexico, on July 16. The second bomb is dropped on Hiroshima, Japan, on August 6. It is followed by a third bomb, which devastates Nagasaki, on August 9. Japan surrenders and World War II ends.
1946	The United States creates the Strategic Air Command (SAC) to deliver nuclear weapons in combat. US proposals for international control of atomic weapons stall in the United Nations (UN). In July, the US demonstrates and tests two atomic weapons at Bikini Atoll in the Marshall Islands. It also passes the Atomic Energy Act of 1946, creating the Atomic Energy Commission (AEC), which transfers control of weapons development from the military to the AEC.
1947	The United Kingdom authorizes the development of atomic weapons and begins its own, independent program under William Penney. The first British nuclear reactor is built.
1948	Under President Harry S. Truman, nuclear weapons development intensifies in the United States. The AEC is ordered to create an "Atomic Bomb Stockpile," new laboratories and facilities are created, and Truman signs an order giving the President of the United States the sole decision to use atomic weapons in wartime. The United States continues atomic tests at Eniwetok Atoll in the Pacific.
1949	Top-secret Soviet efforts, aided by espionage, result in the first successful Soviet detonation of an atomic bomb at Semipalatinsk in Kazakhstan in August. The North Atlantic Treaty Organization (NATO) is formed, and the United States deploys nuclear-capable B-29s to the United Kingdom.
1950	The United States announces that it will develop the hydrogen bomb.

1951 The first postwar atomic tests in the continental United States take place in Nevada. American spies Julius and Ethel Rosenberg are sentenced to death for giving atomic secrets to the Soviets.

1952 The first British atomic bomb, "Hurricane," is successfully detonated off western Australia in the Montebello islands on October 3. The same month, the United States detonates the first hydrogen bomb, a thermonuclear fusion device, "Mike," at Eniwetok Atoll in the Pacific.

1953 The first Soviet attempt to create a hydrogen bomb is tested in Siberia.

1954 The most powerful surface detonation of an American hydrogen bomb vaporizes a small island at Bikini Atoll when the "Bravo" weapon yields 14.8 megatons and blankets more than a thousand square miles with highly radioactive fallout.

1955 The United Kingdom announces it will develop hydrogen bombs. Under Andrei Sakharov, the Soviets develop and successfully test their first true hydrogen bomb in November.

1957 The first British hydrogen bomb is successfully tested at Christmas Island in the Indian Ocean. The UN creates the International Atomic Energy Agency (IAEA). The Soviets announce they have successfully test-launched an intercontinental ballistic missile (ICBM). The prospect of nuclear deployment and attack by missile escalates the Cold War. The first US underground test of an atomic bomb takes place in Nevada.

1958 The United States and the United Kingdom agree to share nuclear weapons design for the first time since the end of World War II. The United States ends atmospheric tests of nuclear weapons and enters into an informal agreement with the United Kingdom and the Soviet Union to halt all tests. This moratorium lasts for nearly three years.

1960 The United States deploys its first operational ICBM, the Atlas D rocket, and the first American Polaris submarines, carrying nuclear missiles, enter service.

1

THE PRE-ATOMIC AGE

Ancient Greek philosophers were the first known scientists to suggest that matter was made up of small, unseen elements, a theory described as "atomism" by Democritus of Abdera in the 5th century BC. Earlier philosophers, and mathematicians such as Pythagoras, had suggested that regular solids were fundamental parts of the universe, and Democritus' teacher, Leucippus, had introduced him to the idea of an atomic system. Democritus, however, elaborated on the earlier concepts and proposed a more detailed system that inspired both followers and disbelievers. Democritus' ideas remained the most sophisticated concepts of atomic structure – and indeed maintained the concept of the atom itself – until modern times.

Democritus' theory was based on the principle that all matter is composed of atoms: solid bits of matter of various sizes and shapes, but so small as to be invisible to the naked eye, and indestructible – the word "atom" comes from the Greek *atomos*, which means "cannot be cut." At an atomic level, atoms created by the disintegration of matter, moving through space, could reform into new matter as atoms were joined together. In this fashion, all that was in the world had been created.

While Democritus' theory, and his followers' adaptations of it, ultimately carried the concept of the atom into the modern era, his own writings were lost in antiquity. Ironically, although his theory was quoted in the writings of his follower Epicurus (themselves quoted and preserved in a 2nd-century AD Roman work), it was rather the detailed attacks of Aristotle (who did not believe in atoms) in the 4th century AD that kept Democritus' ideas alive. Aristotle's arguments were echoed by other ancient philosophers and men of science in antiquity, including Cicero, Seneca, and Galen.

Based on the strength of Aristotle's reputation, which lived on past the end of the Roman Empire, his opposition to atomism also outlasted the ancient era. Arguing, among other things, that Democritus had theorized that there was "no end of the universe, since it was not created by any outside power,"[1] the Catholic Church regarded atomism as misguided at best, heresy at worst.

Adherents of atomic theory rediscovered Democritus in the 13th century, as ancient works saved by Arab scholars were translated into Latin. By the 15th century, some Renaissance scholars braved papal disapproval for discussing atomism. It was not until the 16th century, however, that the concept regained attention as attacks on Aristotle coincided with the repudiation of Catholicism by Luther and others. As science developed in the late 16th and early 17th century, Aristotelian beliefs began to crumble. The invention of the barometer and the air pump in 1634 and 1654 respectively demonstrated that vacuum – a concept Aristotle had condemned – did in fact exist. If it did, then perhaps so, too, did atoms.

French scientist Pierre Gassendi (1592–1655) led the revival of atomism in 1649 when he published *Syntagma philosophiae Epicuri* and argued for atoms, suggesting that they were created by God and were solid, indestructible masses that move by the grace of God to form groups that Gassendi called *moleculae* or *corpuscular*. Gassendi essentially parroted Democritus, but by cleverly insisting that atoms were a gift from God, and a manifestation of His power, Gassendi shifted atomism into an argument that the Church no longer opposed. By 1704, Isaac Newton could write, therefore, that "It seems probable to me, that God in the beginning formed matter in solid, hard, massy, impenetrable, moveable particles, of such sizes and figures, and with such other properties, and in such proportion to space, as most conduced to the end to which he formed them."[2]

By the early 19th century, atomism had re-entered scientific thought, particularly chemistry, where it strongly influenced British philosopher and mathematician John Dalton (1766–1844). As early as 1803, Dalton, after experimenting with gases, put forward a chemical atomic theory that proposed a more sophisticated model than Democritus or Gassendi. Dalton's theory, the basis of modern atomic thinking despite some error, was that

Wilhelm Conrad Röntgen (1845–1923). Röntgen's 1895 experiments with the flow of electrical currents through gas of an extremely low pressure resulted in his discovery of a new type of ray that permeated most objects. He called the new phenomenon "X-rays" because their nature was unknown to him. Röntgen's work inspired the work of French scientist Marie Curie, and led to his receiving the Nobel Prize in Physics in 1921. (Bridgeman Art Library)

atoms combined to form chemical elements. He believed that the atoms in any one element were identical in their masses (an error), but atoms of different elements had different masses. He also believed that atoms could only combine in small, whole-numbered rations (1:1, 2:3, etc.). Dalton based his argument that atoms of different elements had different weights by experimenting with elements to obtain relative particle weight. He was the first scientist to do so. His Table of the Elements, giving them standard symbols, was another great Dalton achievement. Dalton's laboratory work modernized "atomism," and inspired later generations of chemists and other scientists to continue to probe atomic theory. One aspect of that theory, unchanged since antiquity, would be the arena where the greatest breakthroughs would come. That was the concept that atoms were unchangeable, and indestructible. Dalton continued the ancient argument, noting, "we might as well attempt to introduce a new planet into the solar system, or to annihilate one already in existence, as to create or destroy a particle of hydrogen."[3] Future researchers, working with new technology and concepts, would provide the tools to do so.

As the end of the 19th century approached, the Marquis of Salisbury, Robert Cecil, speaking to the British Association for the Advancement of Science in 1894, listed the "unfinished business of science" and posed questions about the atom, namely "whether it is a movement, or a thing, or a vortex, or a point having inertia, whether there is any limit to its divisibility, and if so, how that limit is imposed, whether the long list of elements is final, or whether any of them have any common origin, all these questions remain surrounded by a darkness as profound as ever."[4]

The first light to illuminate that darkness came from the cathode-ray tube. The cathode-ray tube was the initial child of the development in 1855 of a mercury pump by Heinrich Geissler, which produced vacuum tubes of high quality. Others, such as Sir William Crookes, discovered that when one end of a tube was capped with metal, and a battery was hooked up to them, the airless space inside the tubes glowed, passing from the negative plate – the cathode – to the positive plate, or the anode. When the cathode and anode were placed inside the middle of a tube, and the end of the tube was closed off with glass, the glow would become a beam, or a ray.

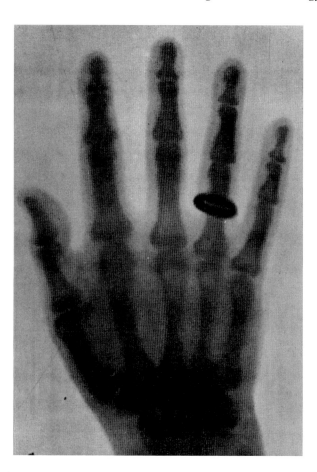

Röntgen captured a series of early images made by X-rays on photographic plates, including one of his wife's hand wearing her ring, which he made on January 25, 1896. Known as Röntgenograms, the plates were visual proof of a hitherto invisible phenomenon. (Bridgeman Art Library)

German and British researchers, working with cathode-ray tubes, learned more about the rays between 1858 and 1894. The rays bend when under the influence of a magnet; otherwise they travel in straight lines. They are formed of particles of some sort of matter, which have a charge. In 1874, James Johnstone Stoney, in calculating the charge, suggested that the unit of charge be called an "electrine." In 1891, he changed the name to "electron."

Then, in 1895, the German physicist Wilhelm Conrad Röntgen, experimenting with covering tubes with screens to determine the nature of the fluorescent light emanating from them, made an amazing discovery. Even when blocked by cardboard, the tube produced a glow on a nearby screen of chemical-coated black paper. Passing his hand in front of the tube to block the glow, Röntgen discovered that it did not completely block it – and, in the dim light, he could see his bones through the flesh of his hand. A new type of ray – not light – was produced by the cathode-ray tube, and the name Röntgen gave it – the X-ray – stuck. Inspired by this, French researcher Henri Becquerel experimented with other fluorescing materials to see if they generated X-rays, and discovered in February 1896 that uranium salt (uranyl potassium sulfate) did when sprinkled on a photographic plate that was left sealed in a darkened drawer.

The phenomena that allowed Röntgen to see through his hand, and leave its marks on an unexposed photographic plate was labeled by French scientist Marie Curie within a few years. Inspired by Becquerel's work, Marie Curie pursued the analysis of rays emitted by pitchblende, the ore from which uranium is extracted, as well as various uranium compounds between 1897 and 1898. Rather than use photographic plates, she used an electrometer (a device invented by her husband Pierre and his brother Jacques to detect extremely low electrical currents) to measure the electrical discharge of the rays in air. Using this delicate instrument in difficult conditions, Curie measured very faint currents in the air after bombarding it with uranium rays.

She later explained:

It was at the close of the year 1897 that I began to study the compounds of uranium, the properties of which had greatly attracted my interest. Here was a substance emitting spontaneously and continuously radiations similar to Roentgen rays, whereas ordinarily Roentgen

In the collections of the Institut de Radium in Paris are minerals and rocks used by Marie Curie in her radiation experiments. Bombarding minerals with uranium rays, Curie discovered that the samples released energy in the form of rays. Deducing that the energy came from atoms, by 1989 Madame Curie had named the rays "radioactivity" based on the Latin word for ray. Among those shown here are carmolite, radium, lepidolite, lurite, toberinite, and rock salt. (Bridgeman Art Library)

rays can be produced only in a vacuum-tube with the expenditure of energy. By what process can uranium furnish the same rays without expenditure of energy and without undergoing apparent modification? Is uranium the only body whose compounds emit similar rays? Such were the questions I asked myself...

In this fashion, Marie Curie determined that the rays were constant, and that minerals with a higher proportion of uranium emitted the strongest rays. Were the rays a product of the atomic structure of uranium? Curie believed so, hypothesizing that they were evidence of the atomic structure of uranium, and that the energy released in the form of the rays came from atoms. While not sure that the energy came from the atoms or from cosmic rays caught by atoms and reflected back (which was not the case), Curie's work suggested that atoms were not solid, elementary particles, particularly if they shed something in the form of rays.

Working with other mineral samples, Curie found that thorium, like uranium, emitted rays. By 1898, Curie felt strongly enough that the rays were an atomic property, and she named it "radioactivity," based on the Latin word for ray. Joined now by her husband Pierre, who set aside his own research to assist her, Marie Curie made another breakthrough:

I found, as I expected, that the minerals of uranium and thorium are radioactive; but to my great astonishment, I discovered that some are much more active than the oxides of uranium and of thorium, which they contain. Thus a specimen of pitchblende (oxide of uranium ore) was found to be four times more active than oxide of uranium itself. This observation astonished me greatly. What explanation could there be for it?... The answer came to me immediately: The ore must contain a substance more radioactive than uranium and thorium, and this substance must necessarily be a chemical element as yet unknown...

Working to chemically separate the ore into separate elements, the Curies isolated two hitherto unknown and highly radioactive elements in 1898, which Marie Curie named polonium and radium. Isolating a sample of sufficient size – one tenth of a gram of pure radium chloride – took the Curies more than three years of backbreaking and expensive work. Eight tons of pitchblende, when processed, ultimately yielded a gram of radium.

Their work, which led to the Nobel Prize for both (and two prizes for Marie, a rare honor), confirmed the cathode-ray research of British scientist J. J. Thomson, who had experimented with cathode rays and discovered that the rays were made up of positively charged particles that he called "corpuscles," but which in fact were the electrons proposed by Stoney. Terminology not withstanding, Thomson deduced that the particles came from within the atoms of the electrodes in the cathode-ray tube, meaning that atoms were not indivisible or indestructible. Thomson's announcement of his discovery and its meaning, in 1897, was the first major development in the evolving view of the atom, and the work of the Curies not only supported but also augmented Thomson's premise.

Marie Curie explained:

> The properties of radium are extremely curious. This body emits with great intensity all of the different rays that are produced in a vacuum-tube. The radiation, measured by means of an electroscope, is at least a million times more powerful than that from an equal quantity of uranium … radium can melt in an hour its weight in ice … we are amazed at the amount of heat produced, for it can be explained by no known chemical reaction … we assume that it undergoes a transformation… No chemical reaction can explain the emission of heat due to radium. Furthermore, radioactivity is a property of the atom of radium; if, then, it is due to a transformation this transformation must take place in the atom itself. Consequently, from this point of view, the atom of radium would be in a process of evolution, and we should be forced to abandon the theory of the invariability of atoms, which is at the foundation of modern chemistry.[5]

While the Curies continued with their work on radium and radioactivity (an initiative Marie continued after Pierre's tragic death in a traffic accident), Thomson and his protégés at Britain's Cavendish Laboratory also pursued their work. Thomson

Pierre Curie developed the ionization chamber to detect and measure radioactivity for his wife's experiments. A highly sensitive device, shown here with two examples, an ionization chamber contained a positive and a negative plate connected by an electrometer (which measures electrical currents). When a radioactive sample was placed in the chamber, air molecules broke down into positive and negative ion pairs, which allowed them to carry electrical current. As the negative ions migrated to the positive plate, and the positive ions migrated to the negative plate, the electrical current flowed through the electrometer, which Curie could then read. The strength of the current was a direct result of the level of radiation. (Bridgeman Art Library)

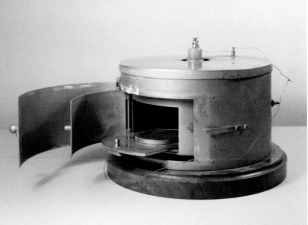

Sir Joseph John Thomson (1856–1940) of Trinity College, Cambridge, discovered the electron in his cathode-ray experiments. His discovery, announced in 1897, was the first major development in the evolving view of the atom. Thomson received the Nobel Prize in Physics in 1906. (Bridgeman Art Library)

proposed a model of the atom that came to be known as the "plum pudding model," in which, as he termed it "a number of negatively charged electrified corpuscles"[6] were surrounded by a sphere of "uniform positive electrification," or, as historian Richard Rhodes has suggested, "like raisins in a pudding." It would fall to one of Thomson's rapidly rising protégés, Ernest Rutherford, to test and ultimately prove another model. Between 1898 and 1911, as Rhodes would later eloquently phrase it, Rutherford "systematically dissected the atom."[7]

As Rutherford studied the rays that the Curies had identified, he determined, in 1899, that there were two types of rays. The first, a high-energy burst of easily blocked and absorbed radiation, which he called alpha radiation, and another, more penetrating type that he called beta radiation. A year later, in 1900, a third, even more penetrating type was identified and named gamma radiation by its discoverer, Paul Villard of France. By examining a radioactive gas emitted by thorium, Rutherford and his assistant, Frederick Soddy, were able to calculate the decay of radioactive materials, and by noting the time it took for half of a sample to do so, determined what is now known as the "half-life" of radioactive elements and isotopes.

As the secrets of the atom were being probed, the concept that the atom possessed a tremendous potential for untapped energy became clear. The work of the Curies had shown how heat was generated by radium, and visitors to Marie Curie's lab could visibly see the results in radiation burns on the scientist's hands. In 1905, German physicist Albert Einstein proposed, as part of his theory of special relativity, mass-energy equivalence, a now-famous formula expressed as $E=mc^2$. While it would take years for science to catch up to Einstein's theory and prove its validity, it suggested tremendous potential for the atom. The formula would later be used during the development of the atomic bomb to determine the energy available in an atomic nucleus, and hence the energy released in a nuclear reaction.

In 1911, Rutherford's "dissection" of the atom determined that the once seemingly impenetrable atom was in fact a series of electrons that orbited a nucleus in space. Shooting rays through a thin piece of gold foil, Rutherford and his assistants noticed that not all energy passed through the foil. He wrote, "considering the evidence as a whole, it seems simplest to suppose that the atom contains a central charge distributed through a very small volume, and that the large single deflexions are due to the central charge as a whole, and not to its constituents."[8] The "concentrated central charge," (later termed the nucleus) set the stage for further refinement, which came quickly.

Shown here in their Paris laboratory, the husband and wife team of Pierre (1859–1906) and Marie Sklodowska Curie (1867–1934) worked together to discern the secrets of the atom, distinguishing alpha, beta and gamma radiation. Following Pierre's tragic death, Madame Curie continued her research, earning the Nobel Prize in Chemistry in 1911 for the discovery of polonium and radium, and for the isolation of pure radium. (Bridgeman Art Library)

In 1913, Neils Bohr, a brilliant Danish physicist and a post-doctoral student of Rutherford's, elaborated and modified Rutherford's model by incorporating quantum mechanical (the study of mechanical processes at the atomic and sub-atomic level) results to describe and delineate the behavior of the orbiting electrons, which Bohr

New Zealand-born Ernest Rutherford, later Baron Rutherford of Nelson (1871–1937) immigrated to Britain as a young scientist to join Trinity College's Cavendish Laboratory. A brilliant protégé of J. J. Thomson, Rutherford expanded on Thomson's work, and between 1898 and 1911 conducted experiments that probed the inner mysteries of the atom. He remained an active researcher even as he mentored and trained many leading scientists (including several Nobel Prize winners). Rutherford received the Nobel Prize in Chemistry in 1908. This portrait, by O. H. J. Birley, hangs in the Royal Society, London. (Bridgeman Art Library)

correctly deduced orbited in circular (and elliptical) orbits like planets orbiting the sun. Bohr also followed up on the work of British physicist Henry Moseley and determined that the central charge was tied to an element's atomic number, or its place on the periodic chart. The potential of the atom was now clear, as was its complexity. Future research into the mysteries of the atom would occupy specialists in atomic physics, who studied the atom's structure, while a new field, nuclear physics, emerged to study the powerful core of the atom.

In 1914, British novelist Herbert George Wells, author of a number of popular works of science fiction, including *The Time Machine, The War of the Worlds,* and *The Invisible Man,* published a new novel in the genre his publisher called "fantastic and imaginative romances." The book, *The World Set Free: A Story of Mankind,* was set in the latter half of the 20th century. Wells, an avid reader, dedicated the book to Frederick Soddy's "Interpretation of Radium" because "this story … owes long passages to the eleventh chapter of that book."

Albert Einstein (1879–1955). Born to a Jewish family, the brilliant Einstein made a series of observations in theoretical physics that gained him not only the Nobel Prize in Physics in 1922 but also paved the way for the development of the atomic bomb. Among them was his theory of relativity, and the now famous formula expressed as $E=mc^2$ which suggested tremendous potential for the atom if its energy could be released. Einstein was the first to realize that an atomic bomb was not only possible, but that its development was probable. (Library of Congress)

Wells' story included passages in which radium, "an element that is breaking up and flying to pieces" showed that the "atom, that once we thought hard and impenetrable, and indivisible and final … is really a reservoir of immense energy." That energy, Wells explains, in the excited tones of a professor's lecture, had enough energy to light a city for a week, or if suddenly released "it would blow us and everything about us to fragments." But the release of energy is a "trickle," and "at present no man knows, no man has an inkling of how this little lump of stuff can be made to hasten the release of its own stores."[9]

The answer is found with the promise of unleashing power to change the world for good, but in the context of a world war in Europe the power is set loose through a new and terrible weapon, which Wells termed the "atomic bomb." Small enough to be dropped by a pilot who throws them out of his aircraft, these weapons explode in "a great ball of crimson-purple fire like a maddened living thing that seemed to be whirling about very rapidly amidst a chaos of falling masonry, that seemed to be attacking the earth furiously…" The atomic reaction is more than a powerful explosive – Wells calls it a "continuing explosive" that "continued a furious radiation of energy and nothing could arrest it." The bomb kept releasing explosive energy:

Niels Henrik David Bohr (1885–1962). Born in Copenhagen, Bohr studied with Ernest Rutherford after receiving his doctorate in 1911. Bohr proposed a new model for atomic structure in 1913, which in its simple form depicts electrons orbiting the nucleus of an atom. The Bohr model remains one of the most powerful iconic images of the 20th century. As director of the Institute of Theoretical Physics at the University of Copenhagen, Bohr received the Nobel Prize in Physics in 1922 "for his services in the investigation of the structure of atoms and of the radiation emanating from them." (Bridgeman Art Library)

Its half period was seventeen days … it poured out half of its energy in its great molecules in the space of seventeen days, the next seventeen days emission was a half of that … and so on. As with all radio-active substances … every day its power is halved, though constantly it diminishes …[it] is never entirely exhausted, and to this day the battlefields and bomb fields of that frantic time … are sprinkled with radiant matter and so centres of inconvenient rays…[10]

H. G. Wells' "scientific romance" gave popular voice to the possibility of unleashing a nuclear genie. But it was a fear that few took seriously, particularly when faced with the horrors of the world war then raging. Ernest Rutherford had been known to joke that "some fool in a laboratory might blow up the universe unawares,"[11] and Frederick Soddy, Well's inspiration, while noting that nuclear power unleashed would give its possessor "a weapon by which he could destroy the earth if he chose," thought it unlikely because "we may trust nature to guard her secret."[12] Even as Soddy wrote this, he and his fellow physicists were hard at work to learn the secret.

FROM NUCLEAR REACTIONS TO NUCLEAR FISSION

Between 1919 and 1939, scientists gradually closed in on the secrets of the atom. In 1919, Ernest Rutherford, now Britain's leading nuclear physicist, published the results from his bombardment of nitrogen atoms by alpha particles. The collision of particles with an atom knocked out a hydrogen nucleus, he determined, and this created a new atom, an isotope of oxygen. This was the world's first artificially induced nuclear reaction, and the artificial transmutation of an element, the long-sought goal of alchemists since medieval times. When news of the achievement reached the public, it astonished the world. The *New York Times*, reporting on Rutherford's work in January 1922, reported that "the dream of charlatans and scientists for nearly a thousand years has been accomplished."

The potential of the discovery was greater than elemental transmutation, however. The *New York Times* quoted British professor O. W. Richardson, who in a late 1921 address to the Mathematics and Physics section of the British Association noted:

But this is only part of the story. It appears that in some cases the kinetic energy of the ejected fragments is greater than that of the bombarding particles. This means that these bombardments are able to release the energy which is stored up in the nuclei of atoms. Now we know from the amount of heat liberated in radioactive disintegration that the amount of energy stored in the nuclei is of a higher order of magnitude, some millions of times greater … than … the combustion of coal … the amounts of energy which have been thus far released … are themselves small, but they are enormous in comparison with the minute amount of matter effected. If these effects can be sufficiently intensified … either they will prove uncontrollable, which would presumably spell the end to all things, or … if they can be both intensified and controlled, then we shall have at our disposal an almost illimitable supply of power which will entirely transcend anything hitherto known… It may be that we are at the beginning of a new age … the age of sub-atomic power.[13]

Rutherford named the split-off portion of the nitrogen a "proton," a major, if not the sole constituent of an atomic nucleus. Within a year, he was thinking that perhaps there were other parts, and in a lecture in June 1920, speculated that another constituent part might exist. That part was the neutron, which Rutherford's former student, James Chadwick, discovered at Cambridge in 1932. Three months earlier, Irène Joliot-Curie, daughter of Pierre and Marie, had noted that penetrating particles formed when she bombarded beryllium with alpha rays. Joliot-Curie thought they were gamma rays, but they were actually neutrons, although she did not realize it.

The neutron, named because it had no electrical charge, was the other constituent of atomic nuclei. More powerful than a proton, a neutron, if fired into nuclei, would split those of even the heaviest elements – something not yet achieved in artificial transmutation. Chadwick's discovery, building on Rutherford's, had provided yet another critical step in the ability to take atoms apart – a step closer to nuclear fission.

This fact was realized, in a flash of inspiration, by Hungarian physicist Leó Szilárd as he crossed a London street in September 1933. A refugee from the Nazis, Szilárd had left his hotel, annoyed by an article in the

Jean Frédéric Joliot (1900–1958) joined the Institut de Radium as assistant to Madame Curie in 1925. The following year, he married her daughter Irène. The Joliot-Curies made a series of crucial breakthroughs, including their work with the projection of nuclei in 1931, but the most significant aspect of their work was the discovery of artificial radioactivity in 1934. They jointly received the Nobel Prize in Chemistry in 1935. After the war, France named him its first High Commissioner for Atomic Energy and in this capacity he directed the construction of France's first atomic pile. (Bridgeman Art Library)

Irène Joliot-Curie (1897–1956) was a brilliant scientist who was the daughter of two brilliant scientists, and the wife of another. After serving as a nurse radiographer in World War I, she returned to her studies at the Faculty of Science in Paris, earning her doctorate in 1925. On her own, and working with her husband, she made a number of key discoveries that paved the way to the discovery of nuclear fission. In addition to her scientific work, she also served France as a commissioner of atomic energy, and actively promoted social and intellectual advancement for women. (Bridgeman Art Library)

New York Times that quoted Rutherford's recent address to the British Association. After discussing the latest developments, including the discovery of the neutron, Rutherford answered a question about prospects for the future. Unlike the more effusive Professor Richardson, Rutherford was dismissive. "We might in these processes obtain very much more energy … but on the average we could not expect to obtain energy," even if high voltage blasts of 30,000 to 70,000 volts were used. Therefore, "anyone who looked for a source of power in the transformation of the atoms was talking moonshine," or nonsense.[14]

Szilárd thought otherwise, and as he strolled, he recalled that neutrons, because they did not interact with whatever substance they passed through, would not stop "until they hit a nucleus with which they may react," that is to say, split.[15] If a chain reaction of neutron collisions split enough nuclei, then an immense release of power would result. Szilárd had read *The World Set Free*, and he realized, like the scientist in Wells' book, that he had just hit upon the means to make an actual atomic bomb, if he found the right material and equipment to do so. Szilárd spent time in his laboratory to attempt to generate a chain reaction, but the materials he was using failed to work. Undaunted, he patented the concept, and in 1936, assigned the patent to the British Admiralty to help keep it secret – and out of the hands of the Nazis.

Meanwhile, in the United States, American physicist Ernest O. Lawrence, at the University of California, Berkeley, eager to build the power needed to push harder at and into the atom, conceived of and designed a new tool, the cyclotron. Lined with electrodes to help give particles recurrent "small pushes" and speed them, Lawrence's circular instrument was more compact than a linear accelerator, also used to speed particles. Testing his first device in January 1931, Lawrence used 2,000 volts of electricity to spin rapidly 80,000-volt protons in the cyclotron. "Atom smashing" had just taken another step forward.

In France, Irène and Frédéric Joliot-Curie, continuing in the tradition of Irène's famous parents, worked as a team, probing the mysteries of the proton. Bombarding elements and tracking the discharges, the Joliot-Curies made a momentous discovery in 1933. Their bombardment of aluminum foil not only transmuted the aluminum into the isotope of phosphorus. It also transmuted it into radioactive phosphorus, the world's first artificially induced radioactive material. This meant, as Richard Rhodes would later note, that scientists now could not only chip off pieces of a nucleus, but they could "force it artificially to release some of its energy in radioactive decay."[16]

In another laboratory, in Rome, another brilliant young physicist, Enrico Fermi, had just completed a theoretical treatise on beta decay (the 15-minute window in which a free neutron decayed to become a proton), and was seeking a new challenge. In January 1934, after reading of the Joliot-Curie discovery, Fermi and his colleagues began a series of experiments, bombarding elements with neutrons. Fermi's breakthrough, in experiments in May and October, was the discovery that neutron bombardment caused nuclear transformation in nearly every element they subjected to the process. At the same time, the experiments also showed that there were different energy levels in neutrons, and in particular, Fermi identified "slow neutrons," or neutrons with low energy levels.

In the bombardment of uranium, hitherto impossible without the use of neutrons, Fermi created an isotope, uranium-239, and a new element with a heavier atomic weight than uranium. This was the first man-made element, the precursor of what the Nobel Prize committee would later recognize as a key step, "the production of elements lying beyond what was until then the Periodic Table."[17] Fermi's work was also another important stepping stone in the development of nuclear fission. But missed by Fermi and his team was a reaction in the uranium which would later be determined to be the first example of nuclear fission.

LEFT: On display at the Institut de Radium in Paris is the apparatus used by the Joliot-Curies to discover artificial radiation. Admiringly described by one of their collaborators, Pierre Savel, as "extremely primitive." In expert hands the equipment allowed the Joliot-Curies to artificially induce and measure radioactivity. (Bridgeman Art Library)

RIGHT: Scottish pioneer of nuclear physics Charles Wilson (1869–1959) invented the cloud chamber to mark the track of alpha particles and electrons. A sealed chamber filled with supercooled, super saturated water, or alcohol vapor, the "Wilson Chamber" allows scientists to visually track ionizing radiation as the ions condense the water or alcohol, forming a mist. (Bridgeman Art Library)

The task therefore fell to scientist Otto Hahn, who was fast closing in on the secrets of fission. Hahn had studied in his native Germany, and in Britain and Canada, where he had worked with Rutherford and made several key breakthroughs, including the discovery of radiothorium and radioactinium. Returning to Germany in 1906, the

Lise Meitner (1878–1968) was a key figure in the discovery of fission. Born in Austria, Meitner graduated from the University of Vienna with a doctorate in 1906, and moved to Berlin to work with Max Planck and Otto Hahn at the Kaiser Wilhelm Institute for Chemistry. Closely collaborating with Hahn, Meitner helped make a number of breakthroughs in the study of radioactivity. Fleeing Hitler's Germany in 1938 because of her Jewish ancestry, Meitner worked in Sweden, and continued to collaborate with Hahn from abroad, between them designing the experiments that proved that it was possible to split the atom to release energy. (Bridgeman Art Library)

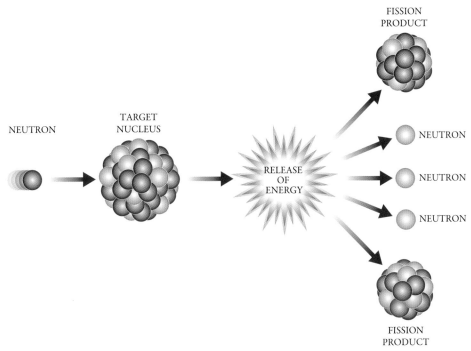

NEUTRON

TARGET
NUCLEUS

RELEASE
OF
ENERGY

FISSION
PRODUCT

NEUTRON

NEUTRON

NEUTRON

FISSION
PRODUCT

Nuclear fission occurs when an atom "splits." A uranium-235 atom struck by a neutron fissions into two new atoms, free neutrons and binding energy. For a chain reaction (and a nuclear explosion) to occur, the free neutrons must strike other atoms and split them.

next year Hahn began a decades-long collaboration with Austrian scientist Lise Meitner. Working at the University of Berlin, the two jointly investigated radioactive transformation, and the qualities of beta rays. With Hahn's student and assistant Fritz Strassman, the two followed Fermi's work closely and inspired by his results, they began their own series of experiments, bombarding uranium with neutrons. Their great breakthrough came in 1938.

That year was a difficult one. Hitler's rise to power in Germany had already seen the forced removal of Jewish scientists and academics, including Albert Einstein and Leó Szilárd, who had fled abroad. Lise Meitner, with Jewish ancestry, also fell under the Nazi definition of a Jew, but as an Austrian national had avoided dismissal – and worse. The *Anschluss* of 1938, with Austria becoming part of the Third Reich, changed her position. One step ahead of the Gestapo, and with the help of Hahn and other friends, Meitner slipped across the Dutch border and made her way to neutral Sweden in July.

With Meitner collaborating via correspondence, the team kept up their work. In December, after bombarding uranium with neutrons, Hahn and Strassman found traces of barium and other elements. The "radium-barium-mesothorium-fractionation" experiment, as it came to be known, demonstrated to Hahn that the bombardment had split (Hahn used the term "burst") the nucleus of the uranium nucleus into the atomic nuclei of the various other elements.

27

"The Evacuation of the Fleet." After target ships were prepared for atomic attack, with instruments and test equipment set in place, and test animals left to their fate, crews left the target ships to board the support ships that departed Bikini lagoon and headed out to sea to await the blast. In this painting by Arthur Beaumont, personnel evacuate the ships for the Bikini Atoll tests. In the center is the veteran battleship USS Nevada (BB- 36), selected to be the aiming point for the air-dropped bomb. The scientists of the 20th century could only have guessed at what their dicoveries would lead to. (US Naval History & Heritage Command)

Hahn and Strassman reported their results in late December in an article in a weekly scientific publication, and sent the results to Meitner for analysis. Working with her nephew, refugee scientist Robert Frisch, who was then visiting her, Meitner agreed that the results showed that the nuclei had been split into their lighter elements, releasing neutrons and photons. Frisch coined a new phrase, "fission," to describe the phenomenon. Hahn and Strassman published an article describing the tests, and Meitner and Frisch separately published on the physics to avoid Nazi censorship. In February 1939, Hahn and Strassman published another article, and predicted, as Frisch had pointed out in the analysis he and Meitner had undertaken, that additional neutrons existed and had been released in the experiment. Reading that, Frederic Joliot-Curie and his team were able to replicate Hahn and Strassman's results – an important scientific proof that the results from Berlin were not a one-off, or in error.

Word quickly spread throughout the international community. Physicists in Europe and in the United States were quick to grasp the implications of fission – a number of them, like Szilárd, had read *The World Set Free*. Now, thanks to Hahn, Strassman, Meitner, and Frisch's work, the possibility of generating a nuclear chain reaction – a self-sustaining and amplifying release of neutrons – was no longer just science fiction. Szilárd, who had secretly patented the concept, knew it. Neils Bohr, looking at the various isotopes of uranium, specifically uranium-235 and uranium-238 (U-235 and U-238), realized how both could be fissioned. Ernest Lawrence's laboratory partner at the University of California, Berkeley, J. Robert Oppenheimer, came to a similar conclusion, realizing that the rapid release of excess neutrons, if a chain reaction occurred, meant that an atomic bomb could be built. That was also very clear to Albert Einstein. Like many of the refugee scientists who had fled Hitler, Einstein also realized, with chilling certainty, that if the Nazis grasped the potential and followed through on Hahn and Strassman's breakthrough, the world was at risk. With that foremost in his mind, and urged on by colleagues, Einstein sat down to write a private letter to the President of the United States.

Frankfurt-born Otto Hahn (1879–1968) was a brilliant chemist who joined Berlin's Kaiser Wilhelm Institute for Chemistry. Closely collaborating with Austrian physicist Lise Meitner, Hahn eventually headed the Institute and was its director until Germany's surrender at the end of World War II, when he was taken into custody by the Allies and interrogated along with other German atomic scientists. Hahn, despite his role in discovering the fission of uranium with Meitner and Fritz Strassman, had not supported atomic weapons development, and was after the war a prominent advocate against nuclear weapons. (Bridgeman Art Library)

2

DEVELOPING THE BOMB, 1939–45

As scientific research into fission continued, the focus was on how many neutrons were released during fission, and how each uranium isotope reacted. In order for a chain reaction to occur, a large number of excess neutrons would have to be produced by fission. Since fission also absorbed neutrons, another critical aspect was ensuring that the ratio between neutrons produced and absorbed was large enough. Another key step was actually creating a controlled chain reaction. This work moved slowly forward, much to the impatience of Leo Szilárd and others, who felt that a desperate race with the Nazis to be the first to develop an atomic bomb was being lost. In fact, the Germans were initially ahead of the American and British efforts, particularly in stockpiling uranium, and the Japanese were also working on solving the problems of uranium refinement and fission to build an atomic bomb.

The fission problem was tackled by Enrico Fermi and a team of other scientists and graduate students. Fermi was now in the United States because his native Italy, allied with Hitler, had adopted the Nazis' racial policies, and Fermi's wife Laura was of Jewish descent. Fleeing Italy, the Fermi family had relocated to America. In March 1939, Fermi, working with Herbert Anderson, was able to determine that on average, two neutrons were produced for every neutron consumed by fission. Experiments found that uranium in water could not produce a chain reaction, but in July 1939, Szilárd wrote to Fermi and suggested that if they suspended the uranium in carbon (graphite) they might be able to produce a chain reaction.

Even as he participated in the discussions over how best to achieve a chain reaction, Szilárd worried, as did many of the refugee scientists, over whether the Nazis had paid attention to Hahn and Strassman's breakthrough and were now pursuing a chain reaction and then an atomic bomb. They were not wrong to think so. The Reich had recently stopped the sale of uranium from recently occupied Czechoslovakia, and there were rumors that a German chain reaction group had been formed. Szilárd decided to enlist Albert Einstein to take action and write to Einstein's close personal friend Elizabeth, the Queen Mother of Belgium. The letter would ask for her help in preventing the world's largest known uranium supply, in the Belgian Congo, from falling into Nazi hands.

Meeting Einstein at the famous scientist's summer home outside New York at Peconic, on Long Island, Szilárd and physicist Eugene Wigner convinced Einstein to write the letter. However, shortly after that meeting, discussions with economist Alexander Sachs, a friend and unofficial advisor to President Franklin D. Roosevelt, led to Sachs's suggestion that Szilárd get Einstein to write to Roosevelt. Sachs would personally deliver the letter and talk with the President. A second meeting with Einstein secured the great man's permission, and after reviewing various drafts, Einstein signed a letter dated August 2, 1939, that Sachs carried by hand into the Oval Office. The letter started by explaining the threat:

> In the course of the last four months it has been made probable – through the work of Joliot in France as well as Fermi and Szilárd in America – that it may become possible to set up a nuclear chain reaction in a large mass of uranium, by which vast amounts of power and large quantities of new radium-like elements would be generated. Now it appears almost certain that this could be achieved in the immediate future. This new phenomenon would also lead to the construction of bombs, and it is conceivable – though much less certain – that extremely powerful bombs of a new type may thus be constructed. A single bomb of this type, carried by boat and exploded in a port, might very well destroy the whole port together with some of the surrounding territory. However, such bombs might very well prove to be too heavy for transportation by air.[1]

The letter went on to suggest that the President "have more permanent contact maintained between the Administration and the group of physicists working on chain reactions in America. One possible way of achieving this might be for you to entrust with this task a person who has your confidence and who could perhaps serve in an inofficial [sic] capacity." That person could "approach Government Departments, keep them informed … and put forward recommendations for Government action, giving particular

attention to the problem of securing a supply of uranium ore for the United States." They could also "speed up the experimental work" on chain reaction, "which is at present being carried on within the limits of the budgets of University laboratories, by providing funds, if such funds be required, through his contacts with private persons who are willing to make contributions for this cause, and perhaps also by obtaining the co-operation of industrial laboratories which have the necessary equipment."

Sachs met with Roosevelt on October 11, 1939. Germany had invaded Poland on September 1, starting World War II, but at that stage the United States was a neutral nation. Roosevelt understood the Nazi threat, but the only action he could, or would take in regard to the potential for the atomic bomb, was to establish a small, secret working committee to meet with Szilárd and other physicists and examine the uranium problem. The initial meeting, on October 21, led to a commitment from National Bureau of Standards (NBS) Director Lyman Briggs to provide $6,000 in funding for Fermi's experiments at Columbia University in New York.

Born in Rome, Enrico Fermi (1901–1954) received his doctorate at the age of 21. After working in Germany, Fermi returned to Italy and in 1927, he was appointed Professor of Theoretical Physics at the University of Rome. Here Fermi became the world's greatest authority on neutrons, building on the work of Joliot-Curies. Fermi and his team discovered slow neutrons, and their results paved the way for Hahn, Meitner and Strassman's discovery of nuclear fission. Fermi received the Nobel Prize in Physics in 1938. A key figure and leader in the Manhattan Project, Fermi relocated to Los Alamos and remained with the project until war's end. (Library of Congress)

BRITAIN TAKES THE LEAD

Despite the steps taken in the United States, official American action was slow, and Szilárd and his compatriots believed, with some justification, that the US government did not understand the seriousness of the situation. Their colleagues in Britain, however, met with a completely different reaction. Otto Robert Fritsch, working with fellow German refugee scientist Rudolf Ernst Peierls, wrote a top secret memorandum in March 1940 that galvanized the British government into action. The same month, after Szilárd had kept badgering Briggs, the US government belatedly released the $6,000 it had promised for Fermi's research.

The Fritsch-Peierls memorandum began with a detailed, and ultimately proven to be accurate, summary of what a uranium-based "super-bomb" would do:

The energy liberated in the explosion of such a super bomb is about the same as that produced by the explosion of 1,000 tons of dynamite. This energy is liberated in a small volume, in which it will, for an instant, produce a temperature comparable to that in the interior of the sun. The blast from such an explosion would destroy life in a wide area. The size of this area is difficult to estimate, but it will probably cover the centre of a big city. In addition, some part of the energy set free by the bomb goes to produce radioactive substances, and these will emit very powerful and dangerous radiations. The effect of these radiations is greatest immediately after the explosion, but it decays only gradually and even for days after the explosion any person entering the affected area will be killed. Some of this radioactivity will be carried along with the wind and will spread the contamination; several miles downwind this may kill people.

While other scientists had thought that a large amount of uranium was necessary to create a bomb, Fritsch and Peierls estimated that after bombarding uranium to create its light isotope, U-235, only a small amount was needed to make a bomb. The "critical size" was "about one pound. A quantity of the separated uranium isotope that exceeds the critical amount is explosive, yet a quantity less than the critical amount is absolutely safe." This revelation meant that a bomb need not be carried in a ship, but could probably be carried by air.

To reinforce the point, the memorandum starkly reminded readers that:

as a weapon, the super-bomb would be practically irresistible. There is no material or structure that could be expected to resist the force of the explosion... We have no information that the same idea has also occurred to other scientists but since all the theoretical data bearing on this problem are published, it is quite conceivable that Germany is, in fact, developing this weapon... Hence it is of extreme importance to keep this report secret since any rumour about the connection between uranium separation and a super-bomb may set a German scientist thinking along the right lines.

Fritsch and Peierls strongly recommended a British atomic program:

If one works on the assumption that Germany is, or will be, in the possession of this weapon, it must be realized that no shelters are available that would be effective and that could be used on a large scale. The most effective reply would be a counter-threat with a similar bomb. Therefore it seems to us important to start production as soon and as rapidly as possible, even if it is not intended to use the bomb as a means of attack. Since the separation of the necessary amount of uranium is, in the most favourable circumstances, a matter of several months, it would obviously be too late to late to start production when such a bomb is known to be in the hands of Germany, and the matter seems, therefore, very urgent.[2]

The British government established its own secret committee in April, and in June the committee asked another German refugee scientist, Franz Simon of the Clarendon Laboratory at Oxford, to look into creating U-235. Simon was able to refine a process of gaseous diffusion to create the enriched uranium isotope for bombs. By turning uranium into a gas, uranium hexafluoride, and then filtering the U-235 out from the heavier U-238 by passing the gas through semi-permeable membranes (barriers that only allowed certain particles to pass through it), U-235 could be condensed and turned into pure metal. By December, Simon had made his report to the committee, explaining the process and providing specifications for a plant to do the work and outlining costs. British physicist James Chadwick, a member of the secret committee, was aghast at the implications, explaining he now "realised that a nuclear bomb was not only possible, it was inevitable. I had then to take sleeping pills. It was the only remedy."[3]

SPURRING THE AMERICANS

In July 1940 a new American committee, the National Defense Research Council (NDRC), headed by Vannevar Bush, who acted as President Roosevelt's science advisor, formed to spur atomic research, albeit with an initial budget of just $40,000. With that money, which was not released until November, the team at Columbia University began construction of a 38-ton uranium oxide and graphite "sub-critical pile" to try to induce a chain reaction. Another group, at the Department of Terrestrial Magnetism at the Carnegie Institution for Science, in Washington, DC (Bush was also its President), turned their attention to determining the "cross section" of U-235 – this work would help establish the probability of a nuclear reaction. American interest in fission, however, was fixed on nuclear power for wartime use, not a bomb. Regardless of final intentions for nuclear energy, the American and British groups shared their research, and in March 1941, armed with the work from the Carnegie Institution, Peierls more accurately recalculated the critical mass for an atomic bomb.

Armed with the new calculations, the British group, codenamed the "MAUD Committee," began work on a series of reports that they shared with their American counterparts. One of the reports, "Use of Uranium for a Bomb," offered a specific plan to build a bomb and estimated the cost at some $25 million. The report urged cooperation between the United States and Britain to develop the infrastructure for a bomb program, and then to build the bomb. The report, although forwarded to the United States in July 1941, went unanswered, and so Marcus Oliphant of Oxford, the initial recipient of the Fritsch-Peierls memorandum, traveled to Washington DC in August to meet with American officials.

To his disbelief, Oliphant discovered that Lyman Briggs, who he called an "inarticulate and unimpressive man,"[4] had not shared the final reports of the MAUD Committee, and had locked them in his office safe. Oliphant then went directly to the American committee. After urging them to action, and demanding an American commitment to building a bomb because Britain, at war, did not have the resources to do so, Oliphant went on to meet with a number of prominent physicists. Inspired by Oliphant's demands, and with a copy of the MAUD Committee report in hand, Vannevar Bush took it to Roosevelt in early October. After a meeting with other key figures later in the month, Bush delivered a report to the President in late November encouraging the US development of a U-235 bomb.

Earlier experiments at Berkeley by physicist Glenn Seaborg, assisted by graduate student Arthur Wahl, had discovered a new element created by bombardment. When a neutron from U-235 hit a U-238 nucleus, it created a short-lived isotope, U-239. As U-239 decayed, it became Pu-239, or "plutonium," the name given to the new element. The possibility of using this element as a material to make a bomb had been encouraged by the British. Despite the fact that calculations showed that the new element would be 170 percent more powerful than U-235, the American team decided on the better-known uranium isotope, which they were then in the process of testing to see what the threshold was for making it go "critical" and start a chain reaction. Fermi and his team's sub-critical experiments at Columbia, ironically, had shown that uranium alone was not sufficiently powerful, and something stronger was needed. That meant processing large amounts of U-235.

As the head of a new "Office of Scientific Research and Development" (OSRD), Bush set into motion a series of projects to continue research under the leadership of Arthur Compton, a Nobel Prize-winning physicist at the University of Chicago. In January 1942, Compton created a new laboratory at the University of Chicago to serve as a consolidated research center. Known as the Metallurgical Laboratory, it would focus on the development of what were then known as "uranium burners" – the nuclear reactors that would generate a chain reaction by "burning" the uranium to create energy. Compton assigned the task of theoretical analysis of fast neutrons to a team led by Gregory Breit, a physicist from the University of Wisconsin.

At the same time, at the University of California, Berkeley, another group, under the leadership of J. Robert Oppenheimer, began the same task. Oppenheimer, a brilliant, unconventional professor, had been invited into the project by Lawrence, who like Szilárd had seen the impending threat of a Nazi nuclear program. The study of neutron behavior was essential – at this early stage, no one was sure that there was not a hitherto undiscovered aspect of atomic behavior that would prevent a chain reaction, and hence a bomb.

J. Robert Oppenheimer
(1904–1967). New York-born,
Oppenheimer studied at Harvard,
switching from chemistry to
physics. Earning his doctorate
from the University of Göttingen,
he returned to the United States,
and within a few years held joint
professorships at the University
of California, Berkeley, and the
California Institute of
Technology.
A brilliant theoretical physicist,
Oppenheimer was at first invited
to work on neutron calculations
for the Manhattan Project, and
soon thereafter was named
scientific director in June 1942.
Oppenheimer resigned as
director of Los Alamos at the
end of the war, but remained
part of the government's
nuclear research until
politically motivated and highly
controversial hearings stripped
him of his security clearance
in 1953, some believing the
decision had more to do with his
concerns over the development
of the hydrogen bomb than
his political leanings.
(Library of Congress)

By the early spring, Enrico Fermi had relocated to Chicago to continue his work
on building a critical mass. At Columbia, Fermi and his team had built successive
"exponential piles" of uranium and graphite to measure the release of neutrons.
The graphite would absorb the neutrons – and in theory control a runaway reaction.
The exponential piles allowed Fermi and his team to increase, slowly and a step at
time, the size of the pile.

A successful pile required a great deal of U-235, and that needed refinement. There were various methods proposed to do this. In March 1942, James Bryant Conant, a chemist, President of Harvard University, and chairman of the NRDC, suggested that the best plan of action would be to develop redundant facilities to produce U-235 and plutonium using every known method, which included gaseous diffusion, electromagnetic separation, centrifuges, and, in the case of plutonium, "breeding" by using atomic piles for bombardment. Only by taking this approach, Conant successfully argued, would the material needed to build a bomb be amassed in the quickest possible time. As Conant's argument carried the day, Glenn Seaborg arrived in Chicago to develop the industrial process to manufacture plutonium.

In May, Breit resigned, and went to work in the US Navy's ordnance laboratory. He believed that the work was progressing too slowly, and he was unhappy with what he perceived to be a sufficient lack of secrecy in the project (his research was shared with Oppenheimer, whom Breit felt was not sufficiently secretive). Compton turned to J. Robert Oppenheimer to take over the theoretical physics team. The 38-year-old Oppenheimer, the son of a German immigrant, had earned his doctorate in physics at Göttingen, Germany in 1927. Oppenheimer joined the University of California, Berkeley, in 1929, moving west from his native New York. At odds with some of his colleagues, and socially awkward, Oppenheimer was sharp, witty, caustic, and brilliant. Within a year of joining the project, Oppenheimer would catapult himself to the head of the newly formed laboratory that would build the atomic bomb.

Oppenheimer's skills as the leader of the theoretical physicists came to the forefront in the summer of 1942, as he spearheaded the efforts of a study group he had assembled at Berkeley. Physicists Hans Bethe, a German refugee scientist from Cornell University, Edward Teller, a Hungarian refugee physicist from George Washington University, John van Vleck of Harvard, Robert Serber, from the University of Illinois, Felix Bloch, a Swiss-born refugee scientist from Germany from Stanford University, and Emil Konopinski of the University of Indiana, all worked with Oppenheimer through the summer of 1942. They developed the basic principles of bomb design, and determined how much U-235 was required for a high-yield nuclear detonation.

THE ARMY STEPS IN

After the slow initial start American response to the German atomic threat, the US effort remained under-funded, somewhat disorganized, and disjointed. Steps to rectify the problems began in the summer of 1942. President Roosevelt secretly approved the project and authorized its initial budget of tens of millions of dollars in June.[5]

The same month, the US Army Corps of Engineers (USACE) established an office to commence the government's part of the project. (The mission of the USACE is still expressed as serving the "Armed Forces and the Nation by providing vital engineering services and capabilities, as a public service, across the full spectrum of operations from peace to war in support of national interests."[6]) When Conant issued a report at the end of August summarizing the summer's work by the civilian scientists, Vannevar Bush, in forwarding it to the War Department, suggested that new leadership was needed. In response, the USACE was handed control of the project. It was the only agency of the US government with broad enough authority, facilities, and expertise in design, engineering, project management, and construction to carry out the bomb project. To carry out the work, in August the Corps created a new office.

The USACE North Atlantic Division, headquartered in New York City, was the initial coordinating office, even though the project was nationwide. To disguise the function of the office and its top-secret mission, it was given the innocuous name of the "Manhattan Engineer District," and the effort to build the bomb, as a result, was dubbed the "Manhattan Project." Initially under the command of Colonel James Marshall, in mid-September, the new district received a new commanding officer.

Colonel Leslie R. Groves was hard working, intelligent, and able to complete large projects rapidly (he had recently overseen the construction of the Pentagon, then the world's largest office building). Groves was also an unpopular officer with a reputation for arrogance and ruthlessness. He later wrote that his initial briefing from a superior was "overoptimistic." The basic research and development had been completed, and "you just have to take the rough designs, put them into final shape, build some plants and organize an operating force and your job will be finished and the war will be over."[7] Assuming command on September 17, he immediately went into action, signing a contract to mine for radium in the Canadian Arctic and purchasing 1,250 tons of uranium ore that the United States had managed to ship out of the Belgian Congo one step ahead of the Germans.[8] Groves also bought up property for the construction of the industrial facilities to manufacture U-235 – all in the first two days on the job. A week later, to give Groves the necessary authority to continue his job, the Army promoted him to brigadier general. With Colonel Marshall and another officer, Colonel Kenneth D. Nichol, as his deputies, Groves began to learn more about the task ahead of him.

At the time Groves joined the project, the procedures for refining uranium – separating the small amounts of fissionable U-235 isotope from the more prevalent U-238 isotope in uranium – were still under development in various laboratories. Lab tests were essential before any one process was selected for massive industrial production. There were three methods under consideration. The first, using a powerful centrifuge to pull uranium apart, was least likely to succeed, and Groves soon killed the research. The next was using "electromagnetic separation," a process that Ernest Lawrence was working on at Berkeley. The third was gaseous diffusion, in which the uranium was converted into the highly caustic uranium hexafluoride gas, and then filtered to capture the U-235 particles, which could then be converted back into metal. Industrializing this method was under active study by scientists Harold Urey and John Dunning and their research was promising.

While Groves evaluated the methods and set about creating the plants to refine the U-235, Enrico Fermi and his team at the University of Chicago worked to determine how best to start – and stop – a chain reaction. In late July, the first shipment of U-235 reached the lab, and a month later Fermi's team had built and tested an experimental pile that brought a self-sustaining chain reaction closer. While the pile did not achieve a sufficient reaction to be self-sustaining, it was clear that a larger pile would do the job. A chain reaction was now assured. From September through to November, Fermi and his team received large shipments of graphite and 3 tons of uranium. In an abandoned squash court at the University's Stagg Field, they began construction of the final pile on November 16, working around the clock in a race to finish.

CP-1, as the final pile was codenamed, was built of graphite that the scientists had cut and shaved into bricks, and loaded with lumps of uranium as they stacked it, layer by layer, to reach the proper mass. Boron and cadmium, both of which possess a powerful capacity to absorb neutrons, were laid into the pile to help control the release of energy. Boron steel rods, inserted into the pile, could be slowly slid out and then back in to control neutron release. After 24 long days and nights, by December 1, before the pile was complete, measurements by constantly monitoring Geiger counters showed that the pile could go critical and achieve a self-sustaining chain reaction if the control rods were pulled out.

After calling a break for lunch on December 2, Fermi and his team reassembled in the squash court. Arthur Compton, a witness to the test, recalled that as he entered the room, 20 scientists had gathered on a balcony as the last checks were made. Volunteers (nicknamed the "suicide squad") stood precariously perched over the pile with buckets of liquid cadmium, ready to sacrifice themselves but nonetheless quench the atomic fire by drowning it should the reaction prove unstoppable. Just before 03:20hrs:

Fermi gave the order to withdraw the control rod another foot. We all knew this was the real test. The Geiger counters ... began to click faster and faster, until their sound became a rattle ... the reaction grew until there might be danger from the rays coming from the pile. "Throw in the safety rods," came Fermi's order... The rattle of the counters fell to a slow series of clicks. For the first time, atomic power had been released, and it had been controlled and stopped.[9]

While only enough power to light a small bulb had been generated, the next important step at the dawn of the atomic age had been taken. A series of new facilities, quickly authorized by Groves, began to spring up in isolated spots around the United States to process U-235 and plutonium on a massive scale, and a new, top-secret laboratory rose in the wilderness of New Mexico to house the scientists who would design and build weapons that would use the newly processed material.

PROJECTS W, X, AND Y

Groves selected an isolated, rural community in Tennessee in which to build the electromagnetic and gaseous diffusion plant. Next to the Clinch River, the plant could tap into the tremendous hydroelectric power of America's Tennessee Valley Authority. Enough power to light a city would be required to run the electromagnetic process alone, as Groves intended to build the world's largest magnets to do the job. Codenamed "Project X," the new facility rose on 1,100 acres 18 miles northwest of Knoxville. Officially known as Oak Ridge, but called "Dogpatch" by its 79,000 residents, it was a "secret city" that did not exist on maps. In the Pacific Northwest, along the banks of the Columbia River, the plutonium processing facility codenamed "Project W," the Hanford Engineering Works, rose on a 400,000-acre reservation. Hanford housed 60,000 workers who built it in a year, and who were then replaced by 17,000 people – the technicians who would make plutonium, and their families.

The third facility, "Project Y," was a centralized laboratory that would be "concerned with the development and manufacture of an instrument of war."[10] Oppenheimer, based on his experience with his summer meeting, had come up with the idea of the lab to end the inefficiency of a number of teams at different universities working on the major problems of the project in isolation from one another. Groves not only accepted the principle of the new lab; on October 15, 1942, he selected Oppenheimer to head it, overruling the concerns of his security officers, who believed that the Berkeley scientist posed an unacceptable risk because they feared he was at best a Communist sympathizer and at worst an actual agent.

A site still needed to be selected, facilities built, and a team of scientists selected. The construction of roads, laboratories, homes for the scientists, and the necessary infrastructure of water and power started for what was initially a small community of a few hundred. The number of scientists, technicians and military personnel kept growing, and construction crews continually worked on additional projects as both staff and laboratory facilities expanded. By the time it was completed, the laboratory, built atop an isolated mesa in the New Mexico desert, would be another secret city, home to 5,800 people. At the end of 1942, Vannevar Bush told President Roosevelt that the total cost of the atomic bomb project would be around $400 million. By the time the project ended, it had cost more than five times that – in all, the United States spent over $2 billion on the Manhattan Project.

Leslie Groves (1896–1970) and Oppenheimer, pictured here at Los Alamos in August 1945. Groves, a career Army officer, was the US Government's choice to head the Manhattan Project when the American drive to develop an atomic bomb faltered under civilian control and the project was assigned to the US Army Corps of Engineers. His partner on this project was the brilliant, conflicted and controversial Oppenheimer. "Oppie" was a seemingly unlikely choice for the position of scientific director of the Manhattan Project because of his associations with and sympathies for Communism and doubts about his loyalties. Oppenheimer oversaw the development of Los Alamos in the New Mexico desert, assembled and managed a diverse and talented team of brilliant scientists and technicians, and successfully delivered the atomic weapon Groves demanded from him. (Library of Congress)

The lab, built on the site of a boy's ranch school at Los Alamos, was ready for occupancy by the initial staff of scientists and their families at the end of March 1943. Within a short time, Oppenheimer and Groves realized that their original calculations of how many people were needed – a hundred scientists – had been a gross underestimate. From that point, the pace of growth never stopped as more recruits and additional buildings expanded Los Alamos constantly.

Groves had demanded that a workable bomb be ready by the summer of 1945. In a series of initial meetings with his team, Oppenheimer and his senior staff developed the basic outline of how the lab would work, and who was responsible for what. To save time, the lab simultaneously began work on research and the engineering needed to design and build a bomb, with key scientists and technicians given overlapping responsibilities. At the same time, laboratories conducted redundant research to overcome hurdles that might crop up in one lab, but not another. Speculative, imaginative research was encouraged, but if it became clear that the line of research was a dead-end, the lab would quickly drop it. Isolated, locked behind a fence for the rest of the war, the Los Alamos lab staff set to their tasks.

The team at Los Alamos determined that two methods of firing off an atomic bomb were likely. The first was firing a sub-critical pellet of enriched U-235 or plutonium into a larger sub-critical mass to initiate an uncontrolled chain reaction. The second, although it didn't seem likely to succeed, was the "implosion method" of squeezing a mass of U-235 or plutonium by use of a controlled explosion to detonate a bomb. While the scientists understood theory, it became clear that an expert in ordnance – the science and art of weapons – was required, and that an expert was needed from the military. The major problem with the "gun method" was that if the two sub-critical pieces did not hit fast enough, the bomb would fizzle – it would produce enough fission to blow itself apart, but nothing more. A small, powerful gun was needed to deliver a strong enough punch.

The military expert selected for the job was Captain William S. Parsons, a visionary and inspirational naval officer who had started his naval career as a battleship gunnery officer before heading into experimental work at the Naval Research Laboratory (NRL). Under Parsons, who arrived in June 1943 with his wife and two daughters, work began on the gun method of firing the bomb – one aspect of the project that was considered a safe bet. With a newly built laboratory, ordnance range, and a team of 200 ordnance experts, Parsons, with his second in-command, Commander Frederick L. "Dick" Ashworth, another naval officer, set to work. By mid-September, the team had fired its first shot of many in a series of gun tests to develop a miniature, high-velocity cannon that would fit inside a bomb, itself small

Capt. William S. "Deak" Parsons (1901–1953) was a visionary and inspirational naval officer with a brilliant career in naval gunnery and scientific development. He was selected to join the Manhattan Project to take the fissionable products of the laboratory and construct a working atomic bomb. Parsons and his team developed the first working bomb, the "Little Boy" weapon, which he accompanied to the Pacific and armed for the attack on Hiroshima. After the war, Parsons was the military's top expert on nuclear weapons, and with a small staff helped lead the development of an atomic program not only for the Navy, but also for the other branches of the Armed Forces until his untimely death from a heart attack. (US Naval Institute)

enough to fit into an airplane. To assist in that effort, Parsons assembled a new team in October to work with scientist Norman Ramsay. Its task was to make the necessary preparations to prepare for combat use the bomb that the rest of Los Alamos was racing to develop.

In November, the production of plutonium in its metal form began in the lab. At the same time, British scientists began arriving at Los Alamos. An earlier decision not to inform the British atomic team about the top-secret atomic bomb work in the United States had been reversed. Following a meeting between President Roosevelt and Prime Minister Winston Churchill in Quebec, an agreement to share the work and the results of the bomb program reopened the door closed more than a year earlier. The agreement, signed on August 19, stipulated that "we will never use this agency against each other," that "we will not use it against third parties without each other's consent," and that "we will not either of us communicate any information about Tube Alloys [the codename for the atomic bomb project] to third parties except by mutual consent."[11]

Key figures in the initial breakthrough research – Britain's best – now joined the growing team at Los Alamos. Among them were Otto Fritsch, Rudolf Peierls, James Chadwick, William Penney, and a young German refugee scientist, Klaus Fuchs.

With them came Neils Bohr, who had recently fled the Nazi occupiers of his native Denmark to neutral Sweden. He was subsequently smuggled into Britain. As part of the British Empire, Canada also joined the effort. Canada was already playing a key role as the supplier of a key ingredient – hundreds of tons of Canadian uranium, the product of sub-Arctic radium mines at Port Radium on the shores of the Great Bear Lake. By the time the war ended, the Americans would have ordered more than 1,500 tons of uranium from Canada.[12]

As 1944 began, work on the gun device proceeded, and by July 1944 the design was complete. However, increasing scientific evidence suggested that it would not work with plutonium. Even as this problem was being grappled with, work at Oak Ridge and Hanford was plagued by a series of problems. The electromagnetic separation equipment had faced a problem in the lack of copper to wind the magnets to carry the current to the huge cores, but that problem had been overcome by the ingenious borrowing of 6,000 tons of silver from the United States Mint – to be returned after the war. Faulty design of the magnets, however, forced an expensive rebuild of the system, and a loss of time the project seemingly could not afford.

An even greater problem existed with the gaseous diffusion plant. The uranium gas was so corrosive that most metal was eaten away, and nothing was therefore available to build a barrier of material strong enough to trap the U-235 in an industrial diffusion process. By the fall of 1944, U-235 production, which should have been in the tons, was at less than a few pounds. The problem would not be solved until it was discovered that nickel was strong enough to resist the corrosive gas. When that breakthrough was made, Groves contracted the job to the Chrysler Corporation. Chrysler turned one of its plants over to a massive effort to build the gaseous diffusion units. Learning that the nickel needed would take two years to mine, Carl Heussner, head of Chrysler's plating lab, ingeniously cut costs and saved time when he developed a method for electroplating steel with the nickel. As Chrysler's workers began their task, the stalled industrial gaseous diffusion process seemed close to fruition.

Plutonium production was beginning, however, and the first full-scale pile – now renamed a "reactor" – was fired up under Enrico Fermi's supervision at Hanford on September 26. Then, without warning, the reactor shut down the following day. Analysis of the problem soon discovered that fission was giving off xenon-135, an isotope that absorbed neutrons even better than U-238 or graphite. Another costly delay, another major expense followed. The reactor had to be redesigned and rebuilt to add more "reactivity" to overcome the xenon. On December 17, the changes proved effective, and the full-scale processing of plutonium began at Hanford.

TURNING POINT

By the first months of 1945, the successful resolution of the processing problem and Parson's group's success with the gun problem had convinced Oppenheimer that sufficient U-235 could be developed to build one uranium-gun bomb by the summer of that year. Furthermore, it was also clear that the Nazis had lost the race to build an atomic bomb. The German conquest of Czechoslovakia and Belgium had given the Nazis access to large amounts of radium, and the conquest and occupation of Norway provided a ready source of heavy water, which acted as a neutron absorbent. But incredibly brave acts of sabotage by European resistance movements, including sinking a ferry containing barrels of heavy water, which were being shipped to Germany, in a deep Norwegian lake, had helped stall the German atomic program.

The disinterest of Hitler, who viewed physics as "Jewish science," and an over-extended German effort to develop a wide range of "super weapons," also helped doom the Nazi bomb. In late 1944, a secret team from Los Alamos, commanded by Colonel Boris Pash, one of Groves' security officers, followed victorious troops as they liberated France and drove into Germany. Interviews with Frederick Joliot-Curie led them to the heart of the German program in Strasbourg, where they discovered that the Germans had not beaten the United States to the atomic bomb – and nor would they.

The Manhattan Project was the seeming winner of the race, as the U-235 bomb was to all intents ready once enough fissionable material was manufactured to arm it. The key question that remained was whether a crash program and retooling of Los Alamos to develop a workable plutonium bomb would also succeed.

3

LITTLE BOY AND FAT MAN

A leading hope of the Manhattan Project from the earliest days was that if a U-235 bomb could be built, then so could a plutonium weapon. Since the initial calculations that Pu-239 would probably have an explosive effect 170 times stronger than U-235, planning for a plutonium bomb had proceeded along the same lines as the U-235 bomb. The gun method of firing a small sub-critical mass into a larger sub-critical mass should result in a nuclear detonation, but it would require the uranium slug to be fired at a speed of 3,000ft per second. As research continued through 1944, however, it became clear to the atomic scientists at Los Alamos that the gun method would not work on plutonium.

At the start of the project, in early 1943, plutonium existed only at a microscopic level. To make a weapon, plutonium had to be transformed into a metal, refined to a high level of purity to ensure that it would reach critical mass and simply not melt down (a process known as pre-detonation), and then be produced in large quantities. Chemists assigned to the project examined various methods of manufacturing purified plutonium and eventually settled on a multi-staged process of precipitation, or using a chemical reaction in a liquid solution to form a precipitate of solid metal. As the initial production of plutonium began, Emilio Segre, a former student of Fermi's and a member of Fermi's team in Italy before the war, began experiments to determine the spontaneous fission rate. Segre, a brilliant physicist and former director of the Physics Laboratory of the University of Palermo, was another Jewish refugee who had stayed in the US after the Fascist government banned Jews from university positions in 1938. After working for

Ernest Lawrence and lecturing at the University of California, Segre joined the Manhattan Project to take a leading role in the Metallurgical Lab.

In June 1943, Segre's initial experiments showed that plutonium should detonate inside a gun bomb. More plutonium became available after November when the Metallurgical Lab was finally able to create plutonium in a metallic form. After further experiments in March 1944 demonstrated an even higher rate of fissioning, and potential problems with pre-detonation, further analysis became essential. In April, analysis of the first samples of plutonium produced at Oak Ridge revealed that the plutonium was likely not to work inside a gun bomb. It was not pure enough, and it would fizzle out in a pre-detonation. The results, however, had come from a limited sample, and so Segre and Oppenheimer kept the report quiet. Segre continued to examine additional plutonium as it became available for testing, to make sure that the results were accurate.

By July, it was clear that plutonium would definitely not work in a gun bomb. On the 4th, Oppenheimer told the Los Alamos staff the bad news. The plans for a plutonium gun bomb were immediately scrapped, and a back-burner effort, implosion, was quickly moved into the lead position. While Parsons had favored the gun method, as sufficiently refined U-235 would work in a gun-based bomb, he now agreed to step up implosion research. Oppenheimer and Parsons quickly reorganized Los Alamos to tackle the engineering and development problems of an implosion weapon. One critical aspect of the shift, in addition to research and development, was the need for a test of the bomb to make sure it actually worked.

The shift to implosion was both a vindication for Seth Neddermeyer, the scientist who had first proposed it as a method of detonation at the beginning of the project, and Oppenheimer's management of the lab. A back-burner project had been allowed to continue, which was exactly what Oppenheimer had planned for when he and Groves had established the unique working atmosphere of Los Alamos. The race was now on, with only a year to go before the deadline for a deliverable atomic bomb.

The concept of implosion called for explosives to compress a ball of plutonium from a sub-critical to a critical mass to start the chain reaction and detonate the bomb. During the first meetings of laboratory staff in April 1943, Neddermeyer, a young scientist transferred from the National Bureau of Standards, suggested the concept. It met with cynical reactions from most of the other scientists, who feared that explosive charges could not be made to perform properly to compress simultaneously a plutonium or U-235 hollow core into a solid ball. They feared that all that would result was a fizzle, or the bomb blowing apart and scattering highly radioactive fragments. Nonetheless, Oppenheimer supported Neddermeyer's pursuit of the problem, and assigned him to work under Parson's ordnance group.

Neddermeyer's first experiments began with test explosions in the back canyons of Los Alamos. Rather than try to blast the complex geometry of a sphere, Neddermeyer encased thick steel pipe in explosives and attempted to crush the pipe equally. He quickly discovered that the pipe was always thrown out of the blast as a twisted, badly warped piece of metal. To compress the pipe thoroughly would also require enough explosives that would rip it apart, ruining the experiments.

As Neddermeyer continued to grapple with the problem, Oppenheimer and Parsons began to push for more results, especially as the first inklings of a Pu-239 gun bomb problem began to surface. When visiting mathematician John von Neumann looked at Neddermeyer's results and at calculations by physicist Edward Teller of the pressures generated in the blasts, he quickly determined that there could only be a very narrow margin for error in the symmetry of the shock waves generated by blasts in order to successfully compress plutonium. That narrow margin meant a variation in the symmetry would shatter the plutonium core, and the bomb would fail. Neddermeyer added six more team members to tackle the extra work required to meet such exact specifications.

At the same time, von Neumann's calculations also showed that if the high-velocity shock waves were generated, a plutonium bomb could be made with an even smaller amount of plutonium than originally believed. Groves and Oppenheimer were by now worried that the failure of the gun method for a plutonium bomb meant that the United States would have only one lower-yield U-235 bomb by the summer of 1945. Even if used in combat, a single bomb would be an insufficient demonstration of America's new atomic power, and it might not only not end the war but also actually spur the Japanese, who were known to have their own nuclear program, into a rushed effort to attack with a bomb of their own.

Oppenheimer asked the theoretical physics team, headed by Hans Bethe, to examine implosion physics more closely, and Teller began to work on more calculations. In January 1944, Teller assumed more responsibility as head of a new implosion theory group. However, he was unhappy with his assignment, believing that Oppenheimer was relegating him to a less important task when his research was centered on a fusion bomb. While the implosion concept was sound, and would ultimately lead to the development of the hydrogen bomb, Oppenheimer believed it would not be developed in time to affect the war, and had placed Teller under Bethe to tackle what Teller saw at best as sidetracking and at worst a breach of faith. In time, Oppenheimer would shift Teller entirely into an effort, not completed at war's end, to create his "super-bomb."

DEVELOPING NEW METHODS OF IMPLOSION

Oppenheimer and Parsons were also having problems with Neddermeyer. The young scientist was taking too long, and he needed more help, a fact that he did not seem to realize. In September 1943, Oppenheimer turned to explosives expert George Kistiakowsky, who arrived at Los Alamos in January 1943. By mid-February, Kistiakowsky had replaced Neddermeyer as the head of the implosion team. Under "Kisty," the implosion team, known as the X Division, focused on making implosion work, while Bethe, still in charge of the theoretical group, assisted. Robert Bacher headed the G Division responsible for building the new weapon (G stood for "Gadget," the nickname for the plutonium bomb) and Parsons, while skeptical of the ultimate success of implosion, oversaw the merging of all aspects into a bomb that could be manufactured, sent off to war, and delivered to a target.

To accentuate the push, more supplies and more bodies were needed. With Groves' approval and the US Army's assistance, enlisted personnel with relevant experience were reassigned to Los Alamos. Known as the Special Engineering Detachment (SED), the draftee scientists and technicians eased a critical shortage in people power. The Manhattan Project was now costing the United States $100 million a month. Results were essential, and obstacles were quickly dealt with, no expense spared.

A key shift in the implosion project came through a suggestion from British scientist James Tuck. After arriving in April 1944, Tuck had suggested using an example from British work on shaped explosive charges designed to crack armor. Tuck believed that high-powered, three-dimensionally shaped charges, used to create "explosive lenses," could generate the powerful series of shock waves necessary for successful implosion. A problem that required solving, however, was achieving simultaneous detonation of the charges. The possible solution was the use of exploding wire detonators in the charges, and the first tests of the detonators took place at the end of May.

The detonation sequence of the Little Boy weapon was simpler than a plutonium core implosion. The bomb was essentially a powerful gun that fired a uranium projectile into a "target" of uranium-235, causing a chain reaction and a nuclear explosion.

The development of the new methods did not necessarily mean success. Over the next few months, an exhaustive program of developing molds and casting explosive charges with fragile explosive compounds discarded tens of thousands of imperfect castings. Over 20,000 lenses that passed quality control were detonated in experiments to develop the simultaneous ignition system and to produce sufficient and equal compression of a plutonium core. As theory and practical application continued at a rushed pace in tandem, the work environment was later described as one in which "in their cubicles the theoretical scientists would sit for many hours working with pieces of colored chalk on a blackboard or with pencil on pads of paper. At frequent intervals one would hear the boom of great explosions on the various proving grounds in the distant canyons." This, said the project's official chronicler, *New York Times* reporter William L. Laurence, represented "in the true sense the explosion of ideas in the minds of men."[1]

One of the explosive ideas that proved to be a further breakthrough came when Robert Christy, another of the British scientists, suggested the use of a smaller, solid core approximately the size of a grapefruit. A smaller, solid mass would theoretically be easier to compress, but it would still require a precise burst to achieve criticality. Squeezed to twice its density, the plutonium would react as the nuclei were shoved closer to each other and free neutrons would punch through the nuclei, releasing more neutrons that in turn would strike more nuclei and release the incredible energy of a nuclear explosion. By the end of December, 1944, the tests of the lenses were progressing sufficiently to suggest that success was around the corner.

To test what constituted the critical mass for an explosion in the uranium bomb, other experiments in another "distant canyon" used a device known as the "guillotine." A wooden frame supported two steel rods that were set into two small blocks of "active material." A smaller block, suspended between the rods, was dropped to come into contact with the other blocks, and then slide past them. For a brief moment criticality, measured by neutron flux, would occur. While this test was dangerous because of the release of harmful radiation for that fraction of a second, another test, conducted under the supervision of Otto Frisch, used a small pile, pushing it to the brink of criticality, essentially modeling the "conditions prevailing in the bomb."

These tests showed that without a doubt the uranium gun bomb would work, and 1944 came to an end, it seemed that a successful method of implosion would be developed, even if by trial and error. To ensure success, however, a test of the Gadget was necessary. In March 1944, Kenneth Bainbridge, a member of Kistiakowsky's explosives group, was placed in charge of group X-2 to "make preparations for a field test in which blast, earth shock, neutron and gamma radiation" were to be measured and studied and to also make "complete photographic records … of the explosion and any atmospheric phenomena connected with the explosion."[2] Bainbridge, a Harvard University physics professor, had previously been in charge of high-explosive development. Described as "quiet and competent" by General Groves,[3] Bainbridge worked closely with the SED and a team of other scientists as he started the massive preparations for the test.

As Bainbridge began his preparations, the issues facing the Manhattan Project other than the questions of implosion were steadily being resolved. The first was both the quantity and the purity of processed plutonium. At the start of the year, Hanford began to produce more plutonium, while at the same time Oak Ridge's gaseous diffusion facilities, built in a rush, went on line. The final tests with U-235 were made, and in February 1945 Oppenheimer ordered the team designing the uranium gun bomb to finalize the design. Parsons turned his focus to planning for the delivery and use of the weapon, which was now codenamed "Little Boy."

At the end of February, Groves and Oppenheimer met with George Kistiakowsky, Hans Bethe, Charles C. Lauritsen, Arthur Conant, and Richard Tolman to examine the best design options for the plutonium weapon. The meeting resulted in a series of decisions. Even through Christy's theory of solid core compression had not yet been proved in a test, the team decided that the use of multiple explosive lenses with a modulated initiator and electric detonators would be used to create simultaneous, converging shock waves to compress the core. With that, all work on other designs for implosion compression was dropped and the design of the plutonium bomb was frozen. The decision was another gamble, because all of the components had problems. Groves had set a deadline of August 1 for a bomb to be ready for combat use, and so the team agreed on a series of deadlines to solve the problems and test an implosion weapon, which was codenamed "Fat Man."

The goals and deadlines were:

March 15–April 15:	The detonators were to have their problems resolved and be ready for mass production.
April 2:	A full-scale mold for the explosive lenses was to be completed and ready for use to cast the lenses out of the explosive compounds selected for the best results.
April 15:	Less than two weeks later, enough lenses were to be ready for multi-point electrical detonation.
April 25:	"Hemisphere tests" were to begin and would measure how the shock waves converged.

By 1945, Los Alamos had developed one working weapon design. The weapon was, at the beginning of that year, the only design that was guaranteed to work. The method was essentially simple: explosive charges were designed to fire a hollow U-235 projectile through a long gun barrel built into the heart of the bomb, which would impact into a U-235 target, inducing a chain reaction and nuclear detonation. "Little Boy" performed with deadly effect over Hiroshima. The weapon shown here is a replica displayed at the National Museum of the United States Air Force at Wright Patterson Air Force Base in Dayton, Ohio. (Alamy Ltd.)

May 15:	A full-scale test of implosion would successfully compress a solid core of metal.
May 15–June 15:	Enough plutonium would be on hand and full-scale spheres would be manufactured and tested for criticality.
June 4:	Molding lenses and assembling the detonators for the field test of the bomb would begin.
July 4:	The field test of the bomb would successfully detonate a plutonium-core weapon.

To meet the deadlines, Oppenheimer established a committee to see the various phases through, including delivery of sufficient plutonium from Hanford, the work at Los Alamos, and the construction of a massive new base to test the bomb. Known as the "Cowpuncher Committee" because in western parlance they were to "ride herd" on the various scientists and technicians and their projects, the committee was Captain Parsons, Charles Lauritsen, Samuel K. Allison, Robert Bacher, and George Kistiakowsky. Parsons had advocated the committee, writing to Oppenheimer that "ruthless, brutal people must band together to force the Fat Man components to dovetail in time and space."[4] Allison, a former member of the University of Chicago's Metallurgical Laboratory and a highly respected member of the Los Alamos team, chaired the cowpunchers. With the committee in place, Oppenheimer then moved into what would be the final phases of the Manhattan Project.

During the first half of 1945, Los Alamos' scientists and technicians raced to complete a workable plutonium core weapon that could be detonated through implosion. The initial weapon, known as "the Gadget," gave rise to the combat version of the bomb, "Fat Man." The "Fat Man" bomb was dropped on Nagasaki, and was later tested at Bikini Atoll in 1946. (Alamy Ltd.)

In March 1945, Oppenheimer split Los Alamos's efforts into two separate projects – "Project Alberta" and "Project Trinity." The same month, another gamble paid off when the first evidence of implosion-produced compression of a solid sphere was observed in a test. By mid-April, Kistiakowsky was sure he had at last achieved optimal results in his sub-scale tests. Another hurdle had passed. To continue the tests with larger-scale cores, in early May the team introduced a Raytheon Mark II X-Unit, protected from the blasts in closely spaced concrete blockhouses, to shoot fast X-rays every ten-millionth of a second to measure the blasts.

TRINITY

Project Trinity was Bainbridge's all-out drive to ready a site to test the Fat Man plutonium-core bomb. Oppenheimer later explained that he had selected the name "Trinity," a choice inspired by poet John Donne – the fourteenth of Donne's *Holy Sonnets* starts: "Batter my heart, three person'd God." The preparations for the test took place at a site selected by Bainbridge after an exhaustive tour of the New Mexico wilderness and approved by Oppenheimer and Groves in the late fall of 1944. The best site would be within a day's drive of Los Alamos, have good weather, and be in as flat an area as possible. The choice was an isolated spot in an area known since Spanish colonial days as the *Jornada del Muerto* (Journey of Death). The test site was an 18 by 24-mile section inside a bombing range of the 2,000-square-mile Alamagordo Air Base. Located 125 miles south of Albuquerque and 30 miles east of the nearest settlement, Carrizozo, then a town of 1,500 inhabitants, the Trinity Site was some 210 miles from Los Alamos. It would be a long day's drive.

There, as a Los Alamos technical history later recounted, Bainbridge raced to "establish under conditions of extreme secrecy and great pressure a complex scientific laboratory in a barren desert."[5] Preparations for the test had languished in late 1944 and early 1945 until the implosion experiments showed promise and the cowpunchers

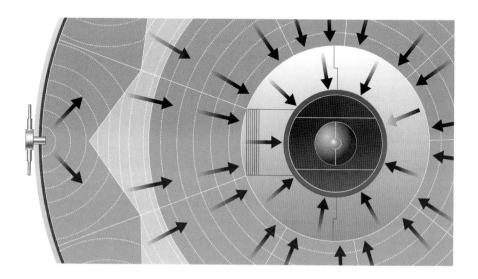

To detonate the plutonium core "Fat Man," shaped charges of fast and slow explosives focused a spherical shock wave to compress the inner components - a beryllium–polonium-210 "initiator" known as the "urchin" and a "pit" of plutonium-239/240. As the metals came into contact, they fissioned and a chain reaction that was controlled and focused by a uranium tamper. About 20% of the pit fissioned, and released energy in the form of a nuclear explosion.

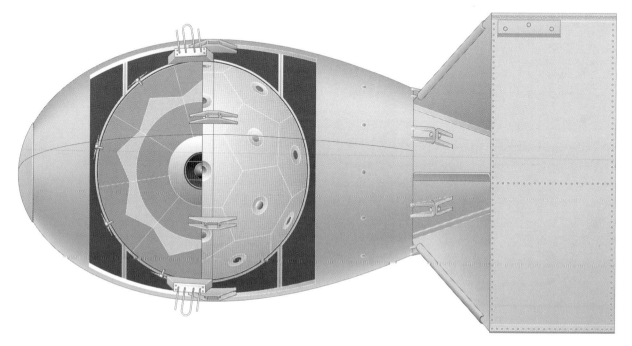

had formed. Spurred on in February 1945, Bainbridge had five months to complete his task before the scheduled date of the test on July 4. Fortunately, preparation of the site had started in December 1944 as workers began to build a series of wood and concrete slab bunkers covered by earth to protect test instruments, motor generators, cameras, and test personnel. A base camp, erected 9 miles southwest of the test site, became the administrative center for the Project Trinity team, with labs, maintenance, repair and support facilities, and living quarters for the military personnel and scientists who worked at the site. By July, the base camp's population had grown to 125 souls who contended with the isolation, heat, alkali-laden water (which forced them to shower with Navy-issue saltwater soap), and an even larger population of scorpions. Boots and shoes needed shaking every morning to liberate unwelcome guests who had crawled into them during the night.

At the test site, Bainbridge selected a flat area termed the "Zero Point" to erect a tower on which the bomb would be detonated. Clustered around Zero were various bunkers. The instrument bunkers were erected 800 yards west and 800 yards north of the Zero Point. Three personnel bunkers were built 10,000 yards from Zero to the north, west, and south. Generator bunkers were built alongside them, and camera bunkers were built next to the north and west personnel bunkers. Later, two more instrument bunkers were built 600 yards northwest and 1,000 yards north, and a small firing bunker was built 500 yards west of Zero Point.

Workers strung nearly 500 miles of communications and signal cables on poles or buried them in trenches to link the various bunkers and instruments. The instruments for measuring the blast's heat, flash, radiation, and shock effects were a diverse assembly of equipment, some of it specially developed at Los Alamos. They included condenser gauges, piston gauges, quartz piezo gauges, crusher gauges, excess velocity gauges, impulse meters, ionization chambers, sulfur threshold detectors, gold foil detectors, gamma ray recorders, electron multiplier chambers, oscilloscopes, coil loudspeaker pickups, geophones, seismographs, spectographs, tracking radar, high-speed cameras, motion picture cameras, and cellophane catcher cameras. While many instruments were placed on the ground at the time of the test, others were suspended from weather balloons or dropped by parachute from observer aircraft.

In May, work on the cross-braced, four-legged steel tower to hold the bomb began. When completed in mid-June, it was 100ft high. At the top was a metal shed to keep the bomb out of the weather. A heavy-duty electrical winch to hoist the bomb up was also installed in the shed. Close by, another tower rose, this one to support a massive steel chamber shaped like a jug. When the test was first proposed, Groves had expressed concern that a pre-detonation would lose the only plutonium the United

States had on hand. A variety of methods to save the plutonium (itself valued in the hundreds of millions of dollars) were studied, among them testing the bomb in water, or burying it beneath a large mound of sand that could then be mined to recover the precious metal in the event of a fizzle. Ultimately, the idea of a massive steel container to hold in the blast prevailed.

The problem was that a steel container big enough to hold the bomb and withstand the detonation of the 5,300lb of high-explosive charges inside the Gadget had never been built before, and contractors approached declined the job until the boiler-making firm of Babcock and Wilcox, in Baberton, Ohio, agreed to take the job. When completed at a cost of over a half million dollars (some accounts claim the actual cost was $12 million), the huge steel jug, nicknamed "Jumbo," was 25ft long and 12ft in diameter. With 14in.-thick steel walls, it weighed 214 tons. Shipped by rail to Pope, New Mexico, crews loaded Jumbo onto a specially designed, 64-wheel trailer that transported it to the Trinity Site. By the time Jumbo arrived, however, confidence in the Gadget was higher, and fear that the atomic blast would vaporize the jug and add its 214 tons of steel to the cloud of nuclear fallout that would follow the blast led to a decision to sidetrack Jumbo. Hoisted halfway up a steel tower 800ft from the Zero Point, Jumbo would bear silent witness to the test.

A third tower, built 800 yards from the Zero Point, was a heavily reinforced wooden platform 20ft high for a pre-atomic test. Known as the "100-ton test," the experiment was intended to test both the detonation of the Gadget and to calibrate the instruments. It used 100 tons of high explosive, packed in cases and stacked atop the tower. To measure the dispersion of radiation, 1,000 curies of radioactive material, produced from a slug sent from Hanford was dispersed in cylinders laced into the stack. The 100-ton test, at the time the world's most powerful explosion, lit up the predawn sky at 04:37:05hrs on May 7. The fireball expanded into an oval before dissipating, and a mushroom cloud of smoke and dust climbed 15,000ft into the desert sky.

The 100-ton test was successful, especially in pointing out logistical and organizational problems such as the need for more people, better communications, and the improvement of the test site's dirt roads, which bogged down vehicles – and hence progress. As a result, 20 miles of roads were paved with asphalt, additional telephone lines and radios were ordered, additional staff were brought in, and a "town hall" was built to better house meetings as the July 4 deadline for the atomic test approached.

By the end of May, enough plutonium had arrived to allow for the final tests of critical mass. Within three weeks, Frisch was able to report that the implosion design would work, and soon after, the lab decided that the bomb would generate a blast somewhere between 4 and 13 kilotons. (A kiloton is the force generated when a

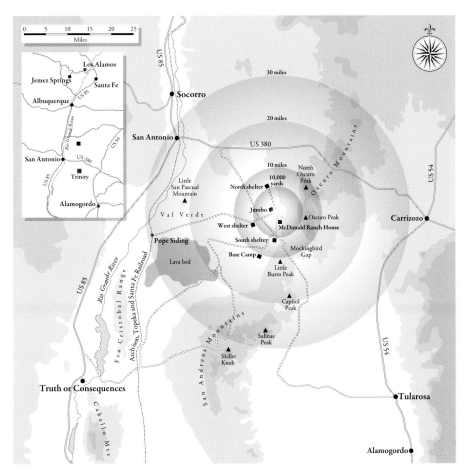

Trinity, where the Manhattan Project first tested the atomic bomb, is in a relatively isolated spot in the New Mexico desert. This map shows the layout of the test site's landmarks. (Artist info)

thousand metric tons of explosive detonates.) A pool was established to take bets on the actual yield, with some scientists betting zero, and others, like an optimistic Edward Teller, suggesting that the yield would be higher at 45 kilotons.

The pool was one means of dealing with the tension everyone felt as the test approached. At that stage, nearly $2 billion had been spent, and reputations were on the line. The war in Europe was over, but the ongoing struggle with Japan continued. A new president, Harry Truman, was in office following Franklin Roosevelt's death on April 12. This change inspired a satirical bit of doggerel that made the rounds of Los Alamos:

> From this crude lab that spawned a dud.
> Their necks to Truman's ax uncurled
> Lo, the embattled savants stood,
> and fired the flop heard round the world.[6]

By June, it was clear that the initial deadline of July 4 could not be met, and a new date, July 16, was set.

At Trinity, final preparations for the test continued up to the day of the shot. After delays caused by inferior castings of high explosive, mostly caused by air bubbles forming inside the explosive as it set, there were not enough lenses ready by July 9. Kistiakowsky, guided by X-ray images, borrowed a dental drill, bored into the castings, and filled the air voids with "molten explosive slurry" to make them acceptable. Enough castings of high explosive were ready on July 10 for the Los Alamos team to begin assembly of two packages, one of which would be fired in a test with a non-fissionable core to see how it worked.

Lieutenant Commander Norris Bradbury, US Navy, one of Parson's team, took on the task of assembling the charges while the plutonium cores were cast. The charges were nestled into place, but despite the careful attention to detail, none fitted tightly. A suggestion to fill the voids with grease was rejected, and instead Bradbury and a team of SED technicians filled the spaces with facial tissue paper and then used Scotch tape to hold the charges together. Equally ingenious and last-minute thinking was also needed with the cores. Coated with nickel to absorb alpha particles and avoid corrosion, the cores soon blistered because plating solution was trapped beneath the nickel and against the plutonium, which gave off heat. The cores required a perfect fit inside the bomb, but stripping the cores was out of the question, as it would expose the plutonium. The blisters were ground down and the irregular surface of the cores was filled with gold foil, leaving each core a brilliant reflective surface.

The core for the Trinity test left Los Alamos on the afternoon of July 12, nestled in the back seat of a US Army Plymouth sedan with scientist Philip Morrison for the long drive to the test site. On arrival, the core was unloaded into the abandoned ranch house of George McDonald, which had lain vacant since the creation of the bombing range in 1942 and the McDonald family's evacuation. The master bedroom, turned into a "clean room" for the bomb's assembly, had its windows sealed with plastic, and now held the workbenches for the scientists and technicians. At Los Alamos, Bradbury's team finished the assembly of the charges into the hemispherical casing of the Gadget, and then lowered a tamper sphere of uranium (which would act as a neutron reflector) inside to fit, as historian Richard Rhodes would later describe it, into the "cavity like the pit in an avocado."[7]

On July 13, just past midnight, an Army 5-ton truck loaded with the high-explosive assembly for the bomb left Los Alamos and drove for eight hours through the night and into the dawn, arriving at Trinity an hour before Bainbridge's team assembled in the McDonald ranch house to start the final assembly. As the cores were laid out,

Lieutenant Commander Norris Bradbury, USN, atop the Trinity tower with the partially assembled Gadget prior to the first test detonation of the atomic bomb. Bradbury, with a doctorate in physics, was in charge of the team that assembled the non-nuclear components of the Gadget. Anxiety was high, and yet Bradbury maintained a sense of humor, writing in his log, "Look for rabbit's feet and four leaf clovers. Should we have the chaplain down here?" (Corbis)

scientist Robert Bacher, the senior advisor, asked the Army for a receipt for the multi-million dollar plutonium that was about to be destroyed. Brigadier General Thomas Farrell, Groves' deputy, signed the receipt:

> I recall that I asked them if I was going to sign for it shouldn't I take it and handle it. So I took this heavy ball in my hand and I felt it growing warm, I got a certain sense of its hidden power. It wasn't a cold piece of metal, but it was really a piece of metal that seemed to be working inside. Then maybe for the first time I began to believe some of the fantastic tales the scientists had told about this nuclear power.[8]

The assembly was ready by the afternoon and the scientists took it by car to the Zero Point, arriving at 03:18hrs to meet up with Bradbury and the rest of the bomb team. Winched off its truck and on skids below the tower, the Gadget was missing one lens, a gap through which the cylindrical plug with the core and its initiator were to fit, tightly, into the heart of the bomb. Everything had been machined to fit perfectly, but as the two assemblies were mated, the plug jammed. As one scientist recalled, consternation reigned until it was pointed out that the core had slightly expanded in the heat of the ranch house overnight, while the rest of the bomb, kept under cover, was cooler. After taking a break to allow the temperatures to equalize, the team found that the pieces fitted together. By late evening, Bradbury had completed the assembly of the bomb, stopping short of inserting the detonators, which would happen the following day after the bomb was winched atop the tower.

On July 14, the team slowly winched the Gadget 100ft up and into the tower, pausing while soldiers piled a stack of mattresses beneath it to cushion the bomb if the winch failed and it fell. Once up, the Gadget's assembly resumed as the detonators were inserted into place, covering the Gadget with an array of wires and plugs. As the assembly progressed, however, bad news came from Los Alamos. The test firing of the other, non-fissionable assembly had produced results that suggested the Trinity bomb would be a dud. Intense discussion, complaints, and several grillings of Kistiakowsky ensued until Hans Bethe reported that a review of the data could not be taken at face value and that a working bomb was still possible if not probable.

By the 15th, everything was at last ready. Tempers were high, tension was perceptible, and Oppenheimer alternately paced, chain-smoked and read as he tried to stay calm. The difficult situation grew worse at 02:00hrs, as a storm hit complete with thunder, lightning, and heavy rain. As the storm continued, Groves postponed

The Gadget detonated at Trinity at 05:29:45hrs on July 15, 1945. A camera captured the world's first atomic explosion at 1/40 seconds. William L. Laurence described it as "a sunrise such as the world had never seen, a great green super-sun climbing in a fraction of a second... lighting up earth and sky all around with a dazzling luminosity." (Los Alamos National Laboratory)

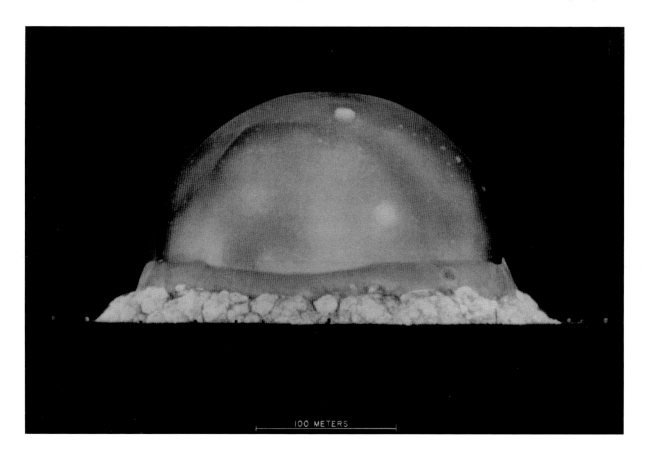

100 METERS

the test to 05:30hrs in the morning when his weather forecaster suggested the storm would end. "You'd better be right on this, or I will hang you," Groves barked.[9]

As test personnel made the last-minute preparations, observers gathered in the bunkers and at a VIP lookout atop Compañia Hill, 20 miles northwest of the Zero Point. At Los Alamos, a group of distant observers hiked and spent the night on a mountain, watching in the distance. Aloft, aircraft stood by with instruments and observers, while at distant places, including a Carrizozo motel room, others waited with instruments. The rain finally stopped and as rockets arced into the darkness to signal the impending shot, and a warning siren wailed, the various groups stood waiting, some hastily slathering on sunblock and donning thick dark glasses to shield them.

Then, at 05:29:45hrs, the Gadget detonated. The world's first nuclear explosion was described by William L. Laurence, the only reporter present:

> …there rose from the bowels of the earth a light not of this world, the light of many suns in one. It was a sunrise such as the world had never seen, a great green super-sun climbing in a fraction of a second to a height of more than eight thousand feet, rising even higher until it reached the clouds, lighting up earth and sky all around with a dazzling luminosity.[10]

Hans Bethe described the detonation as looking "like a giant magnesium flare which kept on for what seemed a whole minute but was actually one or two seconds. The white ball grew and after a few seconds became clouded with dust whipped up by the explosion from the ground and rose and left behind a black trail of dust particles."[11]

The fireball continued to expand, changing colors, followed by a cloud that climbed to 41,000ft as it punched through the clouds above. A "mighty thunder," as Laurence termed it, followed, the ground trembled, and a blast of hot wind swept over the desert, and then came silence punctuated by the exclamations of the assembled scientists and military officials who had watched from a safe distance. The flash and the blast were seen and heard hundreds of miles away.

Determining the force of the bomb was a key aspect of the test. Watching the blast, Enrico Fermi decided to try an informal experiment:

> About 40 seconds after the explosion the air blast reached me. I tried to estimate its strength by dropping from about six feet small pieces of paper before, during, and after the passage of the blast wave. Since, at the time, there was no wind, I could observe very distinctly and actually measure the displacement of the pieces of paper that were in the process of falling while the blast wave was passing. The shift was about 2½ meters,

The Trinity detonation at 15 seconds. The fireball is climbing and expanding, while the cloud from the 18.6 kiloton blast would eventually climb to 41,000 feet. Watching the constantly changing colors as the fireball filled the sky, Oppenheimer thought of the Bhagavad-Gita and Vishnu's terrifying aspect as he assumed his multi-armed form and said "Now I am become Death, the destroyer of worlds." (Los Alamos National Laboratory)

which at the time, I estimated to correspond to the blast that would be produced by ten thousand tons of TNT.[12]

Later, the test instruments showed that the Trinity blast was equivalent to 18.6 kilotons.

As the blast faded, two lead-lined Sherman tanks rumbled to life and drove into the heart of the test area, finding a mile-wide area devoid of life, scorched and swept clean. The tower was gone, leaving only the stubs of its concrete supports. A crater 400 yards in diameter, 25ft deep at the center and tapering up to a 10ft deep depression at the edges, was lined with melted sand that the heat of the explosion had turned into a greenish-gray, highly radioactive glass. Lifted into the fireball and heated to over 14,710°F (8,430°C), the molten glass had rained back into the depression formed by the blast. Termed "Atomsite" and later "Trinitite," the atomic slag was one of many new phenomena observed that morning.

As the bright light faded and the blast echoed, the tension melted. After the cheers stopped, a grim reality set in. "Now we're all sons of bitches," Bainbridge said.[13]

Oppenheimer later recalled, "we knew the world would not be the same. A few people laughed, a few people cried. Most people were silent." He went on:

> I remembered the line from the Hindu scripture, the Bhagavad-Gita: Vishnu is trying to persuade the Prince that he should do his duty and to impress him he takes on his multi-armed formed and says, "Now I am become Death, the destroyer of worlds." I suppose we all thought of that, one way or another.[14]

The incredible display was not lost on the military. General Farrell approached Groves and said, "The war is over." Groves quickly replied, "Yes, after we drop two bombs on Japan."[15] Two days later, over a meal, President Truman and Prime Minister Churchill discussed the success of the joint American-British effort, and agreed to proceed with the combat deployment of the weapon by the Americans as quickly as possible. The bomb was on its way to Japan.

The Trinity blast crater, photographed from the air 28 hours after the test. Four hundred yards in diameter and 25 feet deep, it is coated in radioactive glass formed from fused sand that rained down as a molten rain. The crater from the 100-ton non-atomic test is visible to the lower right. (Los Alamos National Laboratory)

4

DELIVERING THE BOMB

As the Manhattan Project moved closer to developing a working atomic bomb in late 1943, planning for combat deployment of the new weapon began. Despite Einstein's early thinking that an atomic bomb would be too large to be carried aboard an aircraft, developments in both airplane and atomic technology suggested otherwise by the last months of the year. It was clear that the uranium gun bomb would detonate, and Los Alamos scientists and the military were hopeful that a plutonium gun bomb, codenamed "Thin Man," would also work. Accordingly, in October 1943, planning for the delivery and combat use of the weapons began at Los Alamos. One of the first tasks, assigned to a grouping of the Ordnance Division led by scientist Norman Ramsay, was finding an aircraft that could be modified to load and drop atomic bombs.

THE B-29

The aircraft selected was a new long-distance, high-altitude heavy bomber, the B-29. The B-29 "Superfortress" bomber was the response of the Boeing Airplane Company of Seattle, Washington, to a US Army Air Corps (USAAC) Data Request in January 1940 for an aircraft that would serve as a strategic weapon, a very heavy bomber. The sleek, four-engine craft, known as Model 345, came off Boeing's drafting tables as a set of plans delivered to the Army in May 1940. Designated XB-29, the experimental craft then emerged as wind-tunnel models and a full-scale plywood mock-up that impressed the Army sufficiently in May 1941 to order 14 of the model as service test aircraft and 250 production B-29s for combat.

Officially neutral in the rapidly escalating war, the United States was preparing for its inevitable entry into the conflict. In June, as the final design work on the B-29 began in Seattle, President Roosevelt reorganized the Air Corps, merging it with the General Headquarters Air Force to create a more autonomous US Army Air Forces (USAAF), the forerunner of the postwar United States Air Force (USAF). The new USAAF calculated that it would require some 70,000 aircraft for the coming war, and the B-29 was to play a major role as a long-distance heavy bomber. To meet the need for aircraft, the major manufacturers shared the plans for both the B-17 (a four-engine heavy bomber known as the "Flying Fortress") and B-29 bombers to enable mass production on a hitherto unheard of scale. Boeing's planes began to emerge not only from their own factory, but also from the Glenn L. Martin Company, Bell Aircraft, and North American Aviation's factories in Omaha, Nebraska, Kansas City, Missouri, and Marietta, Georgia, with sub-assemblies manufactured by several sub-contractors throughout the country.

The first aircraft rolled out of a Boeing hangar on September 21, 1942. Despite a tragic accident that wrecked a prototype and killed most of its flight crew and military

Shown is in this map are a number of industrial complexes and laboratories that were scattered across the United States. In relative isolation and secrecy, they worked under the control of the top secret Manhattan Project, to develop the atomic bomb. (Artist Info)

observers, the B-29 program pressed forward. By September 1944, there were 647 B-29s in the USAAF's inventory, a number that climbed to 2,242 aircraft by the end of the war the following September. In all, 3,996 B-29s rolled out of Boeing, Bell, and Martin's factory doors. The basic B-29 was 99ft long, with a 141ft 3in. wingspan. Powered by four Wright Cyclone R-3350 radial engines, each with a maximum war emergency horsepower of 2,340, the B-29 flew with a cruising speed of 230mph and a nominal top speed of up to 365mph. Capable of climbing to 31,850ft, the B-29 had a maximum range of between 4,700 and 5,500 miles depending on its load.

The B-29 was built to carry huge payloads of up to 20,000lb of high-explosive and incendiary bombs in tandem, fore, and aft bomb bays. As they rolled out of the factories, the USAAF decided to deploy the aircraft to the Far East and the Pacific, as General Henry H. "Hap" Arnold, the Commanding General of the Air Forces, later explained:

> We did not consider Germany a possible target for the B-29s because we figured that by the time they were ready, the intensive bombardment schedule we were planning with our B-17s and B-24s would have destroyed most of the industrial facilities, the communications systems, and other military objectives within Germany and German-controlled Europe. On the other hand, we figured Japan would be free from aerial bombardment until we could get the B-29s into the picture.[1]

The first B-29 bases outside the United States, therefore, were established in India and then in China, the latter flown in over the Himalayas and built behind enemy lines in the isolated areas still controlled by the Chinese in the spring of 1944. The USAAF's plan was, from mid-1944 when the full production schedule for the B-29 was up and running, to shift to new airbases in the then Japanese-held Marianas Islands to bring the bombers within range of Japan, especially Tokyo. The United States Navy and Marine Corps were tasked with seizing the Marianas, and the invasion of the islands of Saipan, Guam, and Tinian began in July 1944, part of a concerted push that lasted until December. Once those islands were taken, B-29s based there would begin an aerial onslaught to devastate Japan.

In the midst of the rapid build-up and deployment of the Twentieth Air Force, the new air formation devoted entirely to the B-29s with two separate bomber commands within it, the Twentieth and Twenty-First, the Manhattan Project was eyeing the B-29 as *the* plane to carry the atomic bomb to war. In October 1943, when Ramsay's group began their work on selecting an aircraft, the basic dimensions of the bombs Los Alamos planned to build were known – the Thin Man would be 17ft long and

The destruction wrought by firebombing is evident in this aerial view of Osaka, which was leveled by an incendiary raid on March 13, 1945. Robert Haney, an American prisoner of war who survived the attack, described the city as a 25-square-mile "smoldering desert." (Library of Congress)

have a diameter of 23in., and a plutonium core weapon, the Fat Man, would be approximately 9ft long and 59in. in diameter.[2] Only two bombers could handle their size and weight: the B-29 or the British Avro Lancaster, but the Lancaster's bomb bay was determined not to be large enough. It was suggested that "Hap" Arnold had demanded that if an American-built atomic bomb went into combat, an American-built bomber would carry it. Ironically, British-built hardware ultimately carried the atomic bomb in B-29 bomb bays.

By November, Ramsay, working with engineer Sheldon Dike, had selected the B-29. On December 1, 1943, the USAAF ordered Materiel Command at Wright Army Air Field to begin modification of a B-29 that would be flying in from Smoky Hill Army Air Field in Kansas the following day. The directive was titled "Silver Plated Project." In time, it would be shortened into the codename "Silverplate," and the 65 B-29s modified for atomic missions would be known as the Silverplate B-29s. Once modified at Wright to conform to prototype bomb shapes also being shipped to Materiel Command, the first Silverplate B-29 would proceed to Muroc Army Air Field in California for testing. To modify the plane to carry a Thin Man prototype, Materiel Command removed a fuselage structural section between the two 12ft-long bomb bays to make a single, 33ft-long bomb bay with a double set of doors. New

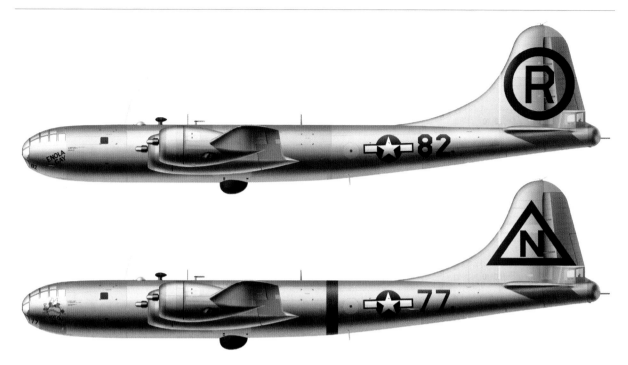

The Manhattan Project needed a special version of the B-29 to create its atomic strike force. Known as the "Silverplate" bombers, the atomic B-29s were a stripped down, faster version with specialized bomb bay doors. Shown here in profile are the two aircraft that dropped atomic bombs in combat, B29-45-MO 44-86292, "Enola Gay," of the 393rd/BS/509th CG, as deployed from North Field, Tinian, August 6, 1945, and B-29-35-MO 44-27297, "Bockscar," of the 393rd BS/509th CG, as deployed from North Field, Tinian, August 9, 1945. Original art by Jim Laurier. (Osprey Publishing)

suspension and release mechanisms for Thin Man and Fat Man bombs were installed, and after more than 6,000 hours of labor, the new Silverplate, itself codenamed "Pullman," flew to California at the end of February 1944.

The first tests began on March 6, and ended on March 16 when a Thin Man bomb released prematurely while the doors were still closed. The crew managed to land the plane safely, and after repairs the plane returned to testing in June. The drops of Thin Man prototypes soon ended, however, with the abandonment of the plutonium gun weapon by Los Alamos, and testing shifted to the Fat Man prototype and to the now nearly completed design for the uranium gun bomb, Little Boy. At 10ft in length and 28in. in diameter, Little Boy was a shorter weapon than the Thin Man. It weighed 9,700lb. The Fat Man, as Los Alamos continued to consider its ultimate configuration, would not change radically in size, but the engineers determined that it would weigh approximately 5 tons, or 10,000lb.

Because the Little Boy and Fat Man bombs could fit into the two-bay configuration of a regular B-29, the aircraft was again modified, with the forward bay set to carry the atomic bomb and the rear bay in the standard B-29 configuration for conventional bombs. The twin, modified glider tow cable attach-and-release mechanisms installed in the plane's first atomic modification, which had failed to work properly in the first tests because the bombs were too heavy, were switched to more reliable British-manufactured Type F release and single-point Type G attachments that did not have the problems of delayed and premature release that had plagued the initial Silverplate mechanisms. With these changes, the Pullman B-29 was returned to the field for further testing in September.

PAUL W. TIBBETS

The Silverplate bombers that followed the first prototype were ordered directly from the Glenn L. Martin Company with the modifications suggested by the Pullman bomber's experience. One of the major issues with all B-29s was engine trouble, and problems with the Pullman's engines had delayed its departure for Muroc. An initial group of 17 aircraft, designated as Project 98146-S, was modified at the Martin plant in Omaha after the order was placed in late August. The first three of the second-phase Silverplate B-29s were ready by October, and were flown to the newly established base for training the newly selected atomic crews.

The commanding officer of the atomic strike force was a carefully selected veteran of the air war in Europe and North Africa, 29-year-old Paul W. Tibbets. Born in Illinois but raised in Iowa and Florida, Tibbets had flown in his first aircraft in 1927 at age 12. Joining the USAAC in 1937, the self-assured, outspoken Tibbets was a superb flier who had risen to the rank of lieutenant colonel through his bravery and command abilities. After a conflict with a superior officer with connections had blocked Tibbets' battlefield promotion to full colonel, Tibbets returned to the United States in February 1943, sent out of the way by friends in high places who knew that Tibbets' abilities as a troubleshooter were needed to move the B-29 project along. Despite the superiority of the aircraft, problems were rife, and the second prototype had just crashed, killing most of the crew. The "big bomber project was a shambles," Tibbets later said.[3]

After a brief stint in Washington, DC, Tibbets was assigned to a new Boeing plant in Wichita, Kansas, to sort out some of the problems. From there, he received new orders to head to Grand Island, Nebraska, to train aircrews in how to fly the B-29. From there he went to Alamogordo for advanced operational training with B-29s. Tibbets had done an excellent job, and the USAAF was pleased with his work, but he was not happy. Following an exciting combat career in Europe and North Africa, Tibbets unequivocally viewed his new assignment in the United States an "emotional letdown."[4] That would change with a summons from General Uzal G. Ent, the commanding officer of the Second Air Force. Tibbets received orders to report to Ent in Colorado Springs.

Arriving at Ent's office on September 1, 1944, Tibbets was first greeted by Lieutenant Colonel John Lansdale, the Army officer assigned to head up security for the Manhattan Project. After a brief conversation in which Lansdale tested Tibbets' honesty by asking him about a youthful encounter with the police, a story Tibbets thought no one knew, but nonetheless confessed to, a satisfied Lansdale took Tibbets into Ent's office. "Deak" Parsons and Norman Ramsay were waiting with the general. Lansdale reported that he was "well satisfied" with Tibbets, and with that Ent told Tibbets he was to be given

Paul Warfield Tibbets, Jr. (1915–2007) was a decorated veteran of the air war in Europe and North Africa. Considered to be the USAAF's best pilot, as well as a man of integrity, Tibbets was selected to test fly the new B-29 Superfortress as the USAAF sought to work out the new bomber's problems. In September 1944, Tibbets received a new command, a top-secret mission to create, train and take into combat the world's first nuclear strike force, a unit that became the 509th Composite Group. Tibbets is shown here in 1945 standing in front of B-29 44-86292, which he named "Enola Gay" in honor of his mother. (The Art Archive)

command of a new, secret combat force that would deliver a "new-type of explosive so powerful that its full potential was still unknown."[5] Ramsay and Parsons then briefed Tibbets on the Manhattan Project and what Tibbets was being asked to do. One problem was specifically developing a method for getting the B-29 to a safe point 8 miles away from the detonation of a bomb. Tibbets calculated that at best a plane would be only 6 miles away after dropping a bomb, but he was confident he could find a solution.

To do his job, the USAAF was assigning an initial force of 15 planes and, in time, more aircraft and 1,768 men. A base, "the farther from civilization the better," would also be provided.[6] Three isolated airfields were available; Tibbets would inspect them and choose one. He would also pick his crews, starting with an available unit, the 393rd Bomb Squadron, then in training at Harvard, Nebraska. The 393rd met with Tibbets' approval, and after inspection he chose Wendover Field in northwestern Utah as his base. Isolated in the middle of salt flats, and with the closest town a small community of a hundred people, Wendover had been a P-47 training base that was in the process of being phased out. Tibbets wasted no time. He established his office on the base on September 8, a week after his meeting with Ent, Parsons, and Ramsay, and only three days later the planes and crews of the 393rd arrived.

From Wendover, backed by the power of the Manhattan Project, Tibbets reached out to select officers and crews "whose superior skills I recognized." Martin delivered the first batch of 17 modified Silverplates in October and November. In time, the force at Wendover grew as 28 more aircraft with additional modifications were delivered and a detachment of 51 scientists and technicians from Los Alamos also joined the 393rd. They were there to participate in the Los Alamos drop test program and to take the bomb into combat with the airmen. In early 1945, as the Trinity test loomed on the horizon and Little Boy was in final preparation, construction crews built weapons assembly and handling facilities and bomb loading pits at Wendover.

On December 17, 1944, Tibbets received orders activating his new command as the 509th Composite Group, a unique self-contained "individual air force" that incorporated all of the support elements it required to fly, maintain, and equip itself. The 509th's organizational structure was:

- Headquarters, 509th Composite Group, the command element.
- 393rd Bombardment (Very Heavy) Squadron, the combat arm of the 509th.
- 320th Troop Carrier Squadron, the air transportation arm of the 509th, flying personnel and equipment in C-46, C-47, and C-54 aircraft.
- 390th Air Service Group, which included the Headquarters and Base Services Squadron, the 603rd Air Engineering Squadron, and the 1027th Air Materiel

Squadron. They oversaw the base's housing, food, finance, personnel and administration, aircraft maintenance and repair, equipment maintenance and repair, and supply.

- 1395th Military Police Company, a force of 133 men who were responsible for the security of the base, aircraft, and the bombs.

In March 1945, the 1st Ordnance Squadron (Special Aviation) joined the 509th to assemble and handle the atomic bombs. They worked closely with the Los Alamos personnel assigned to the 509th, themselves formally designated the 1st Technical Services Detachment.

With his organizational structure set, aircraft and crews in place, and orders in hand, Tibbets set about molding the 509th into a fighting unit and developing the tactics for atomic attacks using the B-29 over the next four months.

"PUMPKINS" AND TRAINING

The newly modified Silverplates featured two bomb bays, the forward bay for atomic bombs, the aft bay configured for additional fuel tanks. A "weaponeer station" was added to the cockpit for the officer who would monitor the bomb in flight and as it fell and detonated. Another modification, stripping most of the guns and armor off the planes, shed 7,000lb of weight. That would speed up the aircraft and enable it to climb higher, all necessary in Tibbets' quest to outrace the bomb's blast. The original engines of the B-29s were not sufficient, and so they were switched to fuel-injected Wright R-3350-41 "Duplex-Cyclone" engines with reversible-pitch propellers that enabled the planes to decelerate in the air or when landing, and to taxi backwards. Also added were pneumatic actuators that quickly snapped the bomb bay doors open and shut.

With his planes modified to better perform their intended missions, Tibbets turned to his crews. His two major concerns were accuracy in dropping the bomb, and flying beyond the reach of the blast. Training for accuracy meant dropping test bombs. The goal was to drop a bomb from 30,000ft and hit a 40ft-diameter target – and not to miss it by more than 200ft. The 509th began training with conventional target bombs, but soon switched to the specially designed "dummy" bombs developed by the Los Alamos team to simulate the size and weight of the anticipated Fat Man weapon. Three separate versions of the ellipsoidal Fat Man shape were developed and tested. Welded into shape from ⅛in. steel, the 10,525lb bombs were packed with concrete or plaster (and occasionally high explosives) and were 128in. long and 60in. in diameter. Because of their shape, the dummy bombs were quickly dubbed "pumpkins," a name they kept throughout and after the war.

Problems with wobbling and accuracy with the first test bombs led to a new design for the tail fin, a box-structure with baffles made of riveted aluminum that restricted airflow and improved the bomb's ballistics. Intensive training, with more than 200 drops of "pumpkins," honed the skills of the 509th's bombardiers. Tibbets also developed a solution and training to deal with the other problem of distance. Given the speed of a B-29, it would take two minutes to fly 8 miles. If a bomb were dropped from 31,000ft, it would fall for 43 seconds before detonating approximately 2,000ft off the ground. The shock wave from the blast, traveling at the speed of sound, or 1,100ft per second, would take another 40 seconds to travel 8 miles. If the B-29 kept flying straight, it would be impossible to travel 8 miles in 83 seconds.

To avoid the effects of the blast, Tibbets developed a maneuver to push his aircraft past the 8-mile range of a detonation. His strategy was to dive and sharply turn the plane once the bomb dropped, facing the aircraft 180 degrees away from the aiming point. The 155-degree turn was a strain on the aircraft as well as a maneuver that required training and skill, but if done properly it would work. If properly executed, the turn would place the plane 6 miles away, with a slant-line distance of 8 miles. The problem solved, the Tibbets maneuver was another intensive aspect of training drilled into the 509th's pilots.[7] Another aspect of training was the challenge of navigating long distances over water and then land, so Tibbets arranged for long-range flights to Cuba's Batista Field, near Havana, sending five B-29s at a time for ten-day-long missions over the Caribbean, making bombing runs on a number of small islands that allowed the pilots to train in the difficult task of shifting from over-water to over-land flying.[8]

PROJECT ALBERTA

As the 509th trained, and as the push for a successful implosion weapon continued at Los Alamos, the "homestretch," as Parsons termed it in a memorandum to Oppenheimer in February 1945, led to the formation of the powerful Cowpuncher Committee and then, in March, Project Alberta, a match to Bainbridge's Project Trinity. Parsons, as head of Alberta, was tasked with getting the bombs turned into weapons that had the proper ballistics to drop on target. He also had responsibility for developing the best methods for meeting several challenges: detonating the bombs after dropping them from an aircraft; getting the bombs and their components safely delivered to an overseas advance base; assembling them there; loading them into the planes; and before then, testing the non-atomic aspects of the bombs, which included loading "pumpkins" with high explosive and dropping them.

Parsons drew together a team of scientists and technicians as well as military personnel for Project Alberta, with Norman Ramsay as his scientific and technical deputy and naval officer Commander Frederick L. "Dick" Ashworth as his operations officer and military second-in-command. Ashworth, the senior aviator at the Navy's Dahlgren Proving Ground, was a recent arrival pulled out of Dahlgren in November and assigned to Wendover to replace Ramsay as the direct technical supervisor of the Los Alamos test program with the 509th. Living in Los Alamos, Ashworth commuted via air to Wendover, and soon got to know the 509th and its men as well as the technical aspects of his job.

Parsons and Ramsay quickly organized their bomb assembly needs – prefabricated buildings, heavy equipment, hand tools, etc. into "kits," or single-item (on a shipping inventory) packages for shipment via rail and naval transports overseas. Everything was done in triplicate for back-up. Parsons, a meticulous planner, also analyzed the potential effect of the bombs to determine the best height for detonation for maximum effect. Hard working and focused, Parsons personally visited the site of a massive explosion that took place on July 17, 1944, when 1,500 tons of high explosives and tons of shells accidentally detonated at Port Chicago, a naval ammunition loading facility on San Francisco Bay. Parsons would later fly as an observer on a B-29 to watch the Trinity test, and made it clear to Groves that he wished to take the bomb into combat himself, to make sure it all worked to plan.

Project Alberta's planning was necessary to take the bomb to the Pacific along with the 509th, and from a forward base in the Marianas to strike at Japan. Even as Tibbets assembled his planes and pilots and began training, the Marianas fell to American forces. In June 1944, the US Navy and the US Marine Corps hit the Marianas, striking Saipan before invading Guam and Tinian. Saipan fell on July 9 with approximately 29,000 Japanese and 16,500 American casualties. The American presence in the Marianas drew out the Imperial Japanese Navy, and in the resulting battles of the Philippine Sea on June 19–21, the US Navy achieved decisive naval victories that crippled the Japanese fleet. The invasion of Guam, a prewar US base, took place on July 21, and effectively ended on August 8. Tinian, the last of the three major islands in the Marianas, offered fierce resistance, and the Marines landed in the face of heavy fire on July 24. Aided by P-47 aircraft that dropped napalm on the Japanese defenders, but facing fierce combat, the Marines secured Tinian on August 1, although there, as with the other islands, isolated pockets of Japanese held out for the remainder of the war.

With the fall of the Marianas, the Twenty-First Bomber Command built new bases to extend their striking power into the heart of Japan. Previously, the Indian and Chinese based B-29 bombers could only attack Kyushu, Japan's southernmost island. From the Marianas, the industrial heartland of Japan, as well as the capital, Tokyo, was now in

OPPOSITE:
Starting in late 1944, the US Army Air Forces used the newly developed B-29s to deliver the first large-scale aerial attacks against Japanese cities. Under the command of General Curtis LeMay, the Twenty-First Bomber Command launched high explosive and incendiary raids that laid waste to some 67 Japanese cities, killing more than half a million and leaving some five million Japanese homeless. In this aerial image taken during a B-29 attack, Tokyo burns on the evening of May 26, 1945. (Library of Congress)

range. The first B-29s to arrive in the Marianas landed at Saipan on October 12, 1944, to escalate the air war. After a photo reconnaissance flight over Tokyo on November 1, the first raid hit Tokyo with limited results due to high winds and the bombers being blown off target.

High-altitude bombing with high-explosive bombs continued to be the Twenty-First's principal tactic, but the reassignment of a hard-driving, cigar-chomping new commander, Curtis LeMay, would see a shift in tactics. Relieving the Twentieth's

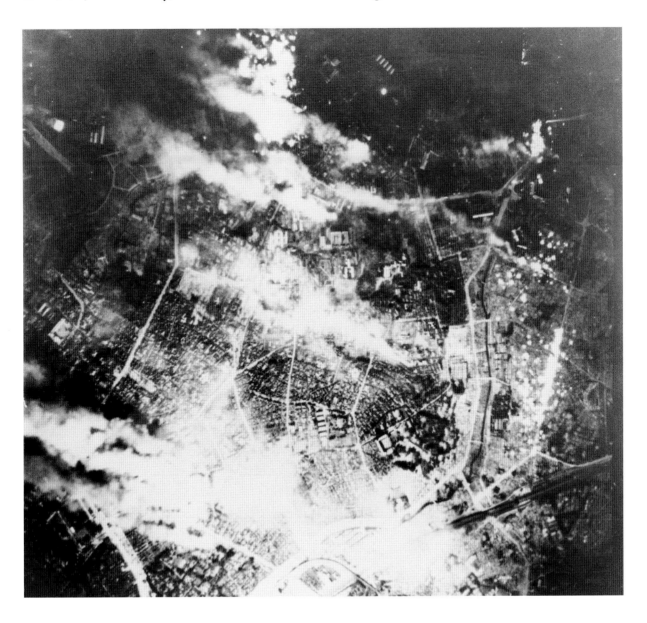

previous commander, Brigadier Haywood Hansell, Jr., on January 20, 1945, LeMay paid close attention to the horrific results of the fire-bombing of Dresden in February. He also weighed the risks to his men and planes against the tremendous sacrifices being made by the US Navy and Marines as they assaulted Iwo Jima in the face of *kamikaze* attacks and the fierce resistance of the Japanese Army, which lost nearly all of their 20,000 defenders while killing over 6,000 Marines and wounding nearly 22,000 others.

LeMay decided that Japanese anti-aircraft fire was not as well organized or effective as air crews were facing over Germany, and that low-altitude flights with planes loaded with incendiary bombs could bring about the Twenty-First's combat objective of wrecking Japanese industry, and breaking the enemy's morale by destroying cities. As the fighting continued on Iwo Jima, on March 9 he launched an incendiary attack against Tokyo with 325 planes loaded with newly developed M69 napalm bombs. Arriving over the city in the darkness of the early morning of March 10, the B-29s unleashed a rain of destruction from the air. When the fires burned themselves out, more than a quarter of a million buildings were gone in a 16.8-square-mile area, and some 83,000 to 100,000 Japanese were dead.[9] Following the attack on Tokyo, Le May's planes struck Nagoya, Osaka, and Kobe. By the end of March, 1,505 sorties by the Twenty-First had hit Japan with millions of pounds of incendiaries. It was, LeMay later said, the beginning of the end for the Japanese. It also marked a new emphasis of the war, as noted by a USAAF spokesman, "the entire population of Japan is a proper military target."[10] By the time of the war's end, over nine million Japanese were homeless, 58 major cities had been devastated, with a loss of more than two million structures, and more than 700,000 had been killed.[11]

SELECTING A FORWARD BASE AND TARGETS

In April, as the air war intensified, the 509th began preparations to head to the Pacific. The war in Europe was drawing to a close, and despite Tibbets' initial thought that his force would divide into two wings, it was increasingly clear that the 509th would carry their new weapon only against Japan. That April, Tibbets set orders in motion to shift planes and crews to Tinian to spur the Manhattan Project into action as the race to meet the deadline for the Trinity test continued. Even as the 509th began to pack, major decisions about their ultimate mission began to emerge.

The death of President Roosevelt on April 12 brought Harry Truman into office. Truman was unaware of the atomic bomb, and on the evening of the 12th, as he took office, Secretary of War Henry L. Stimson briefly told the new President, as Truman later recalled, "about an immense project that was underway – a project looking to the development of a new explosive of almost unbelievable destructive power." Truman learned more from James L. "Jimmy" Byrnes, another Roosevelt confidante, who assured Truman that the "bomb might well put us in a position to dictate our own terms at the end of the war."[12]

After a full briefing by Stimson and General Groves on April 25, two days later an initial meeting of a "Target Committee" to determine where the atomic bomb would be dropped in Japan convened in Washington, DC, at the Pentagon. Groves outlined the priority for selecting which cities to bomb with the new weapon:

> …the targets chosen should be places the bombing of which would most adversely affect the will of the Japanese people to continue the war. Beyond that, they should be military in nature, consisting either of important headquarters or troop concentrations, or centers of production of military equipment and supplies. To enable us to assess accurately the effects of the bomb, the targets should not have been previously damaged by air raids. It was also desirable that the first target be of such size that the damage would be confined within it, so that we could more definitely determine the power of the bomb.[13]

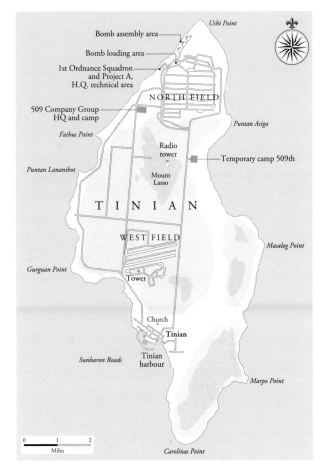

The initial list of target cities under consideration included Yokohama, Nagoya, Osaka, Kobe, Hiroshima, Kokura, Fukuoka, Nagasaki, and Sasebo. It was noted, however, that not all of these would be ideal atomic targets, as the Twenty-First Bomber Command, with a mission of "laying waste [to] all the main Japanese cities," was "systematically bombing out the following cities with the prime purpose in mind of not leaving one stone lying on another: Tokyo, Yokohama, Nagoya, Osaka, Kyoto, Kobe, Yawata & Nagasaki." Yet "Hiroshima is the largest untouched target not on the 21st Bomber Command priority list. Consideration should be given to this city."[14]

The surrender of Germany on May 7 had no effect on the atomic planning – the realization that the Germans did not possess a workable bomb and that the Nazi nuclear effort had stalled, as well as the devastation of Europe, had shifted the emphasis to Japan months earlier. Truman, meanwhile, had approved a larger group, an "Interim Committee" of senior advisors including Vannevar Bush, James B. Conant, Karl Compton, and his

Project Alberta and the 509th facilities on Tinian, where the bombs dropped on Japan were prepared and loaded on to the B-29's. This depiction is based on maps prepared by Project Alberta veteran Harlow Russ. (Artist Info)

soon-to-be-named Secretary of State, Jimmy Byrnes, to advise him on the uses of the bomb. The Interim Committee met for the first time on May 9. One of their first actions was to suggest that a Scientific Panel be formed to advise them. It was suggested that the group be formed with Arthur Compton, Oppenheimer, Ernest Lawrence, and Enrico Fermi as members. That same day, scientist D. M. Dennison, a member of Parsons' team, completed a report on the general procedures for the atomic bombing of Japan. He stressed a range of six days to conduct operations, careful assessment of the weather, the use of visual bombing rather than radar, and the importance of rehearsal runs. This set the stage for 509th sorties over Japan that became known as the "pumpkin missions."

Meanwhile, the Target Committee, now joined by Oppenheimer, Parsons, Richard Tolman, and Norman Ramsay, who served as advisors, met at Los Alamos on May 10–11. Joined by Hans Bethe and Robert Brode for some of the discussions, the group debated a detailed agenda Oppenheimer had assembled, examining how powerful the bomb would be, the best altitude to detonate it, operational considerations, and a list of objectives, including psychological factors in target selection, use against military objectives, and radiological effects. The list of targets had narrowed to Kyoto, Hiroshima, Yokohama, Niigata, and Kokura Arsenal.

The Interim Committee met again on May 14 and 18. The committee's deliberations did not involve America's British allies, an action that was part of the increased American emphasis on security. This mindset was also clear in the discussion over sharing the secret with the Soviet Union, ostensible allies – which was rejected. Also discussed was the role of the bomb in a postwar world. As political implications were debated, a group of scientists led by Leó Szilárd lobbied Byrnes unsuccessfully not to begin what would amount, in their estimation, to a nuclear arms race with the Soviet Union, which they felt would soon have a bomb. Meanwhile, the logistical considerations of bombing continued. The Target Committee, now joined by Tibbets, met again on May 28. Spurred by LeMay's continued success in devastating Japan, the committee narrowed the target list to Hiroshima, Niigata, and Japan's ancient capital of Kyoto. Secretary Stimson, in the wake of another successful raid on Tokyo, which burned out another 16 square miles, called Groves into his office on May 30 to review the target list. With a fretful Groves standing by, aware that the report had not yet been sent up through the chain of command, Stimson bridled at the recommendation that Kyoto be targeted. Mindful of its historical, architectural, and cultural significance, Stimson took Kyoto off the list.

The following day, the Interim Committee, after considerable deliberation and discussion on the moral implications of the bomb, and whether the United States should warn Japan, overruled Stimson's concerns over the destruction of entire cities at Byrne's urging. With Stimson out of the meeting, Byrnes pushed for a "final decision on the question of the use of the weapon" that he would take to the President.[15] That decision was, as Byrnes recommended:

> …and the committee agreed, that the Secretary of War should be advised that, while recognizing that the final selection of the target was essentially a military decision, the present view of the committee was that the bomb should be used against Japan as soon as possible; that it be used on a war plant surrounded by workers' homes, and that it be used without prior warning.[16]

Regardless of the fact that only Little Boy was available as a workable weapon, and the Trinity test was six weeks away, the United States had by then embarked on an unswerving course to use the bomb, and a precedent had been established in which the bomb's deployment was a political process, not a military one. Byrnes, formally invested as Secretary of State on July 3, would take that approach with him to Potsdam as Truman's closest advisor when the President met with Winston Churchill and Joseph Stalin to set the stage for the last acts of the war and the immediate postwar world. While at Potsdam, the report of the successful Trinity test, when it reached the US delegation, brought both relief and determination; feelings shared by Winston Churchill when Truman privately briefed the Prime Minister. Churchill later noted that while the decision was Truman's, as the Americans had the weapon, he had approved of its use against Japan, and that in their discussion that day the question of whether or not to use the bomb had never been raised. There was "unanimous, automatic, unquestioned agreement."[17] The final preparations for carrying the bomb into the Pacific for the 509th to drop it on Japan were underway, and within three weeks the first attack was scheduled.

A vaguely worded exchange between Truman and Stalin over the fact that the United States now had a "new weapon of unusual destructive force" and Stalin's rejoinder that he was glad and hoped that they would "make good use of it against the Japanese,"[18] masked the fact that Stalin was aware of the Manhattan Project thanks to Soviet espionage and had ordered a Soviet atomic program. While still at Potsdam, Truman decided to proceed with the atomic bombing, noting in his diary on July 25 that while this was "the most terrible bomb in the history of the world," it would be used:

> between now and August 10th… The target will be a purely military one and we will issue a warning statement asking the Japs to surrender and save lives. I'm sure they will not do that, but we will have given them the chance. It is certainly a good thing for the world that Hitler's crowd or Stalin's did not discover this atomic bomb. It seems to be the most terrible thing ever discovered, but it can be made the most useful.[19]

Atomic strike routes, to and from
Tinian and Japan, August 1945.
(Artist Info)

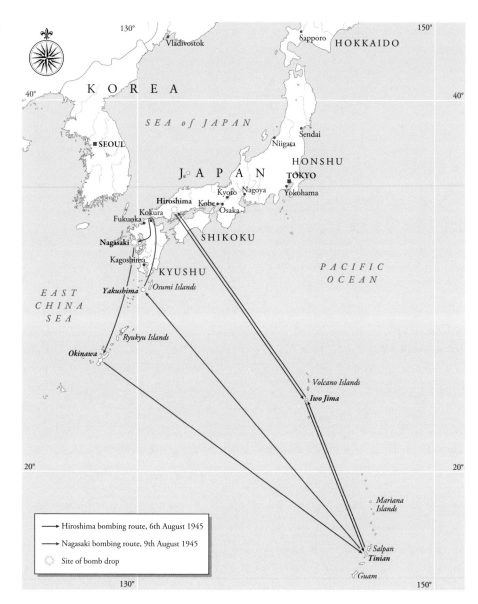

On July 26, as the last components for Little Boy and Fat Man made their way to the Pacific, the Allied leaders issued the Potsdam Declaration, stating the terms for Japan's surrender. It ended with "We call upon the government of Japan to proclaim now the unconditional surrender of all Japanese armed forces," warning that "the alternative for Japan is prompt and utter destruction."[20] LeMay's fire-bombing raids, a planned invasion, Operation *Olympic*, and the atomic missions of the 509th were all calculated parts of the plan for utter destruction.

HIROSHIMA

As Los Alamos raced to complete Little Boy and test Fat Man, and while officials debated where and how to use the atomic bomb, Paul Tibbets and the 509th prepared to go to war. In April 1945, frustrated by the "endless hassling" as the Los Alamos team debated how best to build the Trinity bomb and ruminated over whether it would even work, Tibbets decided to "get moving," as he later explained. "A load of responsibility had been thrown on my shoulders and I decided to exercise the authority that went with it."[1] Without any orders to do so, Tibbets transmitted the secret codeword that triggered the command to ship the 509th overseas. Groves called Tibbets to Washington, reprimanded him, and then quietly and privately acknowledged that Tibbets had "got us moving."

The destination of the 509th was Tinian, now the base for the Twenty-First Bomber Command. In February, Parson's deputy, Commander Ashworth, had flown to the Marianas to deliver a letter from Fleet Admiral Ernest J. King to Admiral Chester L. Nimitz, the commander of the Pacific Fleet. After a long and hot 48-hour flight to Guam, Ashworth arrived soaked in sweat with a "disheveled uniform." Underneath his shirt was a money belt in which Ashworth had concealed the letter. Called into Nimitz's office, Ashworth waited until the admiral's aide left and then "unbuttoned the jacket of my more or less disheveled looking khaki uniform, unbuttoned my shirt and removed from around my waist the fairly well-soaked money belt that contained the letter, all to the amusement of the admiral."[2]

The letter was to the point:

It is expected that a new weapon will be ready in August of this year for use against Japan by the 20th Air Force. The Officer, Commander Frederick L. Ashworth, USN, bearing this letter will give you enough details so that you can make the necessary plans for the proper support of the operations. By the personal direction of the President, everything pertaining to this development is covered by the highest order of secrecy, and there should be no disclosure by you beyond one other officer, who must be suitably cautioned. I desire that you make available to Commander Ashworth such intelligence data as applies to the utilization of the new weapon.[3]

After delivering the letter and securing Nimitz's support, Ashworth evaluated Guam and then flew to Tinian. Project Alberta's team had armed him with a checklist of questions to make sure the advance base in the Marianas would suit their needs. He was to assess weather, terrain, the base's layout and facilities, the ease of transportation, and issues such as the presence of malaria, fungus, and the "amount of ground strafing and bombing."[4] After rejecting Guam as the advance base for the 509th, Ashworth was satisfied that Tinian would work, largely because it was closer by a hundred miles, which could make a critical difference in a fuel-strapped, heavily loaded B-29, and it had existing runways 8,500ft long. Returning to Los Alamos, Ashworth reported back to Parsons and attended a meeting with Oppenheimer and Tibbets to confirm the choice. A detachment of 51 (later increased to 54) Los Alamos scientists and technicians volunteered to go to Tinian and work under Ashworth to assemble and handle the bombs, including loading and flying on the missions as the atomic weaponeers. Officially designated the 1st Technical Service Detachment, they were instead known as the "Destination Team."

The advance base's location was a secret and until the team was dispatched, all they knew it as was the "destination," which became the codename for Tinian. When Tibbets made his unilateral decision to jump-start getting his planes and pilots into the Pacific, Project Alberta began preparations to transport the Destination Team. To move the 509th, Tibbets had to both fly in the planes and send men and supplies by ship. The first shipment of material and men left Wendover at the end of April. The majority of Tibbets' crews arrived at Seattle by rail and were loaded into the waiting Army troop transport SS *Cape Victory* on May 6.

Meanwhile the advance air echelon of the 509th, including Tibbets, flew via California and Hawaii, arriving at Tinian's North Field on May 18. *Cape Victory* arrived on May 29. The remainder of the B-29s and their crews landed at Tinian on June 11. The next three months, Tibbets later recalled, "were among the most frenzied of my military career" as the 509th moved into its advance base, isolated from the rest of the

B-29 crews of the Twenty-First, and began training. Among the issues confronting the 509th was friction between Tibbets and his men with other airmen who were excluded, because of security, from knowing just what the 509th was to do, and resentful of their autonomy and special status. The 509th, apparently, did not do much to counter any resentment. LeMay, although himself privy to the atomic secret, later complained, "The men of the 509th – according to the 509th – were something special. They were the second coming of Christ, and they thought they were supposed to have everything."[5]

"Taunts and jibes," Tibbets noted, followed the 509th as they trained, with a response from some in the 509th that they were there to "win the war." The next salvo was a mimeographed poem, sent around the Twenty-First Bomber Command (and to the 509th) entitled "Nobody Knows":

> Into the air the secret rose,
> Where they're going, nobody knows.
> Tomorrow they'll return again,
> But we'll never know where they've been.
> Don't ask us about results or such,
> Unless you want to get in Dutch.
> But take it from one who is sure of the score,
> The 509th is winning the war.
>
> When the other groups are ready to go,
> We have a program on the whole damned show.
> And when Halsey's Fifth shells Nippon's shore,
> Why, shucks, we hear about it the day before.
> And MacArthur and Doolittle give out in advance,
> But with this new bunch we haven't a chance.
> We should have been home a month or more,
> For the 509th is winning the war.[6]

Undaunted, the 509th went about their training, starting with what Tibbets termed routine orientation flights and dropping conventional bombs on enemy-occupied islands, including the Imperial Japanese Navy base at Truk, as well as Rota, Marcus, and Guguan. On July 20, the 509th went to Japan for the first time, flying a series of missions to familiarize themselves with the route and terrain, and to practice with explosive-filled "pumpkins" that they dropped on Japanese cities. In 12 separate combat missions between July 20 and the 29th, the 509th's sorties of ten aircraft (except for eight planes on the 29th) hit Toyama, Ogaki, Shimoda, Yokkaichi, Fukushima, Niihama, Yaizu, Ube, Kobe, Tokyo, Otsu, Tsugawa, Maizuru, Taira, Osaka, Hamamatsu, Wakayama, Koriyama, Hitachi, Kashiawzaki, and Mushashino with "pumpkins" dropped from 30,000ft. According to Tibbets, one of the pilots, Major Claude E. Eatherly and the crew of B-29 44-27301 "Straight Flush," flew into Tokyo, could not see their targets because of cloud cover, and dropped a bomb by radar on the Imperial Palace. It missed and hit the already ruined Marunouchi railway station near the palace. Eatherly, an excellent pilot but prone to stunts, escaped punishment for trying to bomb a forbidden target, but after the war he caused Tibbets and the 509th much grief when, following his arrest and imprisonment on charges of forgery and breaking and entering, he proclaimed he was committing what he termed "petty crimes" to publicize his guilt for his role in the atomic attacks. Until his death in 1978, Eatherly was a controversial and tragic figure.

PREPARING TO DROP THE BOMB

The shipment of the Destination Team's equipment and facilities was scheduled to arrive at Tinian around June 20, and an "advance party" of four representatives from Project Alberta were sent out on June 17 to meet the shipment. One of them was Harlow W. Russ, a former aeronautical engineer from Lockheed who had joined the project in 1944 to work on the bomb casings. The success of the Trinity test was an uncertainty, but Parsons told Russ before he left that regardless of Trinity's results, Little Boy "would be used in combat and would be used in advance of any Fat Man mission" and that it needed to be ready for use before August 1.[7]

The advance party arrived at Tinian on June 23 to find the bomb assembly and loading facilities 80 percent complete and, as Russ discovered in a briefing, that some 500 Japanese survivors of the battle for Tinian were holed up and hiding on the island. The Little Boy facilities were completed on July 1, and between July 3 and 5 the advance party supervised the transfer and unpacking of the Little Boy assembly equipment. The Fat Man area was completed on July 7, and by the 9th, the Fat Man equipment was in place. Trinity was still a week away, and Tinian was ready for the arrival of the Destination Team and the bombs. With the completion of the Fat Man area, the 509th was at last ready to begin "pumpkin" missions, as the loading pits for hoisting the large bombs into the B-29s had been completed along with the rest of the compound. The pits were necessary because the 5ft-diameter bombs could not fit under the 3ft clearance of a B-29 when it was parked.

After Trinity, the rest of the Destination Team arrived at Tinian, as the focus of the Manhattan Project shifted to the island. By the end of July the Little Boy and Fat Man teams, the project leaders, Parsons and Ramsey, and two military observers, Groves's deputy Brigadier General Farrell and Admiral William R. Purnell, were ready. Tibbets and the 509th continued their practice bombing runs over Japan and the Destination Team worked with the 509th to assemble, load, and drop test models of the two atomic bombs as training exercises.

The first tests used Little Boy models numbered L-1, L-2, and L-5 to test fusing and firing systems. Those drops were made on July 23, 24, and 25 respectively. The next test, with model L-6, was a "dry-run" with a complete and active Little Boy missing only its sub-critical components. The test also involved landing, unloading, and loading the bomb at recently conquered Iwo Jima, where an alternative facility had been built as a back-up. The L-6 test took place between July 29 and 31st, as the bomb was flown to and from Iwo Jima and twice unloaded and loaded in an exchange between two B-29s, one flying as a stand-by, to train the crews in a transfer should the aircraft carrying the nuclear-armed Little Boy be unable to complete the mission and have to abort. The bomb was then dropped into the sea off Tinian and detonated. The Project Alberta team and the 509th were ready to take the atomic bomb into combat.

The cruiser USS *Indianapolis* (CA-35), photographed by Major Harley G. Toomey, Jr., USAF, as it left Tinian after delivering the components for "Little Boy," c. July 26, 1945. Four days later, the Japanese submarine I-58 torpedoed and sank *Indianapolis*, killing most of the crew. (US Naval History and Heritage Command Photograph)

On the day of the Trinity test, July 16, the U-235 pre-assemblies and the projectile that would be fired inside Little Boy to detonate the bomb were loaded onto the cruiser USS *Indianapolis* at Hunters Point Naval Shipyard in San Francisco. The cruiser also carried a 10,000lb crate loaded with the inert parts "for a complete gun type bomb."[8] The projectile was carried in a lead cylinder inside a steel container known as the "bucket" that traveled padlocked to the steel deck of a ship's cabin. On the 26th, three C-54s from Tibbets' "Green Hornet" planes flew out of Kirtland Air Field in New Mexico with the U-235 target rings that the projectile would fire into. After long flights to the west coast, Hawaii, Johnston Island, and Kwajalein, they landed at Tinian on July 28. Also on the 28th, the Japanese government rejected the Potsdam Declaration's demand for an unconditional surrender.

Fat Man's plutonium core and initiator also came by plane, landing on the 28th. The high-explosive pre-assemblies of Fat Man, shipped from Kirtland the same day, arrived at Tinian on August 2. Fat Man test drops began on July 29, and on August 1 Fat Man test unit F13 was dropped. The next unit, F18, was completed by August 4 and the 509th dropped it the following day. With the arrival of the high-explosive sub-assemblies, the team prepared model F33 for a full dry-run test and detonation, but the test did not take place until after the first combat mission with Little Boy.

THE FLIGHT OF THE "ENOLA GAY"

The order to drop the bomb was issued on July 25 by General Thomas Handy, acting Chief of Staff, authorizing the 509th to "deliver its first special bomb as soon as weather will permit visual bombing" after August 3 against one of four targets – Hiroshima, Kokura, Niigata, and Nagasaki.[9] The final assembly of the combat Little Boy, L-11, was completed on July 31. The team was ready to go, but bad weather over Japan delayed the mission until August 6.

Tibbets, previously kept out of the skies over Japan because he was too valuable to lose, had decided, with the approval of his superiors, to command the mission and fly the B-29 that would drop the bomb. He borrowed aircraft 44-86292, a B-29 ordinarily flown by Robert Lewis. For the mission, Lewis joined Tibbets in the cockpit. Tibbets also replaced the bombardier and navigator with two officers he had earlier handpicked for the 509th, Thomas Ferebee and Theodore "Dutch" van Kirk, both of whom had flown with Tibbets' B-17 crew earlier in the war. The final crew of the Hiroshima mission was Tibbets, Lewis, Van Kirk, Ferebee, Parsons, who flew as the bomb commander or "weaponeer," flight engineer Wyatt Duzenbury, assistant engineer Robert Shumard, radio operator Richard Nelson, radar operator Joseph

Stiborik, tail gunner George Caron, electronic counter-measures officer Jacob Beser, and electronics test officer and assistant weaponeer Morris Jeppson.

On the evening of August 4, Parsons watched in horror as the evening combat sorties of the Twenty-First's bombers lifted off on another mission to Japan. Four B-29s in a row had failed to lift off and crashed into a flaming mass of wreckage at the end of the runway. Accidents like this were not uncommon, and in the morning, as word came that the weather was lifting and the atomic mission would take off on the 6th, Parsons spoke with Brigadier General Farrell, worried that if the B-29 carrying Little Boy crashed, "there is the danger of an atomic explosion and we may lose this end of the island, if not the whole of Tinian with every blessed thing and person on it."[10] To avoid that, Parsons proposed that he do the final assembly of the bomb in flight, a procedure he had himself rejected earlier.

Farrell asked Parsons if he had tried the procedure, and was told no, "but I've got all day to try it." The Destination Team loaded Little Boy onto its trailer, and drove it out to the bomb pit. Surrounded by a security screen, the bomb was lowered into

Air and ground crew members gather around and pose beneath the nose of "Enola Gay" at Tinian. The atomic nature of the 509th missions was a secret, leading to rumors and a less than warm welcome for Tibbets and his men. That all changed with the announcement of the successful attack on Hiroshima. (Photograph by George E. Staley, National Air & Space Museum Archives / Smithsonian Images)

After its components arrived, Parsons and his team partially assembled Little Boy for deployment on Tinian. On August 4 they loaded "Little Boy" into "Enola Gay" as an inert weapon for final assembly in the air. That afternoon, "Deak" Parsons practiced the delicate job of final assembly, concerned that an armed Little Boy might detonate if "Enola Gay" crashed on take off. (Getty Images)

the pit on a hydraulic lift. Aircraft 44-86292, now painted with the name of Colonel Tibbets' mother, "Enola Gay," was towed into position over the pit. The bomb crew then slowly raised the bomb into the plane's bomb bay. According to Harlow Russ, "by shortly after noon Little Boy had been loaded into the bomb bay, secured, and all the pullout wires were attached to their hooks in the airplane."[11] With the partially assembled bomb in place, Parsons crawled into the aircraft's crowded interior and began to practice inserting the final components, cutting his bare hands on exposed metal as he sweltered in the hot sun. However, when he finally emerged from the plane two hours later, soaked in sweat, hands bloody and covered in the graphite that lubricated the moving parts inside the bomb, Parsons was confident that he could complete Little Boy once the plane was in the air and on the way to Japan.

The planes would take off in the predawn darkness. That evening, after a normal preflight briefing after mess, Tibbets could not sleep. He played blackjack with a few of his officers until 11:00hrs, when he, Parsons, and Ramsey assembled the men of the flight crews that would fly the combat mission for a final briefing. Until then, none of the men of the 509th knew exactly what their secret weapon was. Tibbets started the briefing with a dramatic statement:

> Tonight is the night that we have all been waiting for. Our long months of training are to be put to the test. We will soon know if we have been successful or failed. Upon our efforts tonight it is possible that history will be made. We are going on a mission to

drop a bomb different from any you have ever seen or heard about. This bomb contains a destructive force equivalent to twenty thousand tons of TNT.[12]

After pausing, Tibbets resumed with a discussion of the tactics and the plan for the mission. Parsons and Ramsey spoke, with Parsons talking about the Trinity test and warning the men to shield their eyes from the flash. After the briefing ended, the crews went to the mess hall for a pre-flight breakfast before heading out to the runway.

Seven B-29s stood by. Three of them were weather reconnaissance planes – "Straight Flush" commanded by Major Eatherly would fly to Hiroshima, "Jabit III" commanded by Major John A. Wilson would fly to Kokura, and "Full House" commanded by Major Ralph A. Taylor would fly to Nagasaki. The three planes rumbled off the runway at 01:45hrs and started for Japan. Four other planes stood by, with "Enola Gay" bathed in lights and surrounded by photographers and cameramen.

The historic occasion of the flight was not lost on the military, and for over 20 minutes the plane and crew were filmed until Tibbets called a halt and started pre-flight preparations. Joining "Enola Gay" on the runway were the planes "The Great Artiste" commanded by Major Charles W. Sweeney, "Necessary Evil" commanded by Captain George W. Marquardt, and "Top Secret" commanded by Captain Charles F. McKnight. "The Great Artiste" carried instruments to measure the blast. The crew of "Necessary Evil" was to observe and photograph the attack, and "Top Secret" was the "strike spare," the plane that would fly as far as Iwo Jima and stand by to take Little Boy to Japan if "Enola Gay" developed problems and had to abort the mission. Despite the US government's quest for post-attack publicity, *New York Times* reporter William L. Laurence, on a secret wartime assignment to the Manhattan Project, was too late to fly on the mission as planned, because he had just arrived on Tinian.

At 02:27hrs Tibbets taxied up onto the runway. Revving his engines, he began a long roll forward using "every inch of the runway" to help ensure that Parsons' fears of a crash were not realized.[13] "Enola Gay" lifted off at 02:45hrs and began to climb on a north-northwest heading of 338 degrees. Ten minutes later, "Enola Gay" passed Saipan at 4,700ft, at a speed of 247mph. Parsons

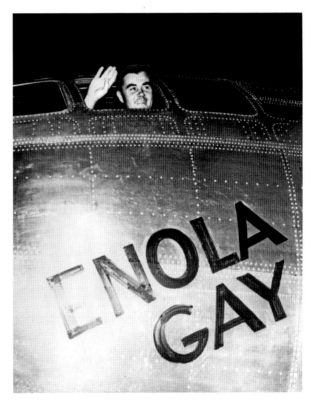

The first atomic mission's secret was released to a selected group of personnel as "Enola Gay" prepared to take off. Surrounded by cameras, the crew prepared for take-off. Colonel Tibbets waved to photographers and film crews as he prepared to taxi and lift off in the early morning hours of August 6, 1945. (Alamy)

and Jeppson climbed into the bomb bay 15 minutes into the flight, and there, with Jeppson reading off the checklist, Parsons delicately and expertly once again performed the final assembly of Little Boy; according to Parsons' log of the mission, at 03:15hrs. The final task was the insertion of a safety feature – "safe/arm plugs." Three green plugs with handles, inserted into connectors on the bomb, disabled the arming and firing circuits. With the bomb prepared, Parsons and Jeppson returned to the weaponeers' station in the forward compartment to monitor the bomb during the flight.

"Enola Gay" and the other B-29s rendezvoused at Iwo Jima at 05:55hrs. Tibbets circled to allow the other planes to gather in formation for the final leg to Japan. "Top Secret" landed on the island to wait for the next few hours. As the sun rose in the sky, at 06:07hrs the strike force was now on its final heading, flying northwest on a 322–325-degree course at 9,700ft. They were headed directly for the southern tip of Shikoku, where the primary target, the city of Hiroshima, lay. An hour ahead of them, the weather reconnaissance planes were just approaching Japan. At 07:30hrs, as "Enola Gay" grew closer, Jeppson climbed back into the bomb bay to switch out the safe/arm plugs, and Parsons turned to Tibbets to let him know that the bomb was now ready. With that, at 07:41hrs Tibbets began to climb to 31,600ft.

Worried by the appearance of clouds as they approached Japan, Tibbets relaxed when a coded radio report from "Straight Flush" came in at 08:30hrs to report that despite some clouds, Hiroshima was clear. The primary target could be bombed visually, as Tibbets' orders specified. Notifying the crew by intercom, Tibbets flew over Shikoku and began the final run across the Iyo Sea toward Hiroshima. The plan of attack called for the bombing to take place at 09:15hrs Tinian time. At 09:06hrs, Hiroshima appeared on the horizon and Tibbets made his way to the initial point, a navigational spot where he turned the B-29 to the west. Flying at 264 degrees, "Enola Gay" was now on the bombing run. Tibbets had expected to run against the wind to assist the bombardier, but a 10mph crosswind was blowing. Ferebee, however, "was an old hand at dropping bombs,"[14] and began to scan the ground below with his Norden bomb sight, looking for the aiming point, Hiroshima's Aioi Bridge.

TARGET HIROSHIMA

One of the planning aspects of the 509th missions to Japan had been flying in small numbers of one, two, or three aircraft at a time. The Japanese, used to larger swarms of bombers, had not seen these flights as a threat, particularly since a number of the missions had been reconnaissance flights. As a result, anti-aircraft and interceptors were not present. On the ground below, the citizens of Hiroshima had woken to another hot summer day and a morning alarm as Eatherly's plane had passed over ahead on its weather reconnaissance. No bombs had fallen, and the Japanese, used to the strange visits of "B-san," had returned to their morning tasks when "Enola Gay" appeared. It was 08:14hrs, Hiroshima time.

At 31,060ft above the city, Ferebee activated a high-pitched radio tone that warned the other planes that the bomb would drop in 60 seconds. As crew slid darkened goggles on to protect their eyes, the tone counted down. When it stopped, the pneumatic bomb bay doors swung open, and Little Boy fell from "Enola Gay" at 08:15:17hrs local time. It fell carrying slogans and notations left by the bomb assembly

In the immediate aftermath the detonation of "Little Boy", the mushroom cloud from the blast climbed 20,000ft from Hiroshima on the morning of August 6, 1945. Staff Sergeant George R. Caron, sitting in the tail gunner's position, had the clearest view of the attack, and captured the scene with his camera. On the ground below the ruins of Hiroshima were engulfed in flames as "Enola Gay" banked and headed back for Tinian. (Photograph by George R. Caron, National Air & Space Museum Archives / Smithsonian Images)

team and the crew, including one note for the "boys of the *Indianapolis*." Returning to sea after delivering the Little Boy components to Tinian, *Indianapolis* was approximately 600 miles off Guam on July 30 when the submarine I-58 intercepted the cruiser. A spread of torpedoes hit *Indianapolis* and sent her to the bottom. The sinking took most of the crew to the bottom; in all, more than 880 men lost their lives, many after they had drifted for days on the open water until sharks, sun, and the sea took their deadly toll.

As Little Boy fell, Tibbets sharply turned the plane 155 degrees and dived 1,700ft to pick up enough speed to throw the plane beyond the deadly zone of the blast. At the same time, "The Great Artiste" dropped three instrumentation packages to monitor the effects of the bomb and radio them back to the scientists on board. Forty-five seconds later, at 08:16:02hrs, radar-activated switches fired the U-235 plug inside the bomb into the target rings and Little Boy detonated 1,903ft above the Aioi Bridge. Ferebee would later joke that he was 13ft off target. From high above, observers saw a "little pin-point of light, purplish-red" that grew into a giant ball of fire. In the cockpit, Tibbets recalled "everything just turned white in front of me."[15] Seconds later, the shock wave, racing at 1,100ft per second, hit the plane. Tailgunner Caron watched it speed through the sky, its leading edge visible as the heated shock front condensed moisture in the air. Tibbets kept the plane level, and then a second shock wave hit. When it passed, Tibbets keyed the intercom and told the crew, "Fellows, you have just dropped the first atomic bomb in history." In his log, co-pilot Lewis wrote, "My God!"[16]

On the ground, the bright flash and the intense heat of the detonation killed, burned, blinded, and maimed as neutrons and gamma particles raced out as deadly radiation. Fifty percent of a nuclear explosion is blast force, with 15 percent radiation and 35 percent thermal effect. Almost everything within a half-mile radius of the hypocenter, or ground zero, was incinerated. Those who survived within that circle of death were shielded from the heat, but even then most died within a day from blast or radiation injuries. More than a mile from the blast, Catholic priest John A. Siemes, a German living in Hiroshima, described the blast from his novitiate window. The sky:

> is filled by a garish light which resembles the magnesium light used in photography, and I am conscious of a wave of heat. I jump to the window to find out the cause of this remarkable phenomenon, but I see nothing more than that brilliant yellow light. As I make for the door, it doesn't occur to me that the light might have something to do with enemy planes. On the way from the window, I hear a moderately loud explosion which

seems to come from a distance and, at the same time, the windows are broken in with a loud crash. There has been an interval of perhaps ten seconds since the flash of light. I am sprayed by fragments of glass.[17]

Other survivors, their stories memorialized in the 1945 bestselling account of the attack, *Hiroshima*, by John Hersey, told of a blinding light, of sudden heat and pressure, and of buildings collapsing on top of or around them.

The flat terrain of the city, the fact that the bomb exploded slightly northwest of the center of Hiroshima, and the largely wooden character of the city's construction meant that the 15-kiloton blast of Little Boy devastated Hiroshima. Described as Japan's seventh largest city before the war, with a population of 340,000, Hiroshima, according to the United States Strategic Bombing Survey (USSBS), was the principal administrative and commercial center of southwestern Japan, and headquarters of the Second Army and the Chugoku Regional Army: "it was one of the most important

The radioactive cloud from the atomic blast drifted over Hiroshima and began to disperse into the wind. This image, said to be from 1,500ft over the city, shows the cloud as it reached into the sky and began to spread. (Roger-Viollet, Paris / The Bridgeman Art Library)

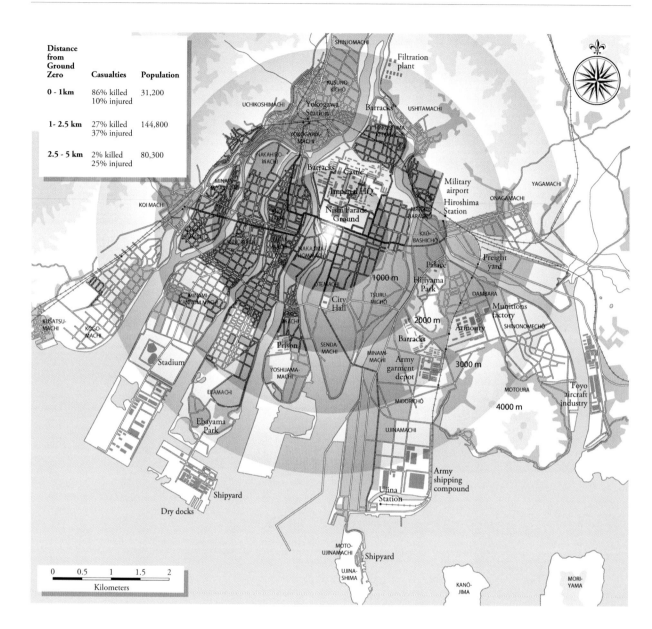

Distance from Ground Zero	Casualties	Population
0 - 1km	86% killed 10% injured	31,200
1- 2.5 km	27% killed 37% injured	144,800
2.5 - 5 km	2% killed 25% injured	80,300

Hiroshima atomic damage and casualties, August 6, 1945. This map is based on the US Stategic Bombing Survey's map (1946). (Artist Into)

military command stations ... site of one of the largest military supply depots, and the foremost military shipping point for both troops and supplies ... during the war new plants were built that increased its [industrial] significance."[18]

The attack immediately killed or injured 60 percent of Hiroshima's population; in time, over 100,000 would die from the effects of the atomic bomb. Radiation sickness, appearing anywhere from immediately to weeks after the blast, would linger. And its effects would last for the lifetime of the survivors.

Nearly 70 percent of the city's buildings were destroyed. The several thousand degrees of heat caused by the fireball, which only lasted for a fraction of a second, nonetheless started fires as far away as 13,700ft from ground zero and burned the unprotected skin of people as far away as 13,000ft. The blast's shock wave, traveling at the speed of sound, imploded wooden structures, gutted buildings, and toppled brick and concrete walls with a peak overpressure of 5psi for a radius of over a mile. Everything within a 2-mile radius was destroyed or seriously damaged. The bomb's result was a smashed city of kindling, with splintered buildings, filled with the dead and dying, that quickly burst into flame as toppled cooking stoves, downed electrical wires, and those fireball fires not snuffed out by the blast were fanned into a maelstrom.

In "Enola Gay," the crew watched in horror while the city "boiled," as Parsons described it:

> The huge dust cloud covered everything. The base of the lower part of the mushroom, a mass of purplish-gray dust about three miles in diameter, was all boiling... The mushroom top was also boiling, a seething turbulent mass ... it looked as though it was coming from a huge burning fire... It seemed as though the whole town got pulverized.[19]

Tibbets watched as fire sprang up everywhere "amidst a turbulent mass of smoke that had the appearance of bubbling hot tar... If Dante had been with us on that plane, he would have been terrified."[20]

The atomic wasteland of Hiroshima in the aftermath of the attack. The streets have been cleared of debris, but the near total devastation of the bomb is clearly visible. On the morning of August 6, 1945, the river was a refuge for the dying, its waters stained red with blood and clogged with corpses as burned and cut survivors crowded the banks. On that morning, over 170,000 people were killed or injured. (Alamy)

The atomic blast's pressure wave and intense heat swept through Hiroshima, leveling 70 percent of the city and leaving a wake of devastation and death within a two-mile radius. The city, a debris filled mass of toppled buildings, and the dead and dying, then burned in a firestorm that uprooted trees, and incinerated survivors as they ran. This image shows the ruins of the city on October 14, 1945, two months later. (Roger-Viollet, Paris / The Bridgeman Art Library)

On the ground, the surviving citizens of Hiroshima were panicked, an exodus described as "aimless, even hysterical" by the USSBS,[21] fleeing as the fires merged, whipped by wind, into a massive firestorm that burned out a 2-mile diameter area of the city. The horrors of the storm were described by Father Siemes:

Beneath the wreckage of the houses along the way, many have been trapped and they scream to be rescued from the oncoming flames. They must be left to their fate. The way to the place in the city to which one desires to flee is no longer open and one must make for Asano Park. Fukai does not want to go further and remains behind. He has not been heard from since. In the park, we take refuge on the bank of the river. A very violent whirlwind now begins to uproot large trees, and lifts them high into the air. As it reaches the water, a waterspout forms which is approximately 100 meters high. The violence of the storm luckily passes us by. Some distance away, however, where numerous refugees have taken shelter, many are blown into the river. Almost all who are in the vicinity have been injured and have lost relatives who have been pinned under the wreckage or who have been lost sight of during the flight. There is no help for the wounded and some die. No one pays any attention to a dead man lying nearby.[22]

As Hiroshima burned, the strike force turned away as the radioactive cloud from the blast swung toward them. The mushroom cloud of smoke from Hiroshima remained visible in the sky until "Enola Gay" was 363 miles away, an hour and a half after the attack. Four hours later, at 14:58hrs Tinian time, "Enola Gay" touched down on the runway it had left.

As Tibbets emerged from the plane to a crowd of some 200 military personnel, General Carl Spaatz, commander of Strategic Air Forces in the Pacific, pinned the Distinguished Service Medal on him. The other crew members, including Parsons, were awarded the Silver Star. The atomic secret was a secret no longer. Laurence was free to begin releasing his stories of the Manhattan Project and its "secret cities," and radio broadcasts and news began to share the incredible news of the atomic bomb with the world.

President Truman, returning home from Potsdam on board the cruiser USS *Augusta*, had his lunch interrupted when the captain of the ship passed him a cable announcing the attack. "This is the greatest thing in history," Truman exclaimed. "It's time for us to get home."[23] The Japanese government released a statement that Hiroshima had been damaged, and that a "new-type of bomb" appeared to have been used, but to the amazement of Tibbets and others no indication of a Japanese surrender was mentioned. It was clear that the enemy would fight on.

At Hiroshima, the night brought no relief for the dying. Surviving doctors and nurses were overwhelmed, and the smell of death filled the air along with smoke. In the morning, on a return to downtown, Father Siemes noted that:

> Where the city stood everything, as far as the eye could reach, is a waste of ashes and ruin. Only several skeletons of buildings completely burned out in the interior remain. The banks of the river are covered with dead and wounded, and the rising waters have here and there covered some of the corpses. On the broad street in the Hakushima district, naked burned cadavers are particularly numerous. Among them are the wounded who are still alive. A few have crawled under the burnt-out autos and trams. Frightfully injured forms beckon to us and then collapse.
>
> Even with relief coming to the stricken city, Hiroshima will be a devastated ruin filled with the dying for many weeks to come.[24]

At Tinian, as preparations began for a second atomic strike mission, this one to carry Fat Man into combat, the United States released a warning to Japan, both in the press, on radio, and in leaflets that B-29s dropped on the country. The message was blunt:

The only structures that remained more or less intact in Hiroshima were reinforced concrete structures, and even these were seriously damaged, especially if they lay within two miles of the hypocenter, or "ground zero." (The Art Archive)

We are in possession of the most destructive explosive ever devised by man. A single one of our newly-developed atomic bombs is actually the equivalent in explosive power to what 2,000 of our giant B-29s can carry on a single mission. This awful fact is for you to ponder and we solemnly assure you that it is grimly accurate. We have just begun to use this weapon against your homeland. If you have any doubt, make inquiry into what happened to Hiroshima when just one bomb fell on that city.[25]

The message then assured the Japanese that "we shall resolutely employ this bomb and all our other superior weapons" unless Japan surrenders. There was no response from the government of Japan, and so the second mission to bomb Japan with atomic weapons proceeded, as Tibbets noted, to "indicate that we had an endless supply of this superweapon" and that Japan would be annihilated under the terms of the Potsdam Declaration.[26] The second attack by the 509th would take Fat Man to the port city of Nagasaki.

6

NAGASAKI

Sixteen hours after the attack on Hiroshima, the White House released a statement from President Truman that outlined more of the Manhattan Project's history while emphasizing the type of weapon and its power:

> With this bomb we have now added a new and revolutionary increase in destruction to supplement the growing power of our armed forces. In their present form these bombs are now in production and even more powerful forms are in development. It is an atomic bomb. It is a harnessing of the basic power of the universe. The force from which the sun draws its power has been loosed against those who brought war to the Far East.[1]

Truman's statement went on to note that the $2 billion project had been a gamble that the United States had won. "The battle of the laboratories held fateful risks for us as well as the battles of the air, land and sea, and we have now won the battle of the laboratories as we have won the other battles."

Truman also made more explicit the threat to the Japanese if they did not surrender:

> We are now prepared to obliterate more rapidly and completely every productive enterprise the Japanese have above ground in any city. We shall destroy their docks, their factories, and their communications. Let there be no mistake; we shall completely destroy Japan's power to make war. It was to spare the Japanese people from utter destruction that the ultimatum of July 26 was issued at Potsdam. Their leaders promptly

B-29 44-27297, "Bockscar," was the aircraft assigned to drop the atomic bomb on Nagasaki. It was a new aircraft which had been delivered to the USAAF on April 19, 1945 and flown to Tinian in June. Built by the Glenn L. Martin Co. at Omaha, Nebraska, the B-29 cost approximately $639,000. (US National Park Service)

rejected that ultimatum. If they do not now accept our terms they may expect a rain of ruin from the air, the like of which has never been seen on this earth. Behind this air attack will follow sea and land forces in such numbers and power as they have not yet seen and with the fighting skill of which they are already well aware.

As Curtis LeMay would later note, "While the Japanese were trying to make up their minds about what to do, the Twentieth Air Force kept up the pressure."[2] On August 7, LeMay sent a force of 153 B-29s against Japan, and followed it on the eighth with a 375-plane incendiary assault on Yawata.

Japan had fought a brutal war in China for 12 years, and more than three years of war with the United States, Great Britain, the Netherlands, and their allies. The Pacific war brought savage battles, atrocities, and an increasing dedication by Japanese troops not to surrender but to die in battle, taking as many of the enemy as they could with them. It was a bitter, racially tinged, and cruel campaign, and troops awaiting the final decision on whether to invade Japan, especially in the aftermath of the bloody battles for Iwo Jima and Okinawa, welcomed all that the bombings brought. The atomic bomb in particular was viewed as a war-ender, a blow rendered so hard that it would crack Japan's will to fight.

News of the Hiroshima attack galvanized the troops in the field, especially those training for the seaborne invasion of the Japanese homeland planned for later that year. The arrival of the bomb brought Allied cheers and hope that the war would be over immediately. Paul Fussell, writing about the impact of the news, was a 21-year-old second lieutenant in a rifle platoon, a veteran of the European war training for the final assault on Japan. The thought of not being obliged to "rush up the beaches near Tokyo assault-firing while being machine-gunned, mortared and shelled" brought more than

With final assembly completed, the "Fat Man" weapon for the Nagasaki mission is shown ready for loading onto "Bockscar." The bomb has been sealed, as shown by the joint in the casing, and the tail fin assembly bolted into place. Signatures cover the tail fin. (Time-Life Photograph / Getty Images)

relief; "for all the practiced phlegm of our tough facades we broke down and cried... We were going to live."[3] However, relief would only come after a second attack, as Japan did not immediately surrender.

The second atomic mission was scheduled for August 11, but an impending five-day storm shifted plans. The Destination Team, already working to prepare Fat Man unit F31 for the next atomic attack, was instead asked to shift their efforts and rush work on F33 for a non-nuclear test run.

On the 7th, as the Fat Man assembly team unpacked the ellipsoidal armor steel casings for F33, they quickly discovered that the casings were warped and the bolt holes did not line up. After a frustrating attempt to beat and reshape the casings into fitting, and a failed attempt to enlarge the bolt holes, which only succeeded in injuring one crew member when the bit jammed and threw him to the concrete floor, the team switched to an unused pumpkin's ordinary steel casing. They fitted it into place and painted it after the high-explosives charges were packed inside. Team member Harlow Russ then added, in black lettering, "JANCFU" on the nose. The first four letters signified "Joint Army Navy Civilian," he later explained, and "the last two letters had the same meaning as ... the standard military vernacular situation description" of SNAFU (Situation Normal, All F****d Up).[4]

When done, they loaded it into the B-29 ordinarily flown by Captain Frederick C. Bock, 44-27297 "Bockscar," but on this test flight commanded by Major Charles

W. Sweeney, the commanding officer of the 393rd. F33's high explosives successfully detonated when "Bockscar" dropped it off Tinian on August 8. F31 would not prove as easy.

The assembly of F31, just after the struggle with F33, also came with trouble that surfaced when the time came to close up the bomb for the evening. The "dog-tired" team had installed the cable for firing the bomb backwards, so that the plugs at each end were female-to-female and male-to-male. The problem was discovered by Navy ensign Bernard J. O'Keefe, who with an Army technician was left to make the final connections in F31 just before midnight. To fix the error would involve waking the rest of the team and spending much of a day taking the bomb apart and putting it back together again. That was what the protocols for the bomb assembly dictated, but there was not enough time to make the August 9 deadline for the mission. Therefore, "rules or no rules," O'Keefe, after swearing the technician to secrecy, stripped off the plugs and re-soldered them on the wire in the correct order. He did so, door propped open as he worked, "keeping as much distance between the soldering iron and the detonators as I could…"[5] The job completed, he sealed F31 and went to bed.

The next day, the Destination Team, none the wiser, rolled F31 out to the bomb loading pit, carefully balancing the bomb as it bounced on its trailer. Stenciled on the casing, instead of "JANCFU" were a number of signatures and notes, just as there had been with Little Boy. The plane selected to drop the bomb was "The Great Artiste," commanded by Charles Sweeney, but the decision to go on August 9 found his plane still outfitted with the monitoring equipment for the instrumentation packages it had dropped at Hiroshima. Sweeney and his crew switched planes with Captain Frederick C. Bocks' crew to once more fly "Bockscar," this time into combat.

The second strike team was:

- 44-27297, "Bockscar," loaded with F31;
- 44-27353, "The Great Artiste," flying as the instrumentation aircraft;
- 44-27354, "Big Stink," commanded by Major James Hopkins, with scientific observers and photographic equipment. Among the observers were RAF Group Captain G. Leonard Cheshire, a member of the British Military Mission to the United States, the official representative of the British government, and Dr. William G. Penney, whose work on the MAUD committee had led to his participation as one of the "British Mission" at Los Alamos;
- 44-86292, "Enola Gay," commanded by Captain George Marquardt on this mission, was the advance weather scout for the primary target of Kokura;

- 44-86347, "Laggin' Dragon," commanded by Captain Charles McKnight, was the advance weather scout for the secondary target of Nagasaki;
- 44-27298, "Full House," commanded by Captain Ralph Taylor, was the "strike standby" that would wait at Iwo Jima in case "Bockscar" developed problems and needed to switch planes.

The combat crew of "Bockscar" were Sweeney, pilot Charles D. "Don" Albury, co-pilot Major Fred Olivi, flight engineer Master Sergeant John D. Kuharek, assistant flight engineer Sergeant Raymond Gallagher, bombardier Captain Kermit K. Beahan, navigator James F. Van Pelt, Jr., radar operator Edward K. "Ed" Buckley, radio operator Sergeant Abe M. Spitzer, and tail gunner Staff Sergeant Albert "Al" Dehart. They were joined on the plane by Frederick Ashworth, flying as weaponeer, electronics test officer Philip Barnes, and Lieutenant Jacob Beser, who flew on this mission as electronic counter-measures officer as he had on the Hiroshima strike.

TARGET NAGASAKI

The primary target was Kokura, an ancient fortified town on the straits of Shimonoseki. Kokura, which had been designated as the secondary target for the earlier Hiroshima mission, was the location of the Kokura Arsenal, a vast factory that provided munitions and poison gas for the Japanese Army. The secondary target was Nagasaki, another ancient town, at the southern tip of Kyushu, that had served as a center for commerce, including Japan's 16th- and 17th-century trade with the Dutch and the Portuguese, and as such the oldest center of Christianity in Japan. It was, as it had always been, an active shipping center, and the setting for a munitions plant that had, among other projects, manufactured the aerial torpedoes Japanese pilots had dropped at Pearl Harbor.

On the evening of August 8, Fat Man F31 slowly rose into the bomb bay of "Bockscar" against "a background of threatening black skies torn open at intervals by great lightning flashes," according to William L. Laurence.[6] Once loaded, the B-29 was towed to the runway and placed under armed guard. Tibbets assembled the crews for a briefing at midnight. William Laurence, present at the briefing, reported that it:

> revealed the extreme care and the tremendous amount of preparation that had been made to take care of every detail of the mission, in order to make certain that the atomic bomb fully served the purpose for which it was intended. Each target in turn was shown in detailed maps and in aerial photographs. Every detail of the course was rehearsed, navigation, altitude, weather, where to land in emergencies. It came out that the Navy

had submarines and rescue craft, known as "Dumbos" and "Super Dumbos," stationed at various strategic points in the vicinity of the targets, ready to rescue the fliers in case they were forced to bail out.[7]

The strike force was to head to Kyushu, rendezvousing at Yakushima, a small volcanic island off the coast, before heading to Kokura. Because of the rough weather, the approach altitude was changed from 9,000 to 17,000ft. A few points made by Tibbets would later come back to plague Sweeney and his crew. He told the crews to wait no more than 15 minutes at the rendezvous before heading on, and he reminded them that the bombardier had to see the target visually in order to drop the bomb. Neither order would be followed.

By 02:15hrs, the flight crews had assembled at the planes, and last-minute checks were underway when Master Sergeant Kuharek, the flight engineer, pointed out to Sweeney that a fuel transfer pump was not working properly. Accounts differ as to whether it was not functioning at all, or required hand-pumping, but the pump was a serious problem. According to "Don" Albury, the co-pilot:

Most B-29s carried a 600-gallon reserve fuel tank in the aft bomb bay. The gas tank was mainly used for ballast, and I don't recall ever having to tap into it on earlier missions. Unfortunately, the fuel-transfer pumps were not working, and the 3,600 pounds of fuel in the back became dead weight. Maj. Sweeney exited the aircraft, and he and Col. Tibbets had a lengthy discussion about the problem. Ultimately, Sweeney made the go decision... Things only got worse from here.[8]

Nearly an hour behind schedule, the mission got underway. The weather planes took off at 02:58hrs, followed by the strike force. "Bockscar" lifted off at 03:47hrs. "The Great Artiste" followed at 03:51hrs, and "The Big Stink" at 03:53hrs.

The planes headed northwest into the storm. On "The Great Artiste," "we were about an hour away from our base when the storm broke," William Laurence later wrote. "Our great ship took some heavy dips through the abysmal darkness around us," and then Laurence noticed "a strange eerie light coming through the window." Staring out into the night, he saw that "the whirling giant propellers had somehow become great luminous discs of blue flame. The same luminous blue flame appeared on the plexiglass windows in the nose of the ship, and on the tips of the giant wings it looked as though we were riding the whirlwind through space on a chariot of blue fire."[9] Static electricity bathed the plane, and Laurence worried that it might detonate the bomb. He was reassured that it would not.

Meanwhile, on "Bockscar," Frederick "Dick" Ashworth had crawled aft at 04:00hrs to switch the safe/arm plugs and arm the Fat Man. Back at his station, he watched the control panel with Barnes. An hour later, around 05:00hrs, the first light of the dawn appeared in the sky, and just before 06:00hrs the sun was up. The planes continued on for another three hours, approaching the rendezvous. There, another problem surfaced as "Bockscar" waited for the other planes:

> "The Great Artiste" found us right away, and we circled waiting for "Big Stink" to show up. We were making small circles at 30,000 feet, and unbeknown to us, it was making big wide circles at 39,000 feet. We never saw one another, and after 40 minutes, "Bockscar" and "The Great Artiste" jumped on the Hirohito Highway and headed for Japan.[10]

On "The Great Artiste" Captain Bock reportedly spotted the "Big Stink," but Sweeney did not, later claiming, as did Albury, that the other B-29 was flying much higher than it was supposed to.

Major Hopkins had flown off without scientist Robert Serber, the only person trained to operate the high-speed camera that was to document the blast. In his haste to board, Serber had failed to grab a parachute, and Hopkins, while taxiing down the runway, ordered the crew to kick Serber off the plane. That, the scientist noted, "was truly idiotic … the plane was supposed to have a mission … to take pictures."[11] Instead, with the plane's engines revving, Serber was pushed out of a hatch and left in the darkness at the end of the runway. Hopkins' stubbornness infuriated Tibbets and the other senior officers when to their surprise Serber walked into their hut an hour later, but "Big Stink" was already gone, operating with the other B-29s on radio silence. Because Serber alone knew how to operate the camera, radio silence was broken for Tibbets to give Hopkins "a little piece of his mind" and for Serber to relay instructions, but in vain. The camera was never used because it was too difficult for the crew to operate.

The weather planes reached Kokura and Nagasaki and reported that while there was cloud cover there was enough visibility to proceed, and so "Bockscar" and "The Great Artiste" departed for Kokura without "Big Stink." At 10:20hrs, the planes arrived to find that smoke drifting from fires at Yawata, a steel mill town firebombed a day earlier, obscured the target. Sweeney made three passes over Kokura, but each time, Beahan reported he could not spot the aiming point. As Japanese aircraft and flak gunners drew closer, it was time to go. At 11:32hrs Tinian time, after 45 minutes over Kokura, "Bockscar" and "The Great Artiste" diverted to Nagasaki. To this day, the Japanese still speak about the "luck of Kokura."

Fuel was low on "Bockscar," and Sweeney and Albury determined that they could make only one pass over Nagasaki. They flew into clouds formed by a weather front blowing in from the East China Sea, and Nagasaki, earlier reported as clear, was now covered by drifting clouds. Sweeney did not want to make the decision to attack alone, and called Ashworth forward. After discussing whether to bomb using radar, with Ashworth initially against it, the weaponeer finally relented. Jacob Beser later commented, "there was no sense dragging the bomb home or dropping it in the ocean."[12] Lining up from their initial point, the crew flew "Bockscar" on a radar approach for 90 percent of the run, until suddenly Beahan shouted that he could see the city through the clouds. It was 11:01hrs Nagasaki time. Switching to visual, Beahan took control the plane and triggered the bomb's release at 28,900ft.

A cloud of smoke and dust punches into the sky above ground zero at Nagasaki on August 9, 1945. The cloud rose 11 miles into the atmosphere before dispersing. Reporter William L. Laurence, watching from a nearby plane, described it as "a flower-like form, its giant petal curving downward, creamy white outside, rose-colored inside. It still retained that shape when we last gazed at it from a distance of about 200 miles." Laurence also described the cloud in a term more familiar to most, "a giant mushroom." Poetic descriptions aside, the cloud from a distance obscured the effects of the blast and heat on the city below. Tens of thousands of people had just died in a matter of seconds. (USAAF photograph, Library of Congress)

Following on "The Great Artiste," William Laurence, who on the flight had mused, "Does one feel any pity or compassion for the poor devils about to die? Not when one thinks of Pearl Harbor and of the death march on Bataan," watched as "out of the belly" of the other plane "what looked like a black object came downward."[13] The crews had pulled their dark glasses over their eyes, and as Fat Man dropped, they counted. Forty-seven seconds later, F31 detonated 1,650ft above Nagasaki's industrial district. It was off target, as Beahan's last-minute glimpse through the clouds had come too late to drop the bomb accurately. The Mitsubishi Steel and Arms Works and the Mitsubishi-Urakami Ordnance Works, where the Pearl Harbor torpedoes were built, took the brunt of the 21-kiloton blast. The explosion swept through the Urakami Valley, the center of Nagasaki's Christian (Catholic) population and site of the Catholic Cathedral. The surrounding hills shielded much of Nagasaki's other residential districts.

The Fat Man was approximately 40 percent more powerful than Little Boy at 21 versus 15 kilotons. The fireball grew as intense as 7,000°F (3,900°C) and obliterated everything living within a 0.6-mile diameter. High winds caused by the blast tore through the city at over 600mph, and the bomb's blast-induced overpressure

The Nagasaki bomb detonated off target (approximately 2 miles away from the planned hypocenter) over Nagasaki's Urakami Valley. The hills that surrounded the valley partially sheltered the rest of the city from the effects of the blast. However, the pressure and heat left a radius of near total destruction of some two miles, and between 40,000 and 70,000 people died instantly. (Ira Clarence Eaker Collection, Library of Congress)

collapsed concrete buildings and reduced wooden buildings to kindling, just as the blast did at Hiroshima. The detonation devastated everything within a 1.2-mile area, with many casualties from flying glass and debris as well as the heat. In all, between 40,000 and 75,000 people died, and as many as 75,000 were injured by the heat, blast, and radiation, according to a 1950 report by the City of Nagasaki.[14]

In the air, Laurence noted that after the initial flash, a bluish-green light still filled the sky as "Bockscar" and "The Great Artiste" sharply turned and dived. A shock wave hit the planes, making them "tremble from nose to tail. This was followed by four more blasts in rapid succession, each resounding like the boom of cannon fire hitting our plane from all directions." Looking down:

> Observers in the tail of our ship saw a giant ball of fire rise as though from the bowels of the earth, belching forth enormous white smoke rings. Next they saw a giant pillar of purple fire, 10,000 feet high, shooting skyward with enormous speed. By the time our ship had made another turn in the direction of the atomic explosion the pillar of purple fire had reached the level of our altitude. Only about 45 seconds had passed. Awe-struck, we watched it shoot upward… As the first mushroom floated off into the blue it changed its shape into a flower-like form, its giant petal curving downward, creamy white outside, rose-colored inside. It still retained that shape when we last gazed at it from a distance of about 200 miles.[15]

There was not much time to linger. "Bockscar" was low on fuel, and after four minutes of observation, the two planes began to head for their emergency landing point, the recently conquered island of Okinawa. Sweeney and Albury worried that they might not have enough fuel to make it, and radioed ahead to alert rescue forces to the fact they might have to land in the sea. Meanwhile, the missing "Big Stink" arrived over Nagasaki, too late to capture the fireball, but in time to photograph the plume of smoke that boiled up from the stricken city. "Big Stink" then headed for Okinawa. All the way, the pilots nursed "Bockscar" along, praying they would make it.

After an hour's flight, the island was in sight. Attempts to raise the tower by radio failed to receive an answer – Okinawa was in the middle of an alert and a number of planes were trying to land at Yontan Field. Sweeney ordered emergency flares fired from the plane, to no effect, and so he ordered every available flare shot out, making "Bockscar" a huge Roman candle as it cut between two planes, one landing, another on final approach, slamming down on the runway at 150mph, 30mph faster than the recommended landing speed. According to Albury:

> At 500 feet, our number-three engine began to suck air, and we felt the effects immediately. Maj. Sweeney and I were too busy even to curse as we fought to control Bockscar's descent. As we touched down, the number-two engine gasped and coughed for the last time as it, too, was starved of fuel. Sweeney and I slammed on the brakes

OPPOSITE
Very little remained standing around the hypocenter. However, some structures were not leveled. This reinforced concrete gate, photographed in October 1945, survived because the force of the Fat Man blast passed through it. Behind it, the ruins of a school established in 1881 as the Kaharkuri English School remains standing, but it was badly damaged with its roof caved in from the blast. (Alamy)

and threw the two running engines' propellers into full reverse. We stopped 500 feet from the end of the runway, and our clock showed it was 1pm. That was the longest nine hours and 11 minutes of my life![16]

Twenty minutes later, "The Great Artiste" and "Big Stink" also landed at Okinawa. When the crew checked the fuel tanks on "Bockscar," other than the unusable 600 gallons in the tail, the B-29 had only 33 gallons left in the tanks. It had been a very close call.

After refueling, and surveying the planes for damage, the Nagasaki strike force took off after a four-hour layover from Yongan Field. They landed at Tinian, hours overdue, at 11:30hrs to a subdued reception. No crowd, fanfare, or medal ceremony as had greeted the crew of "Enola Gay" awaited Sweeney and his crew. They posed for a few photographs and headed off for debriefing. Harlow Russ later commented that the JANCFU acronym he had painted on F33 had been "intended to be facetious, not a prediction."[17] However, there were no public recriminations, and commendations and promotions were forthcoming, although public acclaim and fame never followed the crew of "Bockscar" as it did for that of "Enola Gay." The Nagasaki attack, as a follow-up, never attracted as much attention, even for its survivors and their ordeal.

The atomic wasteland of Nagasaki. St. Mary's Cathedral, also known as the *Urakami Tenshudo* or Urakami Cathedral, the center of Catholic worship in Nagasaki, lies in what was once a residential (and predominantly Christian) neighborhood, 1,000 yards from ground zcro. Completed in 1914, the cathedral was nearly completely destroyed by the blast and was reconstructed in 1959. The remnants of the original church were relocated and now stand in the Nagasaki Peace Park. (Los Alamos National Laboratory)

ON THE GROUND

In Nagasaki, the explosion caught many people by surprise as the mid-day preparations for lunch were underway. Others, alerted by air raid sirens, were taking shelter. Fifteen-year-old schoolgirl Michie Hattori was standing in the entrance to her High School's air raid shelter, "motioning for the pokey girls to come in. First came

Nagasaki atomic damage and casualties, August 9, 1945. This map is based on the US Strategic Bombing Survey's map (1946). (Artist Info)

Distance from Ground Zero	Casualties	Population
0 - 1km	88% killed 6% injured	30,900
1- 2.5 km	34% killed 29% injured	27,700
2.5 - 5 km	11% killed 10% injured	115,200

Only the badly damaged remains of reinforced concrete and brick structures survived close to the hypocenter. The Urakami Valley, with its surrounding hills, sheltered much of the city from more severe damage, and despite the fact that the Nagasaki bomb was as much as 40 percent more powerful than the Hiroshima bomb, the extent of damage and the death toll at Nagasaki was less than at Hiroshima. (Bridgeman Art Library)

the light – the brightest light I have ever seen." Temporarily blinded, Hattori was hit by a "searing hot flash... For a second I dimly saw it burn the girls standing in front of the cave. They appeared as bowling pins, falling in all directions, screaming and slapping at their burning school uniforms. I saw nothing for a while after that."[18] The force of the blast then threw Hattori into the shelter and promptly blew her back out again.

When she regained her sight, Hattori and other survivors made their way toward the school through fires that had started in fallen houses. "Thick smoke and dust filled the air. The fires gave the only real illumination." Hattori heard some of the other girls repeat "jigoku," the Japanese word for hell. They came across a badly burned person crawling in the road. "No clothes or hair were visible, just large, gray scalelike

burns covering its head and body. The skin around its eyes had burned away, leaving the eyeballs, huge and terrifying. Whether male or female I never found out." The victim begged for help, then died.

Survivors made their way to the Urakami River, only to find hundreds of the dead and dying by the river banks and in the water, just as had happened at Hiroshima. Another survivor, 10-year-old Shimohira Sakue, saw "a large number of people at the banks of the river. They were scorched black and struggling to get a sip of water, but most of them died right there on the bank. Hundreds of dead bodies were caught on the rocks in the river."[19] Walking toward her home to find her family, Sakue found the "city was so devastated that we could not even tell where our house had been. All that was left was a field of rubble scattered with blackened corpses." When she reached home, she found her family there had been killed:

> When we finally found the ruins of our house, we dug through the rubble until we found a corpse burnt beyond recognition. The hands were still covering the eyes, with the thumbs plugging the ears. Because the skin underneath was intact, we found when we pulled away the hands that it was our older sister. After that we gathered debris from the ruins of the house and used it to cremate the body. No matter how hard we searched, though, we couldn't find our mother in the rubble. Finally we checked two bodies lying out on the street, and we identified one as our mother by her capped tooth. We had no container for the ashes after the cremations, so we used a blackened kitchen pot to hold the remains of both my mother and sister.

Sakue's older brother, who was farther away from the blast, reunited with her, apparently unhurt. But radiation sickness soon revealed itself. He "began to spit out huge amounts of a yellow liquid. He died later crying that he wanted to stay alive." In this and many other cases, survivors seemingly untouched manifested terrible symptoms within hours, days, weeks, and in time, years after the detonation of Fat Man over Nagasaki.

AFTERMATH

Following the bombing of Nagasaki, the Twentieth Air Force continued to drop leaflets on Japan urging the surrender of the Japanese government. In Tokyo, government leaders were considering surrender, but militarists were urging that the fight continue, hopeful that the Soviet Union, which had remained neutral in the war with Japan, would help negotiate a peace different from the unconditional surrender demanded in the Potsdam Declaration. Those hopes were dashed in Moscow on

August 8, when Soviet Foreign Minister Vyacheslav Molotov called in Japanese Ambassador Naotake Satō, and told him that:

> Taking into consideration the refusal of Japan to capitulate, the Allies submitted to the Soviet Government a proposal to join the war against Japanese aggression and thus shorten the duration of the war, reduce the number of victims and facilitate the speedy restoration of universal peace. Loyal to its Allied duty, the Soviet Government has accepted the proposals of the Allies and has joined in the declaration of the Allied powers of July 26. The Soviet Government considers that this policy is the only means able to bring peace nearer, free the people from further sacrifice and suffering and give the Japanese people the possibility of avoiding the dangers and destruction suffered by Germany after her refusal to capitulate unconditionally.[20]

The Soviets told the ambassador that as of the following day, August 9, they were at war with Japan. At dawn, a massive Soviet assault of over a million and half troops rolled into Japanese-occupied Manchuria, and in a double pincer movement met up at Changchun, cutting off a Japanese retreat into Korea. Over half a million Japanese were taken prisoner.

The Japanese government, on August 10, sent word that it would surrender under the terms of the Potsdam Declaration with one condition, that surrender not "prejudice the prerogatives" of the Emperor. As the United States weighed a compromise, which would leave the Emperor in place but place him under the authority of the Supreme Commander of the Allied Powers, the US government also decided to keep the war "at its present intensity" until the Japanese surrendered. In Japan, a faction of military officers plotted to keep the nation from defeat, even if it meant sacrificing 20 million lives in a national *kamikaze*-style suicide attack or through a *coup d'etat* to prevent the Emperor from surrendering.

On August 10, General Spaatz sent a cable urging a third atomic attack on Tokyo. Groves the same day reported to General of the Army George Marshall that another bomb would be ready for a mission on August 17 or 18. "Jabit III" had already been dispatched to Los Alamos for another plutonium core on August 9, and at Tinian the Destination Team had begun work prepping three practice Fat Man units for test runs. A third combat unit was problematic, despite having components on hand, because the high-explosive assembly had cracked and the bomb had untrustworthy high-explosive cast clock that might not detonate properly. Also there were no detonator chimneys, specially machined lengths of brass tubing, glued into place, that allowed the team to insert and line up the detonators to the exact centre of each lens. This created a "semi-panic," as Harlow Russ later recalled. The clever scientists, engineers, and technicians, using raw material provided by a helpful naval vessel, were able to solve the detonator chimney problem, manufacturing new ones from brass.

In answering Groves, General Marshall had approved preparations for a third attack, but reminded him that "It is not to be released over Japan without express authority from the President."[21] Truman, mindful of the fact that the Japanese were debating surrender, had ordered a halt to the atomic attacks, aware of the civilian toll and not happy with the thought of killing "all those kids," as he confided to Secretary of Commerce Henry Wallace.[22] However, atomic attacks would resume if the Japanese did not surrender.

While Groves, the President and his cabinet, especially Secretary of State Byrnes, considered the role of the bomb as a war-ending strategic tool, debate in the War Department over continued use of the bomb focused on its tactical role:

> The problem now is whether or not, assuming the Japanese do not capitulate, to continue dropping them every time one is made and shipped out there or whether to hold them ... and then pour them all on in a reasonably short time. Not all in one day, but over a short period. And that also takes into consideration the target that we are after. In other words, should we not concentrate on targets that will be of the greatest assistance to an invasion rather than industry, morale, psychology, and the like? Nearer the tactical use rather than other use.[23]

On August 12, as debate consumed two governments, the military forces of Japan and the United States re-commenced hostilities after a brief lull in the fighting. The Twentieth Air Force responded to renewed Japanese attacks by launching more raids against Japan on the evening of the 13th. On August 14, nearly a thousand planes arrived in the skies over Japan. Thousands of tons of bombs rained down in Hikari, Osaka, Marifu, Kumagaya, and Isezaki, the latter two hit by incendiaries as well as high explosives. Other planes dropped mines in the Straits of Shimonoseki and in harbors.

The debate in Japan continued even after the Emperor decided to surrender. A military coup that seized the Imperial Palace in an attempt to stop the broadcast of the Emperor's surrender failed on the evening of August 14, and at noon the next day, the Emperor spoke to his subjects by radio, telling them he had resolved to end the war "by enduring the unendurable and suffering what is insufferable."[24] In reality, his subjects and the victims of Japanese aggression had already suffered, with over two million Japanese dead and millions of Allied casualties, many of them Chinese. Most of Japan lay in ruins, its armies defeated even though Japanese forces continued to fight on in Manchuria, and its navy and merchant marine were for the most part at the bottom of the sea.

In his speech to the nation, Hirohito specifically mentioned the weapon that had helped push Japan to surrender:

> Moreover, the enemy now possesses a new and terrible weapon with the power to destroy many innocent lives and do incalculable damage. Should we continue to fight, not only would it result in an ultimate collapse and obliteration of the Japanese nation, but also it would lead to the total extinction of human civilization. Such being the case, how are We to save the millions of Our subjects, or to atone Ourselves before the hallowed spirits of Our Imperial Ancestors? This is the reason why We have ordered the acceptance of the provisions of the Joint Declaration of the Powers.[25]

The bombs at Hiroshima and Nagasaki had played a powerful psychological role, to be certain, in the end of the war, but they had not won the war. That much was clear to the Army, Army Air Forces, the Navy, and Marine Corps, all of whom had fought a bitter and sustained series of campaigns across the Pacific to victory. While the atomic bombs had not played a major role in combat, however, the unleashing of atomic power had a profound impact, with civilization-altering implications for the postwar world.

REACTION AND RESPONSE

The advent of nuclear power in 1939 and the potential for the new weapon to be used against the United States had spurred the initial development of the Manhattan Project. Fear over what the atomic genie would do when loosed from its bottle had been an ongoing concern of a number of thoughtful scientists and the few political figures who knew about the secret project. That fear was foremost in President Harry Truman's mind when he remarked in a radio address to the country in the aftermath of Hiroshima: "It is an awful responsibility which has come to us. We thank God that it has come to us instead of our enemies, and we pray that He may guide us to use it in His ways and for His purposes."[1]

The initial reaction of many, especially the naval and land forces massing for the invasion of Japan's home islands, was elation. Instead of a protracted and bloody campaign, beach by beach, city by city, island by island, as the war had been waged already, the Japanese simply laid down their arms and the troops that landed came as occupying forces, not as warriors. That fact was not lost on most Americans at home, especially those with fathers, sons, brothers, and husbands in the military. Nor was there thought of revenge.

The *Chicago Tribune*'s editorial cartoon for August 8 illustrated a long fuse running from Pearl Harbor to Hiroshima, which, as it exploded, sent body parts, including a severed human head, into the air. The cartoonist drew the head saying "So Sorry." The *Atlanta Constitution* of Atlanta, Georgia, featured an editorial cartoon depicting a huge explosion in Japan, flinging bodies into the air, captioned "Land of the Rising Sons." The jubilation over the atomic attack was not universal in US news coverage and editorials, but such responses were largely confined to America, as the war in the Pacific had been an intensely personal and emotional conflict since Pearl Harbor. European reaction, especially in *The Times* of London, was more restrained.

The power of the new weapon was obviously not lost in the celebration of victory. The sudden revelation of the top-secret Manhattan Project and the awesome power

A mother and child, dressed in traditional clothing, sit on the ground amid rubble and burnt trees in the ruins of Hiroshima in December 1945. Americans were gradually becoming aware of the human stories and the human toll of the atomic bombings, although it would take a few more years (and the publication of accounts like John Hersey's *Hiroshima*) before a more sympathetic view of the innocent victims of the attack emerged. Many *hibakusha* (the Japanese term for atomic bomb survivors) suffered from radiation-related illnesses, not only in the immediate aftermath, but also in the decades that have followed the bombings. (Photo by Alfred Eisenstaedt / Time & Life Pictures / Getty Images)

of the unleashed atom brought awareness that a new and potent force had been unleashed, and that it represented a change not just in warfare, but for civilization itself. The Dayton, Ohio, *Daily News'* headline was straightforward: "Atomic Bomb, Most Destructive Force in History, Hits Japan." The Las Cruces, New Mexico, *Sun-News* reported, "Single Atomic Bomb Reduces City to Ashes." The *New York Times'* headline was also to the point: "First Atomic Bomb Dropped on Japan; Missile Is Equal to 20,000 Tons of TNT; Truman Warns Foe of a 'Rain of Ruin.'"

In his headline story, Sidney Shalett of the *New York Times* also noted that the new weapon was a double-edged sword:

> The announcement, first given to the world in utmost solemnity by President Truman, made it plain that one of the scientific landmarks of the century had been passed, and that the "age of atomic energy," which can be a tremendous force for the advancement of civilization as well as for destruction, was at hand.

This, he suggested, brought "A Sobering Awareness of Power":

> Not the slightest spirit of braggadocio is discernible either in the wording of the official announcements or in the mien of the officials who gave out the news. There was an element of elation in the realization that we had perfected this devastating weapon for employment against an enemy who started the war and has told us she would rather be destroyed than surrender, but it was grim elation. There was sobering awareness of the tremendous responsibility involved.[2]

The editors of the New York *Herald Tribune* called the announcement of the atomic bomb's existence "more fateful for human history than the whole war itself." On August 7, Hanson W. Baldwin, the *New York Times'* military correspondent, noted that with the atomic bomb, America had "sowed the whirlwind." From the United Kingdom, former Prime Minister Winston Churchill, one of the key players in the project and a staunch supporter of the bomb's use, commented, "this revelation of the secrets of nature, long mercifully withheld from man, should arouse the most solemn reflections in the mind and conscience of every human being capable of comprehension."[3] Churchill echoed the musings of the editors of *The Times* of London, that the atomic bomb, "more surely than the rocket, carries the warning that another world war would mean the destruction of all regulated life."[4]

While the public reaction was a mixture of celebration, reflection, and fear that the bomb might someday be used against the United States, 69 percent of the American public, surveyed in a Gallup poll, supported the atomic bombing of Japan, agreeing that it had been a "good thing," while 17 percent felt otherwise and 14 percent had no opinion.[5] No such survey was taken in war-ravaged Europe. Within the American statistics were a disparate number of views about the future, however, that would manifest themselves in a variety of actions over the next few years. These included the inevitable popular cultural response of writers, musicians, poets, artists, and marketers, and the need to keep the secrets of the bomb from leaking to other countries, especially the ostensible allies, the Soviets – the tensions that would soon erupt into the Cold War were already at play. There were varying opinions and suggestions about international control of the bomb and about the search for peaceful and beneficial uses of atomic power. There were also the intertwined issues of civil defense and the building up of America's atomic strength, issues that were further discussed in the United Kingdom, cut out of America's atomic program after the war, and in the Soviet Union. While outwardly supportive of American efforts to control access to nuclear weapons technology, primarily to thwart diplomatic support for sharing it with the Soviets, British political leaders, including Winston Churchill, feared the consequences of nuclear war. In September 1946, speaking in Zurich, Churchill gave voice to those fears:

> In these present days we dwell strangely and precariously under the shield, and I will even say protection, of the atomic bomb. The atomic bomb is still only in the hands of a State and nation which we know, will never use it except in the cause of right and freedom, but it may well be that in a few years this awful agency of destruction will be widespread and that the catastrophe following from its use by several warring nations will not only bring to an end all that we call civilisation but may possibly disintegrate the globe itself.[6]

The private response of the British government, beginning with Clement Atlee and continuing after Churchill's postwar return to power, was quietly to begin a British atomic weapons program, following the American model that only by having weapons of mass destruction could a nation avert atomic attack. This belief in time extended to other countries, and continues to the present day as the "nuclear club" continues to grow.

However, another significant reaction was the anti-nuclear response, which steadily grew, especially in the era of the "super-bomb." The atomic bombing of Japan reinforced fears of the misapplication of science and technology, beginning with scientists from within the ranks of the Manhattan Project and extending to the public, not only in the United States but also around the world. The development of more powerful fusion

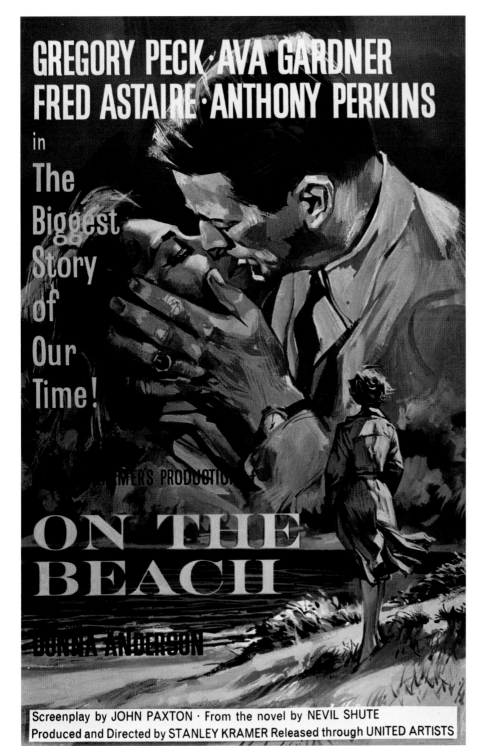

British-Australian novelist Nevil Shute's *On the Beach* (1957) is a bestselling fictional account of the results of nuclear war and the book inspired the film of the same name in 1959. Set in 1963 in the aftermath of a global war, *On the Beach* focuses on how a group of people, among them the commander of the last American nuclear submarine, face death from radioactive fallout that is steadily working its way from the northern hemisphere to the south, eradicating all life. The theme of universal extinction from fallout played into growing concerns and fears over the issue. (Kobal Collection)

On the Beach was directed by Stanley Kramer and featured an all-star cast. Here, in a scene aboard the fictional US nuclear submarine USS Sawfish, Captain Dwight Towers (Gregory Peck) gives explicit instructions to a crewmember he is sending ashore into the atomic-devastated United States who is seeking to determine the origin of a mysterious radio signal in the hope that people have survived the atomic war and radiation. It turns out to be a false alarm, and the crewmember returns with the grim news that everyone is dead. (Kobal Collection)

weapons in the 1950s reinforced and exacerbated nuclear concerns and fears, as evidenced by the February 1958 formation of the Campaign for Nuclear Disarmament (CND) in London.[7] From 1958, in the face of nuclear proliferation and events such as the Cuban Missile Crisis, the anti-nuclear movement expanded globally.

POPULAR CULTURE AND THE BOMB

Historian Paul Boyer, in his book *By the Bomb's Early Light*, documented a number of cultural responses to the atomic bomb, from atomic humor to music, art, and film. Popular 1945–46 songs included "Atom Buster," "Atom Polka," "Atom and Eve," "Old Man Atom," "Atomic Boogie," "You're My Atom Bomb Baby," "Atomic Power," and "When the Atomic Bomb Fell."[8] Boyer notes the first film to incorporate the bomb into its storyline was the nearly completed *The House on 92nd Street*, a September 10, 1945 release by 20th Century Fox about the FBI's infiltration and break-up of a Nazi spy ring. The film was revised before release to have the Nazis seeking atomic secrets, and in 1946 it won an Academy Award for best original motion picture story. It was followed in 1947 by MGM's *The Beginning or the End*, a fictionalized account of the development of the bomb. MGM's promotional book for the film proclaimed that, "It was inevitable that the story of the atom bomb should one day reach the screen … it marks the stoutest challenge ever placed upon Hollywood's film making ingenuity."[9]

Atomic references began to appear both in the media and in advertisements in late August 1945, with "atomic sales" and "atomic results," notes Boyer, and an amazing ad from a Fifth Avenue jeweler:

BURSTING FURY – Atomic Inspired Pin & Earring. New fields to conquer with Atomic jewelry. The pearled bomb bursts into a fury of dazzling colors in mock rhinestones, emeralds, rubies and sapphires... As daring to wear as it was to drop the first atom bomb. Complete set $24.75.[10]

In the same vein, an advertisement in the March 1946 issue of *Mechanix Illustrated* offered for sale "Bomb-Site Jewelry" manufactured from "atomsite," the atomic-fused glass from the Trinity Site. In the New Mexico desert, souvenir stands sprang up, also selling jewelry made from lumps of the still-radioactive atomic slag, as well as the raw product.

In bars, new drinks appeared, starting with a Pernod and gin blend called the "Atomic Cocktail" at the Washington Press Club (sometimes called the Absinthe Fiend); the mix was nothing new, but it was first poured under its new name in August 1945. Not to be outdone, Los Angeles burlesque houses advertised "Atom Bomb dancers," according to Boyer.

Another pop-culture reflection of the new bomb was the "atomic cocktail." Any powerful drink that could lay you out with one glass (or so the thinking went) would qualify, and an odd color to the mix also helped. The Washington Press Club version was a near-glowing green, and it was also potent at half an ounce of Pernod and an ounce of gin. In 1945, American jazz singer and songwriter "Slim" Gaillard recorded the song, "Atomic Cocktail." The song explains that the drink will fall and splash "all around the place," and warns the prospective drinker when they see it coming to grab their suitcase because it will send them through the sky "like air mail." The refrain? "Boom! Atomic Cocktail!" (Kobal)

Popular culture was quick to seize upon the atomic bomb as a positive metaphor, although that view was not universal, and it would change in time. The effect on the world of children was both profound and shallow. One observer commented on a group of children playing at war after the news of Hiroshima, in the usual "rat-a-tat-tat" combat tradition, and how one child ran by, arms outstretched, said boom and ran off. When asked what he had just done, he explained he was the atomic bomb, and he had won. The point was also made in this French children's board game (c. 1945) in which a player moves a bomb carrying plane closer and closer to Japan in order to launch his winning weapon. (Private Collection / Bridgeman Art Library)

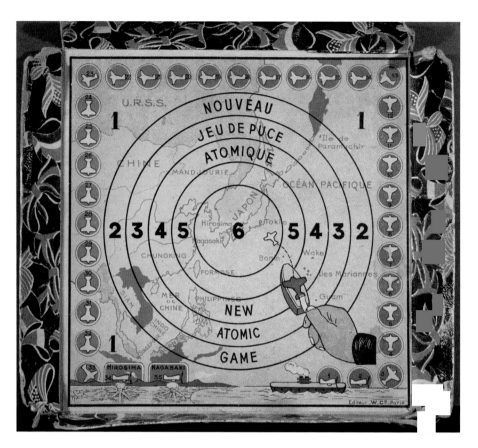

In another arena, the bomb appeared in the first *Superman* comic of 1946, in the January–February issue (#38), which featured Superman in the "Battle of the Atoms." In 1947, Disney released a special cereal box premium 32-page pocket-size book featuring "Donald Duck's Atomic Bomb." Board games featuring the bomb were also released, including one game, from France, in which the players could advance their game pieces into Japan to attack Hiroshima and Nagasaki. American kids could also obtain, for 10 (later 15) cents and a Kix cereal box top, a "Lone Ranger Atomic Bomb Ring." Each aluminum and plastic ring had a four-pronged tail fin complete with a "secret compartment" to hide messages from the enemy. When the tail fin was removed, kids would "See Genuine Atoms Split to Smithereens!" Polonium alpha particles from a small radium sample struck a zinc sulfide screen and after a few minutes, scintillations from the particles appeared on a plastic screen:

You'll see brilliant flashes of light in the inky darkness inside the atom chamber. These frenzied vivid flashes are caused by the released energy of atoms. PERFECTLY SAFE

– We guarantee you can wear the KIX Atomic "Bomb" Ring with complete safety. The atomic materials inside the ring are harmless.[11]

Kix cereal reportedly gave away millions of the rings between 1946 and 1957. While a few European-developed items appeared, like the post-Hiroshima French board game, the US monopoly of the bomb kept the atomic game and souvenir trade almost uniquely American.

INTERNATIONAL CONTROL

The potential spread of atomic technology and the ability of other countries to develop atomic bombs weighed heavily on the minds of American officials. On August 10, 1945, Truman spoke to that concern in a national radio broadcast:

> The atomic bomb is too dangerous to be loose in a lawless world. That is why Great Britain and the United States, who have the secret of its production, do not intend to reveal the secret until means have been found to control the bomb so as to protect ourselves and the rest of the world from the danger of total destruction… We must constitute ourselves trustees of this new force – to prevent its misuse and turn it into the channels of service to mankind.[12]

While the United States and Great Britain would act as "trustees," some government officials, including members of Congress, suggested that the newly formed United Nations (UN), "charged with keeping the peace, be made the custodian."[13] The New York *Herald*, in an August 1945 editorial, also proposed that the atomic bomb needed to be handed to the UN. "The new weapon may well serve to strengthen greatly the forces of civilization… Retained in the hands of the Security Council as a potential punitive weapon, the bomb would have a terrific deterrent effect."[14]

At that stage, only the Americans possessed the "secret" of how to make a working bomb. The Russians, working with espionage-provided knowledge, were still a few years away from building a bomb, and despite their own wartime efforts German and Japanese nuclear scientists had failed to make the necessary breakthroughs that would have led to a workable weapon. The British, staunch allies and leading participants in the bomb effort, nevertheless did not possess comprehensive knowledge of how to create a bomb. Although a joint British and Canadian atomic effort at Ontario was developing plutonium, once the United States excluded Britain from the atomic program at war's end it would take years for the British participants, on their return, to acquire the political will and means to begin a British atomic program. A French veteran of the project would also, in time, take a leading role in developing France's nuclear capacity. But in 1945 these developments were years away. As events would quickly show, most of war-weary, devastated, and financially depleted Europe, especially Great Britain, publicly endorsed the concept of American atomic leadership, even if privately hedging that support with an unspoken "for now."

Eleanor Roosevelt, widow of the former president, reminded Americans that the bomb was the result of the "pooling of many minds belonging to different races and different religions."[15] This precedent suggested a way forward, working "out our difficulties – not by setting up superior races, but by learning to co-operate and using the best that each one has to contribute to solve the problems of this new age." In a nationally broadcast NBC radio "Round Table Discussion" on August 12, University of Chicago Vice President R. G. Gustavson commented, "if the United States tries to sit on this secret, it will make itself the most hated power on the face of the earth."[16]

Other than the Russians and their allies, most Europeans at that immediate postwar stage disagreed with Gustavson. Winston Churchill, for one, was not an advocate of turning the new weapon over to the UN. In his now famous "Sinews of Peace" speech of March 5, 1946, in Fulton, Missouri (where he coined the phrase "iron curtain"), Churchill stated that it would be:

> wrong and imprudent to entrust the secret knowledge or experience of the atomic bomb, which the United States, Great Britain, and Canada now share, to the world organisation, while it is still in its infancy. It would be criminal madness to cast it adrift in this still agitated and un-united world. No one in any country has slept less well in their beds because this knowledge and the method and the raw materials to apply it, are at present largely retained in American hands.[17]

While a number of proponents picked up on H. G. Wells' message in *The World Set Free*, that the advent of the atomic age would lead to world government, the global ideological conflict between the Soviet Union and the United States and their allies ensured that any plans to turn the UN into an empowered, workable world government failed. The issue of communism and its potential influence, not only on proposals for an ostensibly Moscow-driven world government, but even on the sentiments and politics of some of the atomic scientists, gradually emerged as a major issue in how America dealt with the bomb. Concerns that a number of Manhattan Project scientists, including J. Robert Oppenheimer, were at best left-leaning sympathizers and at worst actual agents of the Soviet Union, had spurred a number of investigations and constant surveillance at Los Alamos.

A problem for military and government officials eager to maintain America's grip on its "winning weapon" was the proposal by several scientists not to use the bomb in combat against the Japanese, including Leó Szilárd, who was "horrified" by the attacks. There were also calls by scientists, including Neils Bohr, to share atomic research as part of an international effort to control this dangerous new power. The view of the scientists, which was valid, was that the atomic secret would not stay secret for long, given the nature of science and existing international knowledge of nuclear physics. Both proposals met with suspicion and steps were gradually taken to remove those figures from further work on the bomb. Eventually, Oppenheimer himself would fall victim to the ideological purging of "suspect" atomic scientists in the hysteria of postwar anti-communist witch hunts.

In June 1946, the UN's newly appointed Atomic Energy Commission (UNAEC) met for the first time in New York's Bronx. The American delegate to UNAEC, presidential advisor Bernard Baruch, outlined the United States' proposal for international control of atomic energy. The plan was based on a government committee's report issued in March that outlined how the UN could conduct a survey of all fissionable ores in the world, monitor and control them, license, inspect, and control all nations' atomic facilities, and, through its broad powers of inspection, detect the diversion of atomic resources to military purposes. The United States would not relinquish its atomic resources to international control until it was assured that the UN had a solid plan for carrying out these responsibilities. Even then, considering the atomic fear of its citizens, the United States might continue to develop and build new bombs: "That decision," Baruch said to the UNAEC, "whenever made, will involve considerations of the highest policy, affecting our security, and must be made by our government under its constitutional processes and in the light of all the facts of the world situation... Before a country is ready to relinquish any winning weapons, it must have more than words to reassure it."[18]

American policy was already taking a firm anti-Soviet stance under the direction of President Truman, who saw the Russians as "people from across the tracks whose manners were very bad,"[19] and hence took a hard line with the Soviets from the beginning of his presidency. Secretary of State Byrnes, with the President's backing, was already practicing "atomic diplomacy," or a projection of American will through the sole possession of the atomic bomb. Truman had not shared the secret of the bomb with Stalin at Potsdam (although thanks to Soviet spying, Stalin was aware of the project), and through what historian Gregg Herken terms a "polite subterfuge" – in which Truman only notified Stalin of a new weapon of immense power, but did not mention the use of nuclear fission – US secrecy heightened Soviet suspicions of America's postwar intentions. Byrnes saw, in the atomic bomb, power "to dictate our own terms at the end of the war," and to make the Soviets "more manageable."[20] As he would later joke, Byrnes dealt with the Soviets in negotiations armed with an atomic bomb in "my hip pocket," humor masking the *realpolitik* that now confronted Baruch's proposals to the UNAEC. Following the tabling of the "Baruch Plan," Soviet representative Andrei Gromyko called for a world moratorium on atomic weapon production. Gromyko's proposal did not meet with support, and was rejected by the committee. Ultimately, the Soviet Union and Poland abstained from joining in the committee's December 1946 report on international control of atomic weapons. The rest of the committee, and their governments, publicly supported the *de facto* leading American role, although in time some of them would begin their own atomic programs to challenge America's domination of the atomic secret, including its allies United Kingdom and France.

Devolving into "propaganda harangues," UNAEC debates and discussions dragged on past Baruch's resignation at the end of 1946 and remained unresolved in May 1948 when UNAEC's mandate expired and the UN dissolved the commission.

KEEPING THE SECRET AND SOVIET ESPIONAGE

Despite the decision to reveal the secret of the atomic bomb's development in the immediate aftermath of the Hiroshima attack, the Manhattan Engineer District did not want all of the details released. A memorandum on recommended security requirements, issued on August 8, 1945, by the First Technical Service Detachment reminded the teams at Tinian "it should be clearly evident to all project personnel that intelligent security concerning certain phases of project activities remains a necessity."[21] The memorandum went on to list those areas that remained classified:

Information pertaining to the unit design and details, and character of and details concerning the critical material.

a. Production schedules of critical material, actual or proposed.
b. Proposed tactical uses and/or schedules.
c. Results of tests employing the project weapons or dummies thereof.
d. Data concerning past tactical uses.
e. Communications codes peculiar to the project.
f. Information pertaining to air and water shipments of project supplies.
g. *All* information pertaining to shipments of critical materials.
h. Specific contributions with regard to engineering or design details, or other information contributed by various project installations or by specific project individuals.

i. The operational inter-relationship of project sites.

j. The association of tactical units or the names of tactical personnel engaged in the combat delivery of the weapon to the enemy.

At the same time, Oppenheimer passed along a message to all laboratory members from Robert P. Patterson, the Under Secretary of War:

To the Men and Women of Manhattan District Project:

Today the whole world knows the secret which you have helped us keep for many months. I am pleased to be able to add that the warlords of Japan now know its effects better even than we ourselves. The atomic bomb which you have helped to develop with high devotion to patriotic duty is the most devastating military weapon that any country has ever been able to turn against its enemy. No one of you has worked on the entire project or knows the whole story. Each of you has done his own job and kept his own secret, and so today I speak for a grateful nation when I say congratulations, and thank you all.

I hope you will continue to keep the secrets you have kept so well. The need for security and for continued effort is fully as great now as it ever was. We are proud of every one of you.[22]

Despite Patterson's gratitude and expectation of security, among those who read the message were a small number of participants who had actively violated the project's security and passed atomic secrets to the Soviets. Most notable was German-born scientist Klaus Fuchs, whose regular reports to his handlers enabled the Soviet Union to build their own version of Fat Man and test it by 1949.

The Soviets had learned about the possibility of an atomic bomb's development in September 1941 from British sources, and soon assigned agents and resources to a dedicated program of espionage they codenamed ENORMOZ (enormous). While the US government later claimed it had caught lower-level employees sharing data and had dismissed them, and Army security agents conducted relentless surveillance, tapping phones, and following scientists, a few spies slipped through the net. Fuchs, a member of the Theoretical Division, was the most productive and ultimately the best-known atomic spy at Los Alamos, passing on details of his participation in implosion research, and later, in his postwar career, details of plutonium production and early research into the hydrogen bomb. Another Los Alamos scientist-spy, Theodore "Ted" Hall, remained undetected until the 1950s. Under questioning he never confessed, and his role was not revealed until decades later. Two other Soviet spies, working in Canada as part of the British effort to build a reactor at Chalk River, Ontario, were Allan Nunn May and Bruno Pontecorvo. May, a British national, and Pontecorvo, a Jewish Italian refugee, both passed on observations on their work at Chalk River and reports on their interactions with American colleagues. Pontecorvo, fearful of being arrested following Fuchs' capture, defected to the Soviet Union in 1950. Soviet records, as well as US intercepts of coded Soviet cables, revealed other, unnamed, and as yet unidentified spies at Los Alamos and Hanford.[23]

Another spy was a member of the SED working on the implosion program, Army machinist David Greenglass. A member of the Communist Party, Greenglass passed information to his brother-in-law, Julius Rosenberg, a staunch communist who ran a spy ring. Greenglass' role was discovered in 1950 with Klaus Fuchs' confession and the arrest of a contact, Harry Gold, who had passed messages from both Fuchs and Greenglass to a Soviet agent. With his arrest, Gold implicated Greenglass. Greenglass cooperated with US officials in return for immunity for his wife, an un-indicted co-conspirator, and named his brother-in-law and sister as spies. Arrested in 1950, after a highly publicized trial, the Rosenbergs were convicted of espionage in March 1951. Judge Irving Kaufman, in passing a sentence of death by execution in the electric chair, commented that:

> by your betrayal you undoubtedly have altered the course of history to the disadvantage of our country. No one can say that we do not live in a constant state of tension. We have evidence of your treachery all around us every day for the civilian defense activities throughout the nation are aimed at preparing us for an atom bomb attack.[24]

They were executed on June 19, 1953, seven years to the day after Andrei Gromyko had rejected the Baruch Plan in his speech to the UNAEC. Greenglass received a 15-year prison sentence and served ten years before his release. While a Soviet atomic bomb was inevitable, espionage in the Manhattan Project gave Stalin the weapon more quickly that it would have come otherwise, with some suggesting by as much as 12 to 18 months. What Americans had feared, and in part brought about – an atomic arms race – was taking place.

LIMITING FOREIGN PARTICIPATION

The role of ongoing American efforts to develop atomic power and other weapons occupied the attention of US officials in the aftermath of the war. On August 17, 1945, Oppenheimer, in a brief to Secretary of War Henry Stimson, told Stimson that it was inevitable that more powerful atomic weapons, in larger numbers, were probable, that the United States would not be able to keep the secret of their production to itself, and that no adequate defense was possible.

Oppenheimer would not participate in America's atomic future as director of Los Alamos, however. Eager to return to private life, he resigned as director on October 16, the day he accepted an Army Certificate of Appreciation from General Groves for the laboratory's work during the war. Oppenheimer's views were clear; he had led the laboratory and participated in the bomb project at a time of great "urgency," and with

On January 11, 1949, the *Washington Post* published political cartoonist Herbert Block's "Tick-Tock Tick-Tock." Block personified the omnipresent bomb as "Mr. Atom," and seized upon the announcement that scientists had perfected the atomic clock as a new and more accurate timekeeping device to remind the world that failure to reach an accord on international control of atomic weapons would have devastating consequences. Mr. Atom swings a pendulum (which is an atom with electrons orbiting a neutron) that just misses the head of the unsuspecting newspaper reader. (Library of Congress)

that urgency now passed, the threat of the bomb meant that international control of the new weapon was necessary. In a speech on November 2, 1945, to the Association of Los Alamos Scientists, a group that had formed specifically to influence future atomic policies, he concluded his explanation of these points by noting:

> We are not only scientists; we are men, too. We cannot forget our dependence on our fellow men. I mean not only our material dependence, without which no science would be possible, and without which we could not work; I mean also our deep moral dependence, in that the value of science must lie in the world of men, that all our roots lie there. These are the strongest bonds in the world, stronger than those even that bind us to one another, these are the deepest bonds – that bind us to our fellow men.[25]

Scientists' views on policy, however, while sought, were not going to determine the direction taken by the United States. At the time of Oppenheimer's departure, new Los Alamos director Norris Bradbury inherited a laboratory with an undefined, if not uncertain future.

American policy was clear. It would continue a strong atomic effort, especially as it became obvious that the Baruch Plan had stalled and would likely fail. There was also increased worry over aggressive Soviet advances in Eastern Europe and the belief that these would lead to armed conflict. News that the Soviets were grabbing up Nazi research and scientists, not only from the failed German nuclear effort but also from the V1 and V2 rocket programs, another area of American interest, further raised concern. How American atomic policy would be shaped and administered, however, was less certain.

In October 1945, Congressional legislation to determine America's postwar atomic policy, with language provided by War Department staff and based on the report of the Interim Committee established by Truman in July, was introduced by Kentucky Congressman Andrew May, Chairman of the House Military Affairs Committee, and Colorado Senator Edwin Johnson, Vice-Chairman of the Senate Military Affairs Committee. The May-Johnson Bill had the President's backing. It called for ongoing government leadership in atomic research, with heavy military involvement if not *de facto* control, and sweeping powers including strict penalties for security violations. Opposition from scientists uncomfortable with what they saw as a renewed mandate for the Manhattan Project and Groves' almost dictatorial powers of control dragged into prolonged testimony and debate. As it became clear the bill was stalemated, Truman quietly withdrew his support, but the administration did not offer a substitute. Into the gap stepped newly elected Senator Brien McMahon of Connecticut.

McMahon, chair of both the Senate Special Committee on Atomic Energy and the even more powerful Congressional Joint Committee on Atomic Energy, held hearings through December 1945. The hearings effectively seized the initiative from the Senate Military Affairs Committee, where the May-Johnson Bill now sat stalled. The debates over May-Johnson, according to *Time* magazine's November 19 edition, meant that "Congress was suddenly and humbly intent on learning about atomic power, [and] was sweating at the very thought of legislating about it."[26] On December 20, McMahon introduced a new bill calling for a civilian agency with full-time commissioners to administer America's atomic program and weapons. The bill was opposed by General Groves, who wanted more military control, and hence was more eagerly supported by the scientists who had been opposed to the May-Johnson Bill. It also gained Truman's support by tying control of the agency to the executive branch, and hence the President. When the bill finally passed, ironically, it also provided for a strong military voice in the new agency.

The Senate approved the McMahon Bill on June 1, 1946, followed by the House of Representatives on July 20. Conference committee meetings continued through the summer, and on August 1, 1946, Truman signed the Atomic Energy Act of 1946 into law. The act closed down the Manhattan Project and transferred its facilities and authority to the newly created Atomic Energy Commission (AEC). Headed by a five-person civilian committee, the AEC had two advisory committees, one general and the other a military liaison committee. It answered not only to the executive branch, but also to the Congressional Joint Committee on Atomic Energy. The AEC had inherited a powerful legacy, no longer the sole purview of the military, but operated under firm government control. The AEC also inherited America's atomic arsenal, then only nine Fat Man implosion weapons, when it took over on January 1, 1947. Those nine bombs were all that existed, and were solely the possession of the United States, not even to be shared with the British and Canadian allies who had joined the effort to make them.

One of the provisions of the Atomic Energy Act of 1946 was a strict ban on sharing atomic technology with foreign powers, including allies. Had Roosevelt lived, and Churchill not lost the immediate postwar election and his seat as Prime Minister, the original agreement between Britain, Canada, and the United States might have survived. Instead, Britain, and Canada were both shut out of a program they had spurred and in which they had played a key role. Without the participation of the British mission, and Canadian uranium, the bomb most likely would never have existed. Shut out, the two countries withdrew the last of their scientists who had participated in the Manhattan Project, and pursued their own independent atomic programs.

Beginning in the late 1940s, governments encouraged the concept of Civil Defense and protection against the atomic bomb as the right and responsibility of the public as well as the government. "Fallout shelters" to sit out the aftermath of nuclear war until radiation levels diminished to "acceptable" levels were part of Civil Defense. Here, a group of scouts from the Boy Scouts of America ride on a parade float with a shelter to encourage safety. (The Art Archive)

Canada had not only provided uranium from its northern mines and heavy water from a Manhattan District facility in Trail, British Columbia, but had also participated in the creation of a joint Canadian-British research laboratory in Montreal in 1942. The lab, with the task of designing a nuclear reactor, designed what was known as the Zero Energy Experimental Pile (ZEEP). Work on the ZEEP began in 1944 at Chalk River, Ontario, northwest of the Canadian capital of Ottawa. Chalk River was where two Soviet spies worked, whose discovery would later be one of the factors cited in the American and British split. ZEEP went critical on September 5, 1945, and ensured an ongoing role in nuclear research and development for the Canadians and British after the Atomic Energy Act. While Canada only pursued peaceful uses of atomic power, however, Britain launched its own weapons program, and detonated its first atomic bomb in October 1952.

THE BEST DEFENSE IS A STRONG OFFENSE

In the United States, concern not only over the potential threat from the Soviets, but also the deadly effects of the bomb continued to grow. As Congress debated, *LIFE* magazine's November 19, 1945, issue featured an illustrated article, "The 36-Hour War," which outlined how an attack on the United States by atomic bombs mounted on German V2 rockets would unfold and what the results would be. "The ghastliest of all wars" would be over, as the title suggested, in 36 hours. Large and dramatic illustrations showed rockets streaking over the Atlantic to hit 12 American cities – New York, Chicago, San Francisco, Los Angeles, Philadelphia, Boulder Dam, New Orleans, Denver, Washington, DC, Salt Lake City, Kansas City and Knoxville, Tennessee, killing ten million Americans. While one rocket is shot down, the damage is devastating. From underground rocket-launching sites, the United States retaliates, destroying enemy cities even as enemy airborne troops invade bomb-ravaged American cities. The United States wins the war, but the last two images offered a provocatively frightening view of the costs of victory – an enemy soldier, clad in protective gear, stands in the devastated telephone exchange of a small town, the open-mouthed body of the young, blonde operator sprawled at his feet in a tangle of broken glass and wires, and similarly clad US Army technicians stand in a flattened wasteland taking measurements for radiation in front of the lions of the atomic-blasted New York Public Library. (See pages 169 and 170 for "The 36-Hour War" images.)

The thought of an attack on the United States, given graphic reality, underscored the concerns and fears that had surfaced after news of events at Hiroshima and Nagasaki. What was also emerging was a growing sense of the human toll of the atomic bombings. On August 31, 1946, in a bold move, *The New Yorker* published an account of the Hiroshima attack. Written by journalist John Hersey, the article outlined not what had happened to the city, but instead reported on the experiences of six survivors: Toshiko Sasaki, a personnel clerk; Dr. Masakazu Fujii, a physician who had operated a private hospital; Hatsuyo Nakamura, a mother of three and the widow of a tailor; Father Wilhelm Kleinsorge, a German priest; Dr. Terufumi Sasaki, a surgeon; and the Reverend Mr. Kiyoshi Tanimoto, a Methodist pastor. Hersey had selected the six for his story because they were the most evocative of a series of interviews he had conducted in the bomb-ravaged city. From the start of their day on August 6, 1945, to what their lives were like, injured and stricken with radiation sickness nearly a year later, the article was stunning.

The article took up the entire issue. As the editors wrote in the introduction to the magazine:

TO OUR READERS *The New Yorker* this week devotes its entire editorial space to an article on the almost complete obliteration of a city by one atomic bomb, and what happened to the people of that city. It does so in the conviction that few of us have yet comprehended the all but incredible destructive power of this weapon, and that everyone might well take time to consider the terrible implications of its use.

The New Yorker sold out that day; subsequent editions were quickly published, the article was read and broadcast in its entirety on radio, and the Book-of-the-Month Club reprinted it for free distribution to its members. In October, just two months after the magazine hit the newsstands, Alfred A. Knopf published the article as a book simply titled *Hiroshima*. It has remained in print ever since.

The implications of the book were clear. The *New York Times*, while going on record that it still supported the dropping of the bomb, noted:

What happened to about 100,000 is clear. They died. What happened to the lucky six is an example of what human beings can endure and not die. Every American who has permitted himself to make jokes about atom bombs, or who has come to regard them as just one sensational phenomenon that can now be accepted as part of civilization, like the airplane and the gasoline engine, or who has allowed himself to speculate as to what we might do with them if we were forced into another war, ought to read Mr. Hersey.[27]

Response from various participants in the decision to develop and use the bomb was not long in appearing. Former Secretary of War Henry Stimson published an account of the "Decision to Use the Atomic Bomb" in the February 1947 edition of *Harper's*. Urged to write it by James Conant, Stimson's article was full of detail and was aided by quiet contributions and review from key participants, including General Groves.

Justification for what had happened, while still the subject of debate six decades later, had less interest for most Americans, however. The publication of *Hiroshima*, like the "36-Hour War," made it clear to Americans that when, not if, atomic war came, they would suffer. The effects of radiation had been officially denied despite knowledge to the better by American occupation officials, who stated that Japanese claims of radiation sickness were simply propaganda. Journalists faced a difficult time in gaining access, and the first to reach Nagasaki, George Weller of the *Chicago Daily News*, had to sneak in by outwitting General McArthur's office. Not at all initially sympathetic to the Japanese plight by his own admission, Weller was nonetheless stunned by what he saw. His dispatches mysteriously vanished and until the day of his own death, decades later, he thought they were forever gone. Only recently published, Weller's un-filed and most

Eros and the atom intertwined in the aftermath of the development of atomic weapons. "Atomic burlesque dancers" and an actress labeled the "anatomic bomb" were one manifestation of the phenomena; another was the unofficial christening of the first bomb dropped at Bikini as "Gilda" in honor of the recently released Rita Hayworth film. The film played on the decks of the support fleet to an appreciative military audience who put a new emphasis on the popular term for a woman as a "bombshell" when they stenciled the name and a profile view of Miss Hayworth on the weapon. Another aspect of sexualizing the bomb was the naming of the revealing new French bathing suit, the bikini. (Private Collection / Bridgeman Art Library)

likely suppressed accounts of radiation sickness would have only reinforced the message of Hersey's *Hiroshima*; no one was safe when an atomic bomb detonated overhead.[28]

The thought of no satisfactory defense against the bomb was foremost in the minds of the atomic scientists and the military. It also began to impinge on the consciousness of Congress. In an increasingly tense atmosphere, and concerned that the only potential defense was a strong offense, plans for a postwar "test" of the bomb's military applications moved to the forefront of discussion by the end of 1945.

OPERATION *CROSSROADS*:
THE BIKINI TESTS

In the aftermath of Hiroshima and Nagasaki, the question of what the atomic bomb meant in military terms occupied a great deal of public and government attention. The implications, obviously, were huge. The New York *Herald Tribune*, in a post-Hiroshima editorial, commented: "the victory or defeat of armies, the fate of nations, the rise and fall of empires are all alike, in any long perspective only the ripples on the surface of history; but the unpredictable unlocking of the inconceivable energy of the atom would stir history itself to its deepest depths."[1]

David Sarnoff, president of the Radio Corporation of America (RCA), voiced the fear of many Americans that with the bomb, "No nation will be invulnerable to attack. No Goliath will be safe,"[2] and the *New York Times*, in an editorial went further. "It should make an end of marching, rolling, and even flying armies, and turn most of our battleships into potential scrap."[3]

That view of an obsolete military was not completely shared by the postwar US Air Force. They alone had the means to deliver the atomic bomb in combat, and airpower, as far as Curtis LeMay and his fellow officers were concerned, had not only secured victory, but could also secure the peace. "After looking at the damage done by a relatively few B-29s," Curtis LeMay later reminisced, "I thought to myself that if we'd had such a force in place on December 7, 1941, there probably wouldn't have been an attack on Pearl Harbor. From that moment on, I believed that it would be possible to maintain peace through strength."[4] The USAAF reorganized after the war into three separate commands, one of which, the Strategic Air Command (SAC), formed in March 1946 to "conduct long-range offensive operations in any part of the world," initially absorbed the 509th and its Silverplate B-29s. From these beginnings, following LeMay's appointment to command it in 1948, SAC would become America's airborne nuclear deterrent strike force.

The US Army, Marine Corps, and Navy were less sanguine. For some of them, the words of radio commentator Edward R. Murrow hit very close. "Seldom, if ever, has a war ended leaving the victors with such a sense of uncertainty and fear, with such a realization that the future is obscure and that survival is not assured."[5] The atomic bomb had sparked discussions in naval circles about how ships would fare against atomic attack. The question was raised on the floor of the Senate on August 25, 1945, by Senator McMahon, who suggested:

> In order to test the destructive powers of the atomic bomb against naval vessels, I would like... Japanese naval ships taken to sea and an atomic bomb dropped on them.

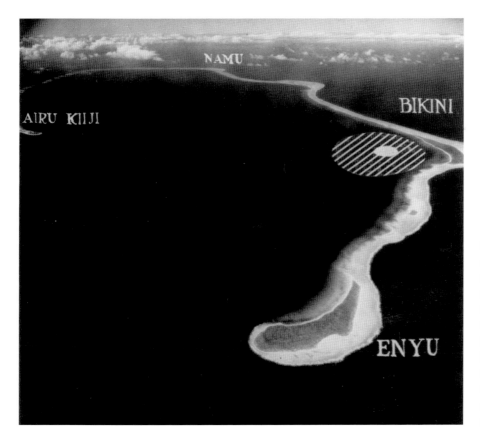

Bikini was selected for the atomic tests because it was relatively isolated from the rest of the world, had a shallow lagoon (essential for divers to examine ships sunk by the blasts) and was under US control. This Operation *Crossroads*-released image shows the atoll and the location where the target ships would be moored. (US Naval Institute)

The resulting explosion should prove to us how effective the atomic bomb is when used against the giant naval vessels. I can think of no better use for these Jap ships.[6]

The idea of dropping the bomb on ships was not new. Discussions at Los Alamos had considered an atomic attack on the Japanese fleet anchorage at Truk, in the Caroline islands of Micronesia, but there were concerns over the Japanese grabbing the weapon if it did not explode. There was also the question of whether or not the depleted Japanese fleet would be a significant target, or a sufficiently visible one. Joined with the delays in producing a working implosion weapon, as well as the rush from Trinity to Hiroshima, these concerns pushed an atomic naval attack off the table.

With the surrender of Japan, the remaining surface ships of the Imperial Japanese Navy, 48 in all, were eyed not only by politicians but also by the American Navy, as targets for destruction. On August 28, 1945, Fleet Admiral Ernest J. King ordered the annihilation of all Japanese naval vessels left afloat. Brigadier General B. M. Giles, a member of McArthur's staff in occupied Tokyo, followed that with a suggestion on September 14 that the atomic bomb be used to sink them. "Hap" Arnold and Curtis LeMay echoed Giles' suggestion, and on September 18, Arnold wrote and asked the Navy that "a number of Japanese vessels be made available to the Army Air Forces for use in tests involving atomic bombs and other weapons."[7]

The request was provocative, given the emerging postwar struggle between advocates of naval and air power over which would constitute the best defense of the United States. Army Air advocates argued that saturation and incendiary bombing had decided the war in Japan, with the B-29-delivered atomic bombs as the *coup de grace*. The use of bombs would decide the next war quickly, as Arnold pointed out in a report that led to *LIFE*'s "36-Hour War." There was no need for a navy if rockets with atomic warheads constituted an offensive arm of a postwar air force. Furthermore missiles designed to shoot down an enemy's approaching atomic rockets were also under the air force's control. This bluntly made a point the Army Air Forces had consistently pushed before and during the war. Naval power, even naval aviation, was obsolete.

The Navy was acutely sensitive on this point, and knew that it was more than a matter of inter-service rivalry. Their survival might very well be at risk. Senior officers also remembered the USAAC's sinking of the captured German battleship *Ostfriesland* off the Virginia Capes in 1921 by aerial bombs in a staged test arranged by maverick USAAC officer Billy Mitchell. The Navy had responded to the threat of aviation by incorporating it into its service in the 1920s and 30s. The build up of fast carrier forces during the war had also shown that when confronted by change,

Admiral W. H. P. Blandy, commander of Joint Task Force One, the military command tasked with Operation *Crossroads*, briefs US Secretary of Defense James Forrestal on the American atomic bomb tests at Bikini. *Crossroads* was to be the first scientific tests and political demonstration of the new weapon by the United States. (National Air & Space Museum/Smithsonian Images)

especially following the devastation of the fleet at Pearl Harbor by Japanese carrier aircraft, the US Navy was capable of meeting the challenge and incorporating new technology, strategy, and tactics. The Navy prepared to meet the Army Air Forces head-on. They would move forward to test the bomb against ships. They called in "Deak" Parsons to draft a report on the matter.

If conducted by the Navy, the tests would prove "that ships were not excessively vulnerable to atomic attack," and that "Navy carrier aircraft could be just as useful and valuable as Air Force bombers for the delivery of atomic weapons."[8] While the existing Fat Man bombs were too big to fit into anything other than a B-29, Parsons, as the head of the Manhattan Project's push to take the bomb into battle, was already thinking ahead to re-designing the bomb from a laboratory weapon, designed and painstakingly assembled by scientists, into a combat weapon, manufactured in large numbers and readied for use by military technicians. Soon to be appointed a rear admiral for his exceptional work at Los Alamos and Tinian, Parsons was also thinking ahead to shipborne atomic weapons, including torpedoes, and atomic power for naval vessels.

Secretary of the Navy James Forrestal, questioned by Congress in August 1945 about the implications of the atomic bomb, answered that the Navy was and would

remain an important part of America's defense, and would incorporate the bomb, as "control of the sea by whatever weapons are necessary is the Navy's mission."[9] The day after Forrestal's testimony, the *New York Times*, reporting on naval opposition to suggestions to merge the War and Navy Departments into a new Department of Defense, noted that the Navy was amenable to joint operations regarding "scientific developments." The *Times* predicted "it would not be at all surprising" within the next six months to see an agreement "to test the effects of the new atomic bomb against warships."

> There has been some speculation … whether the atomic bomb might cause the bottoms of steel ships to disintegrate and thus sink the entire fleet … some Navy authorities say they would like to see such a test conducted against some of our old battleships for, if the atomic bomb works this way, they want to know it.[10]

Based on his experience and knowledge, "Deak" Parsons knew better. The Navy also had plenty of ships. The 1,200-vessel US Navy of August 1945 was planning to scale down to a 400-ship postwar force. With a number of vessels in reserve, as well as a certain number of combat-damaged, hastily repaired vessels that might better be scrapped, the Navy responded positively to the Army Air Force's request in October. Admiral King agreed to support the atomic bombing of captured Japanese ships along with "A few of our own modern naval vessels … included in the target array" as part of a coordinated operation under the control of the Joint Chiefs of Staff.[11] The Navy also suggested an underwater detonation of the bomb as well as an aerial drop.

On October 24, the *New York Times* reported that the Navy was prepared to test the atomic bomb against ships dispersed at sea as well as a fleet "massed at anchorage as in Pearl Harbor on December 7, 1941." The formal announcement of the tests, however, did not come until December 10, when the *Times* reported that while details were yet to be worked out, it would be a joint Army-Navy test. The USAAF "have been working aggressively to get a leading role in the experiment to make sure it will not be an all-Navy affair." At the same time, naval officers were clear on the message they wished to send to the American public and politicians. The US Navy would survive in the coming nuclear age.

JOINT TASK FORCE ONE

Parsons, as chief of the "Navy Atomic Bomb Group," which included himself, Ashworth, and another promising officer from the Dahlgren Proving Ground, Horacio Rivero, was an obvious choice to head up the Navy's evolving atomic program and the tests. However, Parsons felt he did not have the necessary rank and hence the authority to get the job done. He recommended that the job go to an old friend, Rear Admiral William Henry Purnell "Spike" Blandy. Blandy, an "imaginative but thorough planner and a resourceful, energetic combat leader," had spent much of his career in ordnance.[12] After an earlier career in battleships, destroyers, and as head of the gun section of the Bureau of Ordnance, Blandy became Chief of the Bureau of Ordnance in 1941.

Under Blandy, the Bureau of Ordnance had worked to develop the VT (variable time) or proximity fuse for anti-aircraft guns. Using radio waves in a "mini-radar" configuration inside a shell, the new fuses detected when they were close enough to an enemy airplane to detonate

Admiral William Henry Purnell Blandy (1890–1954), was placed in command of the Bikini tests, with Parsons as his deputy. A no nonsense officer, Blandy commanded the respect of the military establishment and politicians. Bridling at media criticism of him as an "atomic playboy," Blandy responded: "The bomb will not start a chain-reaction in the water converting it all to gas and letting the ships on all the oceans drop down to the bottom. It will not blow out the bottom of the sea and let all the water run down the hole… I am not an atomic playboy… exploding these bombs to satisfy my personal whim." (US Naval Institute)

In response to criticism that the atomic tests would destroy still valuable vessels, Joint Task Force One prepared this chart depicting the ships that would be used as targets at Bikini. It summarizes their types while making the point that their scrap value in a shrinking, postwar Navy was less than half a new ship. (US Naval Institute)

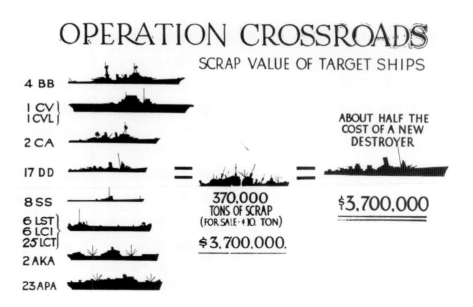

and destroy it. The officer who had spearheaded the effort to develop the fuse, and the one who took it into combat in the Pacific to test it, had been "Deak" Parsons. Blandy had backed Parsons and the fuse in 1941–43. Following the success of the VT fuse, Parsons' next assignment was the Manhattan Project. The proximity fuse would follow him there, and become a trigger for the atomic bomb. Parsons had not forgotten Blandy, or the admiral's influence when the VT fuse needed it. "Spike" Blandy, fresh from his last wartime assignment as commander of all pre-invasion activities for the Iwo Jima and Okinawa campaigns, now assumed the Navy's atomic mantle as a newly promoted vice admiral and deputy chief of naval operations/special weapons. Sidney Shalett of the *New York Times* had a better title for Blandy, whom he tagged the "Buck Rogers of the Navy."[13]

On December 22, 1945, military planners submitted recommendations to the Joint Chiefs of Staff for the atomic tests. The report outlined three atomic detonations, one in air, one in shallow water, and the third a deep-water explosion, and recommended placing the tests under the control of the Joint Chiefs with an independent evaluation board pulled from the ranks of the Army, Navy, the Manhattan District of the Corps of Engineers, and civilians. The Joint Chief approved the plan, and sent it to the President through the Secretary of War and the Secretary of the Navy. On January 10, 1946, President Truman concurred with his cabinet officers, and created Joint Task Force One (JTF-1) to conduct the tests, placing Blandy in command. While Congressional authorization for the tests would not come until June 1946, Blandy and his team sprang into action because the first test was set for that summer.

One of Blandy's first actions, on January 12, was to name the tests Operation *Crossroads*. He explained that he chose the name "because it was apparent that warfare, perhaps civilization itself, had been brought to a turning point in history by this revolutionary weapon."[14] Blandy's orders were to determine "the effects of atomic explosions against naval vessels in order to appraise the strategic implications of the application of atomic bombs including the results on naval design and tactics." JTF-1 was also to assess the "military, lesser military and principal scientific and technical objects," such as determining what the bomb would do not only to ships, but also to crews and equipment. They were also to determine the best means of decontaminating ships and to gain "sufficient data … to permit naval architects and engineers to design more resistant ships."[15] To carry out the tasks, Blandy immediately named Parsons, now promoted to rear admiral, as his deputy, and began assembling a fleet of ships not only to support Operation *Crossroads*, but also to serve as targets. Among them would be captured Japanese ships.

The German cruiser *Prinz Eugen*, one of the few German naval vessels acquired by the United States at war's end, ended up as a target ship at Bikini. Little brother of the famous battleship *Bismarck*, *Prinz Eugen* had participated in the sortie out of the Baltic and into the North Sea when *Bismarck* sank HMS *Hood*, and had survived the war only to die a slow death, radioactive and leaking, at the end of Operation *Crossroads*. (US National Archives)

The Japanese battleship *Nagato* was one of two Imperial Japanese Navy ships selected for use at Bikini. Battle-damaged and effectively a "dead" ship, *Nagato* was put back into commission by a US Navy crew and made her way to Bikini, arriving finally under tow to die beneath the atomic bomb. The former flagship of the IJN was selected to serve as much as a symbolic sacrifice as a scientific target. (US Naval Historical Center)

The tests were appealing, especially to political leaders, for more than technical reasons. They were a demonstration to the world, particularly the Soviet Union, of the United States' wealth and power at a time when the nation in the aftermath of the war was assuming the role of global leader. In April 1946, Blandy stated in a national radio broadcast that the upcoming tests would "help us to be what the world expects our great, non-aggressive and peace-loving country to be – the leader of those nations which seek nothing but a just and lasting peace."[16] Commentator Raymond Gram Swing more bluntly stated that Operation *Crossroads*, "the first of the atomic era war games ... is a notice served on the world that we have the power and intend to be heeded."[17]

Another potent statement was using the bomb to destroy ships of the once-feared Imperial Japanese Navy. The tests backed up the US image as a powerful nation by symbolically emphasizing America as the principal victor in the war. The inclusion of three captured warships – the Japanese battleship *Nagato* and cruiser *Sakawa*, and the German cruiser *Prinz Eugen* – as atomic targets was an echo of earlier triumphant victory parades of conquering heroes in ancient Rome. One early 1946 newspaper account, accompanied by an *Associated Press* photograph of 24 battered-looking destroyers and submarines, crowed that "Trapped Remnants of Jap Fleet Face Destruction in United States Navy Atom-Bomb Tests."

The use of Japanese warships as atomic targets was a "symbolic killing" of the enemy's ships with the same weapon that had forced his capitulation. The battleship *Nagato* particularly fulfilled that role. The onetime flagship of the Imperial Japanese Navy and the scene of operational planning for the Pearl Harbor attack, *Nagato* had been "captured" as a bombed-out derelict in Tokyo Bay in September 1945. The capture, a press event staged by military press officers, symbolized "the complete and final surrender of the Imperial Japanese Navy."[18] Sinking the same battleship with an atomic bomb now ritually "destroyed" the Imperial Japanese Navy in a more potent manner than prosaic scrapping or scuttling at sea. The battleship's intended fate was so important that at the tests American support vessels moored alongside carefully tended *Nagato* as "there was some danger that the captured Japanese ships ... might actually sink ... if they were left unattended..."[19]

A massive publicity effort also unfolded, with an invitation for media to attend, the assignment of a "press headquarter ships" (USS *Appalachian*), live radio feeds, and specially prepared media packets, lectures, and tours. "No effort was spared in making this the best reported as well as being the most reported technical experiment of all time."[20] In all, 114 US radio, newspaper, magazine, and news service reporters attended the first test, and 75 stayed for the second test. Ten foreign reporters also attended the tests.

Operation *Crossroads* was as much a political spectacle as it was a scientific test. While the Hiroshima and Nagasaki attacks were relatively undocumented, the blasts at Bikini were witnessed by tens of thousands of military personnel, as well as official representatives from other countries (including the Soviet Union) and reporters. Here VIP observers are shown "lit up by the light of an atomic bomb." (Smithsonian Images)

Throughout the first eight months of 1946, hundreds of articles and features dominated the newspapers and magazines, newsreels, and radio broadcasts, and plans were made for live radio transmission of the tests. Mindful of the ongoing debate over international control, the United States also invited the members of the UNAEC to send two observers to the tests. Ten nations accepted, including the Soviet Union.

The intense effort to publicize the tests, however, was focused more on a domestic rather than a foreign audience. Blandy stressed in interviews and news statements that the purpose of *Crossroads* was defensive, but derived from the perspective that the best defense was a strong offense through nuclear capability. As he had said at the beginning of the tests, testing the bomb on warships would "improve our Navy," because "We want ships that are tough, even when threatened by atomic bombs; we want to keep the ships afloat, propellers turning, guns firing; we want to protect the crews so that, if fighting is necessary, they can fight well today and return home unharmed tomorrow..."[21]

He went on to stress that:

The tests stand out clearly as a defensive measure. We are seeking to primarily learn what types of ships, tactical formations, and strategic dispositions of our own naval forces will best survive attack by the atomic weapons of other nations, should we ever

Los Alamos sent a number of scientists and technicians to participate in the atomic tests at Bikini. The widely held view of many was that the tests were a spectacle and not a true scientific test. Here the Los Alamos contingent is shown gathered at Bikini. (Los Alamos National Laboratory)

The crew of the target ship *Prinz Eugen* departs their ship for the first atomic test, removing numbered tags to ensure that no man was left behind. (US Naval Institute)

have to face them. By no stretch of the imagination can such steps of caution and economy be taken as a threat of aggression. If, because of such a false assumption, we failed to carry out these experiments, to learn the lessons which they can teach us, our designers of ships, aircraft and ground equipment, as well as our tacticians, strategists and medical doctors would be groping their way along a dark road which might lead us to another and worse Pearl Harbor.[22]

Thoughts of disaster and of atomic holocaust filled some news accounts. Others focused on other less serious aspects, including the decision of a French bathing suit designer to name his new creation, the "bikini," for the islands.

PREPARATIONS FOR THE TESTS

After studying a number of sites in the Caribbean and Pacific, JTF-1 selected Bikini Atoll in the Marshall Islands to conduct Operation *Crossroads*. The atoll, 6 miles wide with a shallow, 180ft-deep lagoon encompassing some 200 square miles of water, lay 2,400 miles west of Hawaii and 4,500 miles from San Francisco. A former German colony absorbed by the Japanese overseas empire after World War I, the Marshalls had fallen to the United States and formed the core of what would become the strategically important US Trust Territory of the Pacific Islands. Bikini was "ideal" for the tests because it was not only under US control, but also had a small population of 167 people, who could be relocated. It was also isolated, and the shallowness of the lagoon meant that divers could recover test instruments from sunken ships.

With Bikini's selection in January 1946, JTF-1 rushed to prepare it for the tests, even as it raced to find enough military personnel and scientists as well as ships. Ultimately, 37,000 officers and enlisted men from the Navy, along with 5,000 civilians and Army and Army Air Forces troops, formed the *Crossroads* commitment of 41,963 men and 37 women. Congress authorized the Navy to use 33 combat vessels as targets, but additional vessels were needed to fill out the target array, so the Navy added a large number of merchant-type attack transports and landing craft. In all, 94 ships steamed to Bikini as targets – 2 aircraft carriers, 5 battleships, 4 cruisers, 12 destroyers, 8 submarines, 19 attack transports, 41 landing craft, 2 yard oilers, and an advanced repair dry-dock. The target fleet's oldest ship, the 1912 battleship *Arkansas*, had fought in World War I. Most of the ships were veterans of major engagements of World War II, including Pearl Harbor, Midway, the battle of the Coral Sea, the Aleutians Campaign, Tarawa, the invasion of the Marshalls, the battles off the Philippines, including Leyte, and the D-Day landings at Normandy.

Among the equipment exposed to nuclear blast, heat and radiation at Bikini were the standard weapons of the Army, Marine Corps, Navy and Air Force. Here, journalists examine a variety of weapons installed on the deck of a target ship prior to the "Able" Test of July 1, 1946. (US Naval Institute)

To ensure that every possible angle was captured on film, the aerial drop of the "Able" bomb at Bikini was filmed by manned and drone aircraft circling above the atoll. Here, camera crews aboard a B-29 film the test. (Smithsonian Images)

To further test the bomb, the military loaded 22 of the target ships with fuel and ammunition and installed 220 tons of equipment, ranging from tanks, heavy and light artillery, tractors, and airplanes to mortars, radios, fire extinguishers, telephones, gas masks, watches, uniforms, canned foods, and frozen meat. They mounted swatches of cloth on plywood sheets to face the blast. Crews landed and placed 71 target airplanes on the ships, including two seaplanes moored in the water. To measure the atomic blasts, scientists and technicians installed 5,000 pressure gauges, 25,000 radiation measuring instruments, 750 cameras, and 4 television transmitters, and 5,000 rats, 204 goats, 200 pigs, 200 mice, and 60 guinea pigs joined JTF-1 to stand in for the absent crews as living test instruments.[23]

At Bikini, crews blasted coral, bulldozed sand, and placed huge concrete mooring blocks in the lagoon while building temporary quarters, instrument towers, and camera bunkers on the shore. In March 1946, after assurances that they could return, and that their islands were required "for the good of mankind," the 167 people of Bikini were loaded aboard a Navy Landing Ship, Tank (LST) along with the thatched roofs and wooden frames of their residences, plus belongings and outrigger canoes, and taken to Rongerik, an island 128 miles away. For them, "there would be no returning," said *National Geographic* writer Carl Markwith. "Civilization and the Atomic Age had come to Bikini, and they had been in the way."[24]

Initially planned for May 15, the tests were postponed until July 1 by President Truman, so that Bernard Baruch's planned presentation of the US proposal for international control of atomic weapons to the UNAEC would have taken place. The additional time did not diminish the quick pace of *Crossroads* preparations. In May and June, the target vessels, as well the other ships of the 242-vessel *Crossroads* fleet, arrived at Bikini. On Kwajalein, USAAF crews from the 509th Composite Group, along with scientists and technicians from Los Alamos, created a Tinian-like facility to serve as the base for preparing and loading a Fat Man bomb into the B-29 assigned to *Crossroads*.

The 509th, reassigned to Roswell Army Air Field in New Mexico, had become part of the newly established SAC in March 1946, and in May the *Crossroads* contingent of the 509th had departed for Kwajalein. The B-29 selected to drop the *Crossroads* bomb was 44-27354, or "Dave's Dream." In March 1946, practice bomb runs were initiated to select the crew for Bikini. A B-29 carrying pioneering atomic test

"Dave's Dream" lands at Kwajalein after dropping its atomic bomb at Bikini. The "Able" bomb had missed its target, missing USS *Nevada* by more than 1,500 yards. Instead of a welcoming ceremony, the crew was hauled in for an intensive debriefing. (Smithsonian Images)

bombardier David Semple, who had flown in the earliest test runs at Muroc, crashed in New Mexico, killing all of the crew. When the winning crew, commanded by Major Woodrow "Woody" Swancutt, was selected, they named their plane in Semple's honor.

A full-dress rehearsal of the first test, scheduled for June 23, was postponed for a day. On June 24, the initial test bomb run was called off because clouds obscured the target, the battleship USS *Nevada*. The second run found the target unobscured, and "Dave's Dream" dropped a high-explosive bomb just off *Nevada*'s starboard side. The success of the test run cleared the way for dropping a combat-loaded Fat Man. The target array was 78 ships, with 24 of them within a 1,000-yard radius of *Nevada*. The Navy moored the others so that they spread out in geometric lines, bow and stern on, broadside to the blast, "so that individual ships of each major type would be placed in positions ranging from close … for major damage … to appreciable distances … for light damage."[25]

TEST "ABLE," JULY 1, 1946

At 05:55hrs on July 1, "Dave's Dream" took off from Kwajalein, followed by observation, photographic, and instrumentation aircraft and radio-controlled "drones": Navy F6F Hellcats and Army B-17 Flying Fortresses that would dive into the atomic cloud to measure radioactivity. Climbing to 32,000ft, "Dave's Dream" reached Bikini at 08:03hrs. Bikini had been abandoned for the test; 15 miles out to sea, the support

The initial detonation, Test "Able," Bikini, as captured from the air, July 1, 1946. (Smithsonian Images)

fleet waited and watched. At 08:59hrs, bombardier Major Harold H. Wood released the bomb, which fell for 48 seconds before detonating 518ft above the lagoon just 50 yards off and slightly to starboard of the bow of the attack transport *Gilliam*. The bomb had missed its intended target, *Nevada*, by 2,130ft, an error that angered officials and resulted in the interrogation of the crew of "Dave's Dream" when they landed.

Observers out to sea watched as "a whole hemisphere of air catches fire, ten, twenty times the size of the first burst. Through the goggles it looks fiery red … [and] seems to cover the whole target fleet."[26] Caught in the incandescent fireball and battered down into the water by the shock wave, *Gilliam*, "badly ruptured, crumpled, and twisted almost beyond recognition," sank in 79 seconds.[27] The blast swept the nearby transport *Carlisle* 150ft to one side as its superstructure and masts were nearly wiped off its decks. It began to burn, and sank in 30 minutes. The destroyer *Anderson*, hit hard by the blast, burst into flame as its ammunition exploded. While burning fiercely, *Anderson* capsized to port and sank by the stern within seven minutes. The destroyer *Lamson* sank 12 minutes after the blast, its hull torn open. The Japanese cruiser *Sakawa*, badly battered, burned fiercely and sank the following day.

After radiological monitors determined that the radioactive cloud had blown out to sea, and the lagoon was safe to re-enter, the support fleet steamed back into Bikini lagoon that afternoon. They found a number of damaged ships, some still on fire, including the aircraft carrier *Independence*, "an impressive edifice of junk" that the bomb had blown into "a cocked hat,"[28] with a badly warped and buckled hull, and the submarine *Skate*, its topsides stripped off by the blast and its conning tower bent. However, those expecting massive damage, or the destruction of the entire fleet were disappointed, among them the press. Atomic scientists who had feared this reaction to what they knew would be less than cataclysmic results had their fears confirmed. As wags began to call Bikini "No Atoll Atoll" or "Nothing Atoll," a sense of relief as well as disappointment began to change the perceptions of many, including some of the military. That perception changed with the second test.

TEST "BAKER," JULY 25, 1946

The second test took place three weeks later. The Navy re-moored the target ships around a Landing Ship, Mechanized (LSM) that suspended the bomb 90ft below the surface of the water in a casing made from the scrapped conning tower of a submarine. When the

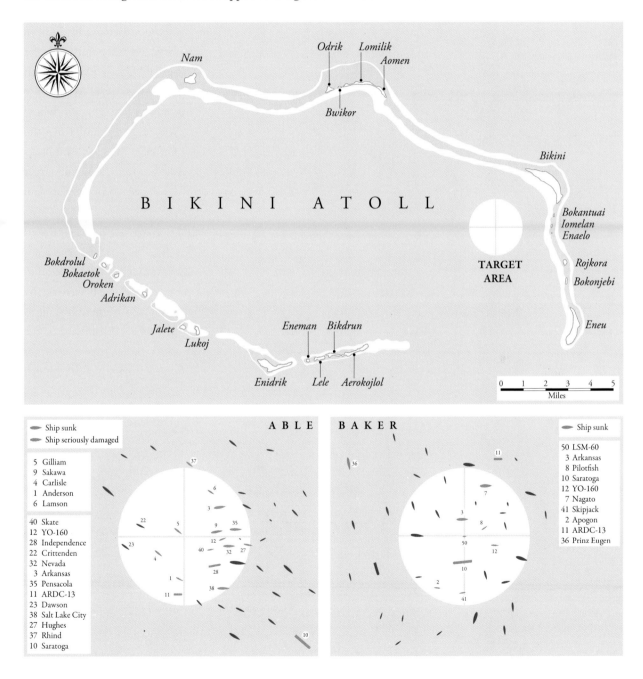

155

The water column displaced by the "Baker" blast contained over a million tons of seawater. It climbed at a rate of 11,000ft per second, and was 975ft in diameter. The falling column of water washed highly radioactive water and steam over and into the otherwise undamaged target ships, contaminating them. (US Naval History & Heritage Command)

burst erupted from the lagoon at 08:34hrs on the morning of July 25, a mass of steam and water mounded up into a "spray dome" that climbed at a rate of 2,500ft per second into a column. The center of the 975ft-thick column was a nearly hollow void of superheated steam that rose faster than the more solid 300ft-thick wall of water at the perimeter, climbing 11,000ft per second and acting as a chimney for the hot gases of the fireball. The gases, mixed with excavated lagoon bottom and radioactive materials, formed a cauliflower-shaped mushroom cloud atop the column. The battleship *Arkansas*, caught in the upward blast, was crushed, capsized, and sunk in less than a second.[29]

The blast created "atomic tidal waves" that smashed into the ships. The first wave, a 94ft-tall wall of radioactive water, lifted and smashed into the aircraft carrier *Saratoga*. The carrier's hull was twisted, the flight deck partially collapsed, and *Saratoga* sank within seven and a half hours, slowly settling by the stern. *Nagato*, its hull broken open, sank two days later. Beneath the lagoon, the incredible pressure of the bomb's burst crushed three submarines that settled onto the seabed, leaking air bubbles and oil.

Observers were far more impressed with the visual spectacle of the "Baker" test. Just the same, "Baker" only claimed nine more ships in its detonation. William L. Laurence, the dean of atomic reporters, found that the tests had shifted public attitudes:

> Before Bikini the world stood in awe of this cosmic force … since Bikini this feeling … has largely been supplanted by a sense of relief unrelated to the grim, reality of the situation… [The average citizen] had expected one bomb to sink the entire Bikini fleet, kill all the animals … make a hole in the bottom of the ocean and create tidal waves … everyone participating in the test would die. Since none of these happened, he is only too eager to conclude that the atomic bomb is, after all, just another weapon.[30]

On some contaminated target ships, Navy crews scrubbed them with brooms and brushes in a futile effort to remove fallout and reduce the level of radioactivity. Here a crew labors in vain to clean the decks of the cruiser *Prinz Eugen*. When radiation monitors discovered that *Prinz Eugen* was too radioactive to be safely crewed, Blandy ordered the cruiser to be towed to nearby Kwajalein Atoll, where it later developed a leak and sank. (US Naval Institute)

However, as the crews prepared for the third and final test, "Charlie," radioactive contamination of the target fleet ended Operation *Crossroads*.

RADIOACTIVE RESULTS

During the "Baker" test, a boiling mass of radioactive water and steam penetrated nearly every target ship left afloat and contaminated the lagoon water. Radioactive material adhered to wooden decks and paint, rust and grease. For weeks after the tests, the Navy tried to wash the fallout off with water and lye, and sent crews aboard contaminated ships to scrub off paint, rust, and scale with long-handled brushes, holystones, and any other "available means," but they could not remove the radiation. Radiation monitor David Bradley later wrote that:

Aircraft that flew through the atomic cloud to obtain samples were contaminated. Here, a crew scrubs down an irradiated plane. (Smithsonian Images)

I made a careful survey of the deck, finding the intensity to vary a great deal in a matter of feet… When the survey was completed, the Chief turned his booted, sweating, profane and laughing crew loose… Yet when the hydraulics were done and the deck rinsed clean, another survey showed the invisible emanations to be present… The portly Chief stood watching the dial on my Geiger counter, completely bewildered.[31]

The target vessels were contaminated with varying levels of radiation, some so high that ships could not be boarded for long. The destroyer *Hughes*, for example, could only be safely boarded for eight minutes before the crew received the maximum recommended dose.

The problem escalated with the discovery that the support ships were also becoming contaminated. Radiation in the seawater irradiated growth on hulls and salt water lines inside ships began steadily to register increasing dosages. Worried about inadequate numbers of radiological monitors, insufficient equipment, and a "cumulative hazard," Blandy acted on the advice of his radiation experts and cancelled plans for a third test and ordered badly damaged ships sunk on August 10.

As Operation *Crossroads* steamed away from Bikini, it towed a battered, irradiated fleet of targets to nearby Kwajalein, and then to Pearl Harbor, Bremerton, Washington,

Despite the best efforts of the overworked radiation safety officers, crews of the target and support ships were exposed to varying and at high levels of radiation. Here, the atomic damaged USS *Skate* (SS-305) rejoins the fleet with its crew standing on its deck after the Able test. After monitors detected high levels of radiation, the crew abandoned *Skate*. Towed back to San Francisco Bay after the tests, *Skate* was studied and then scuttled off the California coast in October 1948. Even after surviving the blast and heat of two atomic bombs, the majority of the Bikini target fleet succumbed to radiation. (US Naval Institute)

and Hunters Point and Mare Island in California. There crews stripped them of ammunition and left them to rust. Ultimately, all but a handful of the *Crossroads* target ships were scuttled after being placed "off-limits" at various naval bases. One ship, the German cruiser *Prinz Eugen*, capsized and sank at Kwajalein Atoll under these circumstances. At the same time, animals taken from the target ships began to die, in increasing numbers, even those that had been locked far below, behind layers of armor. The lesson was not lost on the scientists and the military, who in the aftermath of the tests

Following the atomic tests at Bikini, the US Navy scuttled some contaminated target ships and sent others to various locations to gradually "cool down" or undergo further decontamination efforts. Two attack transports, USS *Crittenden* (APA-77) and USS *Gasconade* (APA-85) and two submarines, USS *Skate* (SS-305) and USS *Skipjack* (SS-184), were sent to San Francisco and Mare Island Naval Shipyards along with the heavily damaged and irradiated carrier USS *Independence* (CVL-22). Here, *Gasconade* and *Skipjack* sit in dry dock at Hunters Point, San Francisco, as crews sandblasted and acid-washed them to reduce their radiation levels. (National Park Service)

noted that "from a military viewpoint, the atomic bomb's ability to kill human beings or to impair, through injury, their ability to make war is of paramount importance."[32]

Starting in 1948, the Navy began taking the *Crossroads* target ships to sea and sinking them. The explanation was that the sinkings were part of training exercises and tests of new weapons. That year Dr. David Bradley, M.D., radiological safety monitor at Bikini, published his journal of the tests as *No Place to Hide*. It stayed on the *New York Times* best-seller list for ten weeks. *No Place to Hide* was a forceful book that told the "real" message of Bikini. Operation *Crossroads*, "hastily planned and hastily carried out ... may have only sketched in gross outlines ... the real problem; nevertheless, these outlines show pretty clearly the shadow of the colossus which looms behind tomorrow." Bradley's metaphor was the target ships rusting at Kwajalein, many of them seemingly undamaged but "nevertheless dying of a malignant disease for which there is no help."[33]

The "cure," being enacted as Bradley's book was printed, was the sinking of the contaminated ships. In a February 1949 column, *Washington Post* columnist Drew Pearson termed the tests a "major naval disaster." He reported that "of the 73 ships involved in the Bikini tests, more than 61 were sunk or destroyed. This is an enormous loss from only two bombs."[34] Thus, Pearson reinforced David Bradley's conviction of the radioactive menace that *Crossroads* had revealed. Pearson, like Bradley, pointed to what he viewed as a military effort to keep the true lesson of *Crossroads* – the virtual destruction of the target fleet by radioactivity – from being fully apprehended by the public. Yet the story had ultimately leaked, combining with the fears of radiation first raised by Hersey's *Hiroshima*.

For the military, the results of *Crossroads* had been "inconclusive" for the Army and Navy. Neither achieved the "knockout" they had hoped for. The Army argued that while the blasts had only sunk a handful of ships, the bomb's contamination had proved ships to be vulnerable; the Navy responded that the fleet's tight anchorage at Bikini was not a realistic scenario for wartime, when "properly dispersed" ships "executing evasive maneuvers and utilizing their own defenses, would be far less vulnerable ... than, for instance, fixed air bases."[35]

Following each test at Bikini, radiation monitors equipped with Geiger counters surveyed the lagoon, as well as any target ship as teams boarded to retrieve instruments, test animals, or attempt to wash down the ship to reduce its level of radioactivity. The magnitude of the task was such that there were simply not enough monitors or equipment to handle the job, especially in the aftermath of the "Baker" test of July 25, when nearly every target ship, and many support ships, were contaminated by radioactive seawater and lagoon bottom sediments. (US Naval Institute)

One of the victims of the "Baker" blast was the World War I battleship USS *Arkansas* (BB-33), which lay moored in close proximity to the bomb. The blast pounded *Arkansas*, capsizing it while lifting its stern into the air as the bow dug into the seabed. The falling column uplifted water and pulverized coral and sand then smashed the ship into the lagoon floor, 180ft down, and buried *Arkansas* in thick, radioactive silt. (US Naval History & Heritage Command)

In the aftermath of Bikini, both services continued their efforts to incorporate additional atomic bombs into their arsenals, arguing for larger numbers of smaller, more deliverable and diverse weapons. Mindful of the effects on their crews, the military also adopted plans for passive radiological defense, strengthening hulls and equipment to withstand shock and developing fallout wash-down systems to try to reduce radiation levels. These changes came with the understanding that "the seamen of tomorrow must be prepared to accept radioactivity as part of the hazards of their living and be ready to live and fight and save their ship even though they know they are doomed to slow death."[36] To help counter that message, as military forces worked to perfect the delivery and punch of atomic weapons, the government developed a program of civil defense to convince a frightened public they could survive an atomic attack.

NUCLEAR PROLIFERATION AND DETERRENCE

In the aftermath of the Bikini tests, the failure of the Baruch Plan, and the passage of the Atomic Energy Act of 1946, the United States embarked upon a program of nuclear deterrence and a concomitant focus on civil defense to reassure Americans that the nation could survive an atomic attack. An atomic bureaucracy, administered by the newly formed Atomic Energy Commission (AEC), built up the scientific, technical, and industrial aspects of the United States' atomic program, while the armed forces further integrated nuclear weapons and atomic power into their strategies and tactics.

Other countries also challenged the American nuclear monopoly, beginning with the Soviet Union. Soviet nuclear research, greatly aided by espionage, had begun in 1943 and picked up speed in 1945. Under the direction of Stalin's Lavrenti Beria, head of the NKVD (Stalin's secret police), with Igor Kurchatov as scientific director, the Soviet program built its first reactor in Moscow in 1946. Working with the plutonium produced, Kurchatov's scientific team built the first device, an exact copy of a Fat Man, codenamed RDS-1, or *Pervaya molniya* (First Lightning). The 22-kiloton device successfully detonated on August 29, 1949, at the Semipalatinsk Test Site in Kazakhstan. The initial production of a Soviet bomb had been achieved with dangerous shortcuts. It took the Soviets another two years of refinement before their second detonation, a 38-kiloton bomb tested on September 24, 1951.

An American B-29 sent aloft to monitor the Soviet Union for radioactive byproducts in the atmosphere, part of a top-secret program named AFOAT-1, detected the First Lightning test not long after it happened, and alerted US officials. As the radioactive cloud from the test moved north, US ground facilities also picked up traces of the test, confirming that the United States was no longer the sole possessor of the atomic secret. The official public reaction was a Presidential statement:

> We have evidence that within recent weeks an atomic explosion occurred in the USSR. Ever since atomic energy was first released by man, the eventual development of this new force by other nations was to be expected. This probability has always been taken into account by us... This recent development emphasizes once again, if indeed such emphasis were needed, the necessity for that truly effective and enforceable international control of atomic energy which this government and the large majority of the members of the United Nations support.[1]

The other response, kept secret, was a report from the General Advisory Commission of the AEC, which recommended "an intensification of efforts to make atomic weapons available for tactical purposes, and to give attention to the problem of integration of bomb and carrier design in this field," but stopped short of recommending the pursuit of "super-bombs" of greater power.[2] While such weapons were potentially feasible, they had not yet been proven, and even if so:

> It is clear that the use of this weapon would bring about the destruction of innumerable human lives; it is not a weapon which can be used exclusively for the destruction of material installations of military or semi-military purposes. Its use therefore carries much further than the atomic bomb itself the policy of exterminating civilian populations.[3]

The committee recommended against creating a more powerful weapon. Recommendations notwithstanding, the super-bomb proposal, advocated by Edward Teller and other scientists, as well as the military, was seen as an inevitable Soviet development if the United States did not create it first. And so, on January 31, 1950, President Truman approved and announced an American program to develop a super-bomb. That weapon, developed by Teller and Stanislaw Ulam, used a staged detonation sequence with a fission bomb igniting tritium-deuterium to achieve fusion and a generate a thermonuclear blast measured not in kilotons but in megatons. This method was perfected and tested within the next four years. The super-bomb would become better known as the hydrogen bomb, or H-bomb.

Onetime atomic ally Britain also pushed its own atomic weapons program.[4] It was spurred by the Soviet bomb and concern that a Soviet-dominated Eastern Europe could pose as much of a threat to Britain as the Nazi-occupied continent once had. Initial British discussions over an atomic weapons program began in August 1945 with a special sub-committee, established by newly elected Prime Minister Clement Attlee, examining Britain's options. Frozen out of ongoing American development by the Atomic Energy Act, Britain began its own program in late 1946 under the direction of William Penney, the Manhattan Project veteran who had flown on the Nagasaki mission. The government asked Penney to prepare a report on the feasibility of a UK atomic weapons program in October 1946; at the same time, atomic facilities, notably a reactor at Harwell, Oxfordshire, were constructed to start processing plutonium-239. Penney's report was positive, although the British veterans of the Manhattan Project did not possess a complete, detailed understanding of every step involved in atomic weapons production, only those areas each scientist had worked on. Nonetheless, Penney was optimistic. The Attlee government authorized the British atomic program in January 1947, and under the codename of High Explosive Research (HER), began work at Fort Halstead, Kent. The HER program later moved to a former RAF base at Aldermaston, Berkshire, which became the Atomic Weapons Research Establishment (AWRE) in 1950. Aldermaston remains the site of the United Kingdom's now renamed Atomic Weapons Establishment.

The formation of the North Atlantic Treaty Organization (NATO) in 1948 and the subsequent basing of atomic-capable B-29s in Britain did nothing to calm British concerns about external threats, and the bomb program continued quietly. The reactor at Harwell, codenamed "GLEEP" (Graphite Low Energy Experimental Pile), was the first nuclear reactor in Western Europe. It went critical in August 1947. The British also built plutonium-producing reactors at Windscale (Sellafield, Cumbria) in 1947, and started loading nuclear fuel in them in 1950; by July 1952, Windscale had produced enough weapons-grade plutonium for Britain's first nuclear weapon.

On October 3, 1952, British scientists successfully detonated the first British atomic bomb, codenamed "Hurricane," which they had armed with British and Canadian-manufactured plutonium. The bomb was loaded in the frigate HMS *Plym*, which steamed to the isolated Montebello islands, 80 miles off the Indian Ocean coast of Western Australia. For the test, the Royal Navy moored *Plym* in shallow water nearly a thousand feet off the island of Trimouille. The 25-kiloton blast obliterated the frigate, left a crater in the seabed, and swept over the island and its assembled test instruments. The official film of the test, *Operation Hurricane*, made it clear to British audiences and the world what Hurricane's success meant:

That lethal cloud rising above Montebello marks the achievement of British science and industry in the development of atomic power, but it leaves unanswered the question of how shall this new-found power be used – for good or evil, for peace or war, for progress or destruction. The answer doesn't lie with Britain alone, but we may have a greater voice in this great decision if we have the strength to defend ourselves and to deter aggression.[5]

In November 1953, the "Blue Danube," a plutonium-core implosion weapon, and Britain's first combat atomic bomb, went into service.

As the British effort pushed forward, France also sought to develop the bomb. Despite the pioneering work of the Curies and the Joliot-Curies and other scientists, French atomic research had lagged because of the Nazi occupation during World War II. At the end of the war, General Charles de Gaulle, President of the provisional French government, established the *Commissariat a l'Energie Atomique* (CEA), a civilian atomic energy authority that would oversee all aspects of a French nuclear program, with Frederic Joliot-Curie as High Commissioner. Dr. Bertrand Goldschmidt had before the war worked as Marie Curie's last assistant before her death, and as a Free French scientist had worked at Montreal, Canada, as part of the British-Canadian team associated with the Manhattan Project. He returned to France in 1946 to continue developing solvent extraction of plutonium, and took a leading role in France's nuclear ambitions.

The first French reactor, built at the Fort de Chatillon outside Paris, went critical in December 1948, and within a year had started extracting plutonium using Goldschmidt's tributyl phosphate solvent method. Despite continued development of nuclear power and the construction of additional reactors, French development of a bomb was slow, however, due to internal politics and a belief in non-proliferation. Quiet efforts within the government and military to develop atomic weapons came with French military reversals in Vietnam, and in late 1954 the French Prime Minister authorized an atomic bomb program.

After the Suez Crisis of 1956, plans to develop an independent French nuclear deterrent gained more political and military backing, but it was not until Charles de Gaulle returned to power in 1958 that the first French bomb was completed and tested. The first, a powerful 60–70-kiloton burst codenamed *Gerboise Bleue* (Blue Jerboa) was detonated at the Reganne oasis in the Algerian portion of the Sahara Desert on February 13, 1960. France was now a nuclear power, and would continue to hone its nuclear sword in a series of tests in Algeria and then in French Polynesia.

THE AMERICAN RESPONSE, 1948–60

In the decade between 1948 and 1958, American nuclear policy and practice changed dramatically in response to the loss of the atomic monopoly, increased paranoia over Soviet intentions and communist infiltration of the United States, and the atomic fears of the public. Concern over atomic attack had diminished after Bikini, despite the fact that the tests had highlighted the issue of radiation sickness, but in the aftermath of the announcement of the Soviet bomb, nuclear fear once again became an issue for US leaders.

The United States' nuclear arsenal in 1948 consisted of a handful of Fat Man bombs, and these laboratory-produced weapons were slow to assemble. "Deak" Parsons had argued for mass-produced combat weapons, and as the Navy's Director of Atomic Defense, had participated in the creation of the Armed Forces Special Weapons Project (AFSWP). The AFSWP had then acted with Los Alamos to shift the lab's Z-Division, formerly the Ordnance Division headed by Parsons, to a new, separate laboratory at Sandia Base in Albuquerque, New Mexico. Working at Sandia in 1948–49, Parsons was able to modify a naval carrier aircraft to carry atomic weapons, and pushed through the development of the Mark 4 atomic bomb, which was essentially an easier to assemble, mass-produced version of the Fat Man. This step allowed the United States to increase its atomic arsenal from the nine Fat Man bombs it had on hand to more than 500 weapons over the next decade. With an "in-flight insertion" nuclear core that allowed weaponeers to arm a bomb in the air, the new bombs were also safer to carry on SAC's broad-ranging missions. SAC, relocated in 1948 to Offut Air Force Base near Omaha, Nebraska – a more central location in the country – had assumed an expanded role under Curtis LeMay, and was now flying extended patrols in the newly developed Convair B-36 "Peacemaker," an intercontinental bomber that could carry both atomic and, in time, thermonuclear weapons.

The increased capacity of both weapons and vehicles to deliver them did not lead to another combat use of the bomb by the United States. Additional atomic tests, such as Operation *Sandstone* (1948) at Enewetak Atoll in the Pacific, with three detonations, and Operation *Ranger* (1951), with five detonations of new types of bombs, dropped by aircraft at the newly opened Nevada Test Site, brought the bomb back to the American mainland for the first time since the war, and helped develop new combat fission weapons. Additional tests in the Pacific, such as Operation *Greenhouse* (1951) and Operation *Ivy* (1952) at Enewetak, helped develop the H-bomb, with the last 1952 test, "Ivy Mike," firing off the first hydrogen bomb, a massive 65-ton structure on the island of Elegulab on November 1. The blast from "Mike", at 10.4–10.6 megatons in force, was more than a thousand times more powerful than Hiroshima, and obliterated the island, leaving a 2-mile-wide crater a half-mile deep in the atoll. At the same time, however, despite reverses in the Korean War in 1950–51, where American and UN troops were pushed back by intervening Chinese forces, Truman resisted suggestions to use the atomic bomb to resolve the conflict. While nuclear-capable planes flew training and combat missions over the Korean peninsula, the bomb was not an ideal weapon to deal with the conflict and Truman may have balked at again using the bomb against Asians.

Instead, new policies for dealing with communist "aggression," including an American first-strike option, and responding to conflict wherever in the world by focusing on the Soviet Union if it proved to be the instigator, were developed. This locked the United States and the Soviet Union into a cycle of arms build-ups, creating weapons of greater reach and power, and in larger numbers, as part of a strategy of mutual deterrence and "mutually assured destruction." In 1954, the United States fired off its first combat-ready H-bomb, the 14.8-megaton "Castle-Bravo" weapon at Bikini, vaporizing another island and sending a thousand-mile swatch of fallout into the Pacific. The Soviets, who had first tested thermonuclear technology in 1953 at Semipalatinsk, followed with weapons developed by physicist Andrei Sakharov, detonating their first true H-bomb in November 1955. Not to be outdone, the British tested their first H-bomb in May 1957 with an air-dropped weapon on Christmas (Kiritimati) Island in the central Pacific.

New technologies for delivering the bomb followed quickly. Efforts to develop atomic "rockets" and missiles based on German V1 and V2 technology had been foreseen by military planners since the end of the war, notably in "Hap" Arnold's well-publicized report on the "36-Hour War" in late 1945. It was not until 1957 that the first strategic nuclear weapon on a rocket appeared, when the Soviets developed the first long-range, intercontinental rocket capable of being armed with a nuclear warhead. The 280-ton R-7 rocket failed to reach its target in its first tests, but in early October 1957, using an R-7, the Soviets successfully launched an orbital probe which they named *Sputnik* ("satellite") into orbit, much to the consternation of the United States. While the initial Soviet claim of a rocket had largely been ignored, the "Sputnik crisis" spurred American rocket and missile development.

With its military problems ironed out in 1958, the R-7 entered production and was ready for combat use in 1959. The same year, the United States deployed its first operational intercontinental ballistic missile (ICBM), the "Atlas D" rocket. The Atlas rockets, developed by Convair for the USAF, sprang out of a postwar rocket program for military purposes that had languished until reinvigorated by news of the Soviet program. At the same time, the United States also took atomic missiles to sea, when the Regulus missile, essentially a winged, unmanned aircraft fired from a submarine's deck after being taken out of a specially fitted hangar, was introduced. The 500-mile range of the Regulus gave way to new missile-firing boats at a time when the Navy was also building more nuclear-powered submarines following the 1955 success of

THE 36-HOUR WAR CONTINUED

NEAR WAR'S END ENEMY AIRBORNE TROOPS COME IN

Said General Arnold: "Airborne troops have become one of the most effective units of a modern fighting force.... Fully equipped airborne task forces will be able to strike at far distant points and will be totally supplied by air."

In spite of the apocalyptic destruction caused by its atomic bombs, an enemy nation would have to invade the U.S. to win the war. The enemy's airborne troops would be equipped with light rocket weapons of great destructive power (*above*, *rear*) and devices such as goggles which make troop-directing infrared signals visible. The enemy soldier above

is repairing a telephone line in a small U.S. town.

By the time enemy troops have landed, the U.S. has suffered terrifying damage. Some 40,000,000 people have been killed and all cities of more than 50,000 population have been leveled. San Francisco's Market Street, Chicago's Michigan Boulevard and New York's Fifth Avenue (*see opposite page*) are merely lanes through the debris. But as it is destroyed the U.S. is fighting back. The enemy airborne troops are wiped out. U.S. rockets lay waste the enemy's cities. U.S. airborne troops successfully occupy his country. The U.S. wins the atomic war.

34

"The 36-Hour War," an illustrated article in the November 19, 1945 edition of *Life* Magazine, was the first depiction of unleashing the "winning weapon" on the victors. After an initial atomic attack on American cities, enemy troops occupy bomb-damaged cities as in this atomic ravaged telephone exchange with a dead operator sprawled on the floor. (*Life* magazine, 1945. Author's Collection)

BY THE MARBLE LIONS OF NEW YORK'S PUBLIC
LIBRARY, U. S. TECHNICIANS TEST THE RUBBLE
OF THE SHATTERED CITY FOR RADIOACTIVITY

their first; USS *Nautilus*. In June 1959, the US Navy launched its first true ballistic missile submarine, USS *George Washington*, the lead boat in a series of Polaris-missile-carrying undersea craft that could cruise, surface, and fire a nuclear weapon from a location close enough to the Soviet Union, giving little to no warning to the Soviets in time of war. The Cold War was in full force, and for the first time global nuclear war and the potential annihilation of the planet was possible.

DUCK AND COVER

While developing its nuclear stockpile, the US government adopted a dual program of civil defense and increased surveillance to detect enemies "from within." Through the early 1950s, a series of increasingly vehement pushes to find and expose communist sympathizers and actual agents occupied official and public attention. Civil defense measures included the publication of official books to reassure the public that they could survive an atomic attack if they took precautions, and to downplay fears of radiation. Efforts to disparage books like Bradley's *No Place to Hide* included a 1949 book by Ralph Lapp, a Manhattan Project physicist and Pentagon advisor as part of the Office of Naval Research, entitled *Must We Hide?* Lapp's book, seen by historian Paul Boyer as "quasi-official," dismissed the fears raised by Bradley, arguing that radiation was dangerous, but also "one more of the hazards of contemporary living … we have adequate instrumentation to permit accurate evaluation of any radiation hazards that may exist."[6] Lapp also argued that the continental United States was big enough so that most Americans would avoid the direct results of atomic attack.

Following Lapp, in 1950 the US government published *How to Survive an Atomic Bomb*, written by Richard Gerstell, who like David Bradley, was a former radiation monitor at Operation *Crossroads*. "There is definitely some place to hide," Gerstell wrote, laying out in text and illustrations a practical guide to surviving an attack, including how to take shelter, using canned foods after an attack, and avoiding risks such as fallout. Fallout and radiation "is not likely to hurt you" if precautions were taken. The government had taken steps to help. "A new and proven military science has arisen. Radiological defense, which consists of the detection and avoidance of radioactive hazards, is something which, in a quiet but effective way, the Government has been perfecting for several years."[7]

A steady public relations campaign followed, with an emphasis on public and private blast and fallout shelters, the latter well stocked with emergency supplies to wait out the aftermath of an atomic attack, and mass-produced radiation detectors including Geiger counters and smaller, pencil-shaped dosimeters. A 1949 film featuring actress and singer Doris Day included a newly written song about Geiger counters, all part of

OPPOSITE
Ultimately, the "36-Hour War" concludes with an American victory, but a costly one, as technicians measure radiation in the ruins of downtown Manhattan, in this case standing in front of ruins of the New York Public Library at Fifth Avenue and 42nd Street. The iconic marble lions that guard the Library's entrance, "Patience" and "Fortitude" provide a shocking point of reference for American readers. (*Life* magazine, 1945. Author's Collection)

the move to lighten the nation's mood about radiation that noted that the new invention was "clicking," and that because it was "ticking" she "knew" where the clicking was coming from – radiation.

Other steps included the 1951 implementation of CONELRAD (Control of Electronic Radiation), a national emergency warning broadcast system, and regular drills, especially for schoolchildren. A January 1952 film, *Duck and Cover*, used an animated turtle to teach children to take evasive maneuvers if they saw the flash of an atomic detonation. The film opened with a song:

There was a turtle by the name of Bert
and Bert the turtle was very alert;
when danger threatened him he never got hurt
he knew just what to do...
He ducked!
And covered!
Ducked!
And covered!

He did what we all must learn to do.
You.
And you.
And you.
And you!
Duck, and cover![8]

The film then depicted children taking the "right" steps to protect themselves in the event of atomic attack. Millions of American children saw the film through the 1950s and early 1960s, and participated in regular "duck and cover" drills.

In the United Kingdom, the British nuclear defense effort included the government instituting the Civil Defence Corps in 1950. A 1963 booklet, *Advising the Householder on Protection against Nuclear Attack*, was followed a year later by a series of informational films, the *Civil Defence Information Bulletin*, which were produced and released in 1964. The *Bulletin*'s seven films acquainted viewers with the effects of nuclear weapons, how to prepare for attack, including setting up a "fallout room," and other defensive measures similar to the American "duck and cover" drill. Updated nuclear defense manuals, published by the UK government in 1980 under the title, *Protect and Survive*, were accompanied by a 20-episode series of short, animated features.

Resistance to government messages of reassurance surfaced at the same time as the first atomic defense programs. In Britain, the 1958 establishment of the CND in response to news that the UK government was launching a program to develop hydrogen bombs was a particularly powerful counter-message. In the United States, resistance to Civil Defense drills was encouraged by the Catholic Worker Movement and antiwar activists, some on the grounds that there was no real "defense" against the bomb. Protests included not going to fallout shelters during atomic drills; in one case, the *New York Times* of May 7, 1958, reported, "9 PACIFISTS SEIZED IN DEFYING ALERT." They were not alone, as the anti-nuclear movement grew in size in the 1960s.

A growing number of popular cultural messages reinforced the anti-nuclear movement, among them post-apocalyptic books and stories. In one famous, 1950 short story by author Ray Bradbury, *There Will Come Soft Rains*, an automated, robotic home of the future continued to function after the death of its owners (and presumably all people on earth) following an atomic attack. Another powerful story was a book by British author Nevil Shute, *On The Beach* (1957), which had an even greater impact when United Artists released it as a feature film with Gregory Peck and Ava Gardner in 1959. All life on earth slowly succumbs to radiation poisoning in the book and in the film. Other works offered a slightly more optimistic view than *On The Beach*, with some survivors in a post-attack world, such as Pat Frank's *Alas, Babylon* (1959), or Walter M. Miller's 1960 book *A Canticle for Leibowitz*, in which one nuclear holocaust is in time followed by another, ultimately completely destructive atomic war.

While government civil defense strategies stressed survival in the atomic age, the American, British, and French governments pushed peaceful uses of atomic energy, a theme that dated from the earliest days of nuclear physics and the discovery of X-rays. In addition to medical uses, atomic power and the manufacturing of atomic planes, cars, and trains were advocated. AEC Chairman David Lilienthal, who worked very hard in his term of office to make the atom seem friendlier to Americans, not only likened radiation to sunshine, he also encouraged efforts to "Free the Atom" (the title of an article he wrote in the June 17, 1950, edition of *Collier's* magazine) for business. The French, with the world's oldest atomic research program (dating to the Curies), created the CEA in 1945, and French efforts to build reactors, as well as use radionucleides in medical treatment, commenced. Non-military British nuclear power efforts commenced later, although significantly, when the Calder Hall nuclear power plant at Cumbria went online in August 1956, the first reactors to deliver electricity in commercial quantities.

With all of these efforts, the United States, and the world, slowly passed from the early era of the atom into a new, and darker, age in which fission and fusion held the power not only to change civilization, but to end it. That fear, expressed at the beginning of the age, had not been a possibility until the early 1950s and the creation of the H-bomb. More than six decades have passed since the first atomic explosions of 1945 heralded the arrival of this new age, and in those decades profound scientific, military, and sociological changes have occurred. Apart from nuclear accidents, the atomic genie has not escaped the bottle, although the same fears of more than 60 years ago continue as more nations seek to join the ranks of nuclear powers, while others, notably the United States, seek to forestall or stop them. There is no end in sight for the atomic age, only continuing ripples in the pond from the first stone thrown into it on July 16, 1945.

10

LEGACIES OF THE BOMB

The atomic age has inspired a cultural response on a global scale. In addition to the numerous books, stories, films, and artistic depictions of nuclear energy, weapons, radiation, and atomic attack, the iconic power and symbolism of the split atom is also evident in the variety of more naïve souvenirs. These include radium tonics (radioactive drinks to cure illness), and the use of use of radium "glow-in-the-dark" paint to create luminescent dials on watches, clocks, and instruments. They also include games and toys that date from the earliest days of humanity's encounters with radiation to more potent depictions of nuclear consequences that range from the terrifying to the ridiculous, including the popular figures of "The Hulk," the comic book and film persona of gamma-ray-mutated scientist Bruce Banner, and "SpongeBob SquarePants," an apparently mutated sponge that lives with his friends at "Bikini Bottom," which is presumably Bikini Atoll. The "radiation craze" of the early 20th century has waxed and waned in response to the various phases of the nuclear age, and continues in the 21st century in a different form. No longer a radiation craze, humanity's fascination with the power of the atom is represented by an attraction and repulsion that is manifested not only by souvenirs, but also by a growing interest in "atomic tourism," as well as determined efforts to preserve and interpret significant sites in the history of the atomic age.

The various sites and settings of the early atomic age have, in large measure, become tourist destinations and museums as part of the human response to the changed circumstances of the world in the atomic era. Some laboratories remain active centers of research, such as the Cavendish Laboratory at Cambridge, where Maxwell, Rutherford,

Thomson, Aston, Chadwick, Blackett, and Wilson, among others, made some of the earliest and most significant discoveries. Overcrowded, the "Old Cavendish" was supplemented with the "New Cavendish" Laboratory in 1974, although the famous old buildings and labs within it still stand and remain in use.

There are many sites that retain structures, buildings and physical traces of activities associated with the dawn of the nuclear age, some highly visited, like Hiroshima and Nagasaki, some still closed for security and safety, such as much of Los Alamos or Enewetak, and some sites that exist in relative isolation, such as Tinian's North Field, where the 509th was based. Shown here is one of the two concrete-lined bomb pits that allowed crews to raise the weapons into the B-29 bomb bays. Since this photo was taken in the 1980s, the pits have been excavated and covered over with Plexiglas covers to allow visitors to look down into them. (US National Park Service)

In Paris, Marie Curie's laboratory at no. 11 on the now appropriately named rue Pierre et Marie Curie, where she worked between 1914 and 1934, is part of the Institut Curie, the Curie and Joliot-Curie legacy institution dedicated to continuing the work of the family in research, teaching, and cancer treatment. Also featuring the artifacts and

This stone and concrete monument stands at the hypocenter at the Trinity Site. The top plaque reads "TRINITY SITE Where the world's first nuclear device was exploded on July 16, 1945." The plaque below it notes that the Secretary of the Interior named the site a US National Historic Landmark in 1975. (Photograph by James P. Delgado)

The stump of one of the legs of the 100-foot high Trinity test tower remains in place at ground zero. (Photograph by James P. Delgado)

papers of Irène and Frédéric Joliot-Curie, the museum started as a simple display of the director's office of the Institut following the death of Frédéric Joliot-Curie in 1958; it grew to include artifacts in cases, and finally, in 1967, Marie Curie's office and lab was opened for private, limited tours. Disassembled and decontaminated, Marie's lab was reopened in 1981 for public tours. Not all early pioneers have their own museums. The equipment and notebooks from Otto Hahn and Fritz Strassman's 1938 work to confirm fission are displayed at the Deutsches Museum in Munich, for example.

In the United States, early laboratory sites remain largely unheralded or have vanished. Columbia University's Pupin Physics Laboratory, where Enrico Fermi first worked after fleeing Italy, and where the uranium atom in the United States was first split in January 1939, is a National Historic Landmark, but not a museum – it remains an active university facility, albeit with parts of one of the country's first cyclotrons still in its basement. Ernest Lawrence, inventor of the cyclotron, is commemorated at the University of California, Berkeley, by the Lawrence Hall of Science, a large science center and learning resource that includes displays on Lawrence and his work. The university founded the Hall of Science following Lawrence's death in 1958 as a "living memorial to his genius."[1]

Stagg Field at the University of Chicago, where Enrico Fermi led the team to build CP-1 and there induce the first self-sustaining nuclear reaction, was demolished in 1957 to make way for a new library. The site, at S. Ellis Avenue between E. 56th and 57th Streets in Chicago, is a National Historic Landmark and is commemorated by plaques and a 12ft-tall bronze sculpture by Henry Moore, entitled "Nuclear Energy," which was dedicated on the 25th anniversary of the successful experiment in 1967.

Los Alamos, still an active government-run laboratory, is a largely off-limits and classified facility, including a number of historically significant areas and structures, although portions are open to the public. The Los Alamos Historical Museum, run by the Los Alamos Historical Society, features important papers and artifacts from the Manhattan Project era. The lab's Bradbury Science Museum, named for Los Alamos' second, long-serving director Norris Bradbury, features artifacts, videos, and other memorabilia documenting the history of the Manhattan Project and Los Alamos' role, as well as two life-sized statues of J. Robert Oppenheimer and Leslie Groves. The museum's Defense Gallery includes bomb casings and displays on the lab's current work.

In Albuquerque, the Department of Energy's National Atomic Museum featured extensive displays and a diverse and significant collection of artifacts, including outdoor displays of bomb casings, an 11in. atomic artillery gun, missiles, and a B-29 and a B-52A bomber. The National Atomic Museum, renamed the National Museum of Nuclear Science, relocated in March 2009 to a new and expanded facility in southeast Albuquerque. The museum has served as a gathering place for tours heading to Trinity Site, which is open twice a year, in April and October, for public tours. Caravans of cars organized by the Alamogordo Chamber of Commerce also make a 170-mile round trip, and unescorted private cars can head in for the biannual visit. Visitors are greeted by the McDonald Ranch, restored by the National Park Service (NPS), the remains of Jumbo, the stub of a footing for the Trinity tower, and a stone cairn marking ground zero in the center of the fenced-in crater. Much of the Trinitite is gone, bulldozed and removed, although an area of the green glass is covered by a shelter to show what once lined the crater.

One of the Trinity test instrumentation bunkers slowly deteriorates in the New Mexico desert. A variety of devices were installed by Los Alamos scientists and technicians to record and measure the effects of the world's first atomic explosion. (Photograph by James P. Delgado)

Trinity was the centerpiece of the "Atomic Bomb National Monument" proposed by Senator Carl Hatch of New Mexico in March 1946. The legislation, never passed by Congress, would have placed the site, "Enola Gay," and an atomic museum at Trinity under the control of the National Park Service (NPS) as the "Atomic Bomb National Monument." While Congressional approval of the monument never happened, the NPS did take steps to protect the site, including requesting a 100lb box of Trinitite for future museum display, acquiring the documentation of Trinity Site by the Historic American Buildings Survey, and designating the site as a National Historic Landmark in 1975. The first public tours of Trinity Site took place in 1953, and since then thousands have visited the still remote setting of the first atomic explosion.

In 2004, Congress approved the Manhattan Project National Historic Park Study Act, which the President signed into law on October 18, 2004. The NPS is currently reviewing sites at Los Alamos, Hanford, and Oak Ridge. At Oak Ridge National Laboratory, the world's oldest surviving reactor, the 1942-built graphite reactor was decommissioned in 1963 after 20 years of operation. Preserved, it is a National Historic Landmark and is now open for tours as part of regular public bus tours of the laboratory. In August 2008, the Secretary of the Interior designated Hanford's 1943-built B reactor, where the plutonium for Trinity and the Nagasaki Fat Man was made, as a National Historic Landmark, making it possible for the reactor to be saved and opened to the public as part of a park or museum. Much of the rest of Hanford's massive plant, now closed as it has ceased to be an active nuclear facility, has been demolished as part of a post-Cold War clean up.

The two B-29s that carried the bomb into combat have also been saved and are on public display. "Bockscar," set aside after the war, is preserved and displayed at the National Museum of the US Air Force in Dayton, Ohio. Transferred to Davis-Monthan Army Air Field in Arizona for dry, desert storage in August 1946, just a year after its atomic mission, "Bockscar" remained there for 15 years, its title formally transferred to the Air Force Museum, at Wright-Patterson Air Force Base. In September 1961, a crew flew the still-operational B-29 to the museum, where it has remained on display since.

Signs warn visitors as they approach the Trinity Site. The White Sands Missile Range notifies visitors to the site that "Radiation levels in the fenced, ground zero area are low. On an average the levels are only 10 times greater than the region's natural background radiation. A one-hour visit to the inner fenced area will result in a whole body exposure of one-half to one millirem." (Photographs by James P. Delgado)

"Enola Gay," however, faced a more difficult time as a museum display. After participating in Operation *Crossroads*, it flew back to the United States and was laid up at Davis-Monthan. It remained there until July 1949, when Paul Tibbets flew it to Park Ridge, Illinois, for a special ceremony where the Smithsonian Institution received title to the aircraft and accepted it at Orchard Place Air Field. It remained in storage there until 1952, when the City of Chicago selected the field as the site of O'Hare International Airport.

Flown then to Pyote Air Force Base in Texas and, in 1953, to Andrews Air Force Base near Washington, DC, "Enola Gay" languished in outdoor storage until the Smithsonian partially disassembled it for storage at the Smithsonian's Suitland, Maryland, Paul E. Garber Preservation, Restoration, and Storage Facility. There, the plane remained in pieces for 23 years, until restoration and reassembly finally commenced in 1984 and proceeded for the next decade. The forward portions of "Enola Gay" were moved to the National Air and Space Museum on the Mall in Washington, DC, in 1995 as part of a controversial display commemorating the end of the war and the atomic bombings of Japan. They remained there until 1998, when the Smithsonian returned the pieces to the

The McDonald Ranch, the site of the Trinity test bomb's assembly, has been both documented and restored by the US National Park Service. Barely visited, it sits in isolation in the desert. Due to its remoteness it sometimes appears as if Trinity happened yesterday, not decades ago. (Photograph by James P. Delgado)

The atomic-damaged ruins of the Hiroshima Prefectural Commercial Exhibition Hall, constructed in 1915 are the most prominent landmark in Hiroshima Peace Park, which occupies the center of the blast-damaged area of the city. In 1966, the City of Hiroshima decided to retain the building and its dome as a monument, and since then, two separate projects have been undertaken to preserve the structure. In 1996, it was designated as part of the World Heritage Site by UNESCO. (© Rolf Richardson/Alamy)

Garber facility for final reassembly of the entire aircraft. After more than 44,000 hours of work, "Enola Gay" was again in one piece and ready for display in the new Steven F. Udvar-Hazy Center near Washington Dulles International Airport, which opened in December 2003.

ATTACK SITES

Tinian, the site of the 509th's advance base for the atomic strikes against Japan, is part of the Commonwealth of the Northern Marianas Islands. The former base is gone, leaving only the airstrips at North Field, where "Enola Gay" and "Bockscar" once roared off from and later touched down following their missions. Overgrown and abandoned, the only monuments of note are the two atomic bomb loading pits. Filled in for many years and marked by simple signs, they were excavated by the government for ceremonies marking the 60th anniversary of the attacks, and remain open and under cover.

Hiroshima and Nagasaki, rebuilt in the aftermath of their devastation, each mark and commemorate the attacks. A surviving bomb-damaged structure, Hiroshima's Prefectural Industrial Promotional Hall, sits 490ft from ground zero. The ruins were preserved by the city and designated as the Hiroshima Peace Memorial. It is now a UNESCO World Heritage Site. The ruins sit inside Peace Memorial Park, which

A woman prays at the Hiroshima Peace Memorial Cenotaph. Designed by Kenzo Tange and built in 1952, the cenotaph is said to provide shelter for the souls of those killed by the bomb. The words "Let all the souls here rest in peace, for we shall not repeat the evil" are inscribed on the cenotaph. The ruins of the Exhibition Hall can be seen through the arch of the cenotaph as visitors pray. The stone chest inside the shelter contains volumes with the names of all persons killed by the Hiroshima bomb, including the names of *hibakusha* who have died in the intervening years. More than 77 volumes with more than 258,000 names are now inside the chest. (Photograph by Chris Ballentine © Paul Thompson Images/Alamy)

Nagasaki Peace Park occupies the site of the hypocenter of the bomb's detonation on August 9, 1945. A prominent feature in the park is the Nagasaki Peace statue, a 9.7m high figure created by Nagasaki sculptor Seibou Kitamura A cenotaph in front of the statue holds the names of those in Nagasaki who died as a result of the atomic bombing of Nagasaki. (Photograph by James Montgomery, © Jon Arnold Images Ltd. / Alamy)

occupies the site of the leveled downtown core of old Hiroshima. There are numerous memorials and monuments, a burial mound for 70,000 unidentified victims, a memorial cenotaph, and a Peace Hall and museum filled with artifacts that include many personal effects of the bomb's victims. Development of the park and its buildings and monuments began in the 1950s, and the site today is a gathering place for quiet reflection as well as the annual Peace Memorial Ceremony, described by the City of Hiroshima as an annual event held each August 6 to "console the souls of those who were lost due to the atomic bombing as well as pray for the realization of everlasting world peace."[2] The mayor of Hiroshima reads a peace declaration, "conveying Hiroshima's wish for the abolition of nuclear weapons and the realization of eternal world peace." The declarations have at times been controversial. At 08:15hrs, a giant "Peace Bell" in the park is rung, sirens sound, and a moment of silence follows.

Nagasaki also features a Peace Memorial Park, established on the 10th anniversary of the attack in 1955. The park features a central monument marking the hypocenter, or ground zero, monuments, memorials, and statues, including a large 33ft-high bronze figure by Nagasaki sculptor Seibou Kitamura depicting peace. A fountain of peace also sits inside the park to help the souls of victims who died searching for water, a common plight for many survivors who struggled in the aftermath of the attack. The fountain includes an inscription from one survivor, a young girl who later remarked that "I was thirsty beyond endurance. There was something oily on the surface of the water, but I wanted water so badly that I drank it just as it was."[3] Like Hiroshima, Nagasaki also holds an annual peace ceremony on August 9.

The ceremony at Hiroshima ends at night with an annual ritual that represents the souls of the dead, as thousands of paper lanterns are set adrift on the Motoyasu River. Brightly lit, they slowly move away as the current gently carries them out to sea. It is a ceremony that has been adopted in other countries, and each August 6 and 9, paper lanterns drift on other waterfronts not only to remember the bomb's impact in Japan, but also to make a point about the global threat of nuclear weapons.

BIKINI

The other atomic site of the dawn of the atomic age is Bikini Atoll, the setting for Operation *Crossroads*. After years of subsequent tests, Bikini is abandoned, its shores

Bikini Atoll's islands are covered with concrete bunkers from decades of nuclear testing. Many of them date from the era of the hydrogen bomb. This reinforced concrete bunker on the Bikini Island is one of many, empty now except for creeping vegetation and geckos. (Photograph by James P. Delgado)

The sunken ships of Bikini Atoll are filled with irradiated test equipment, instruments, and, in the collapsing hangar of USS *Saratoga*, aircraft. This SBF-4E "Helldiver" remains in place as it was secured for the "Baker" test of July 25, 1946. Along with several other aircraft, it sank with the ship. (US National Park Service, photograph by Larry Murphy)

littered with rusting machinery and cables, its islands covered by thick concrete bunkers. The bottom of Bikini's lagoon is pocked with nuclear blast craters and the sunken ships of *Crossroads*. In 1989 and 1990, archaeologists from the NPS' Submerged Cultural Resources Unit returned to Bikini with the US Navy to relocate the sunken fleet and conduct a detailed study of the ships in the first major archaeological assessment of a nuclear testing site.

The team surveyed 11 vessels during two field seasons, including the wreck of the former German cruiser *Prinz Eugen*, a *Crossroads* target vessel, at nearby Kwajalein Atoll. The majority of the fieldwork at Bikini focused on the US aircraft carrier USS *Saratoga*. Other vessels surveyed to varying degrees were the battleships USS *Arkansas* and *Nagato*, the attack transports USS *Gilliam* and USS *Carlisle*, the submarines *Apogon* and *Pilotfish*, the yard oiler YO-160, the floating dry dock ARDC-13, and a landing craft, LCT-1175. In addition to documenting gross physical damage to the ships, the team also measured residual radiation, which was negligible (less than 10 microcuries), assessed unexploded non-nuclear ordnance left aboard for the tests, and documented the presence of test instruments for measuring blast, heat, and radiation effects.

The sunken ships of Bikini Atoll are, in their isolation from the rest of the world in a depopulated land, evocative artifacts – the material record of Operation *Crossroads* as well as the fundamental human behaviors that brought the world itself to a crossroads. The crushed hulls, toppled masts, and abandoned test instruments at Bikini preserve the reality of Operation *Crossroads* in a manner that can never fully be comprehended through

The bridge of USS *Saratoga* is a popular destination for wreck divers who explore the sunken carrier at Bikini Atoll. Instruments, equipment, and engraved instructions and signs remain in place more than 60 years after the blast waves of the "Baker" atomic detonation damaged and sank *Saratoga*. Among the items left on the bridge is a thick pair of dark glasses used by observers to watch the "Able" detonation of July 1. Discarded, they lie in the silt covering the bridge's deck. (US National Park Service, photograph by Larry Murphy)

written accounts, photographs, or even films of the tests. Drawn by this and the challenge of diving on a collection of significant vessels in relatively shallow yet "expert" depths, hundreds of divers have visited Bikini since the early 1990s. Now a dive park administered by the Bikini Council, Bikini, provides accommodation, a dive boat, and guided dives to surface zero and into the heart of ships sunk by the atomic blasts of 1946. Ongoing deterioration of some of the ships creates unique challenges for the tour operation and divers; the most notable change of the last decade being the slow collapse of USS *Saratoga*, whose massive superstructure is slowly capsizing to one side as its decks also give way.

Ultimately, Bikini, like the still-radioactive B reactor, the Trinity Site, the A-bomb dome at Hiroshima, or other sites of later atomic tests, are reminders of the true legacy of atomic weapons if the arsenals honed after 1945 are ever fully unleashed. In 1947, the final report on Operation *Crossroads*, written for the Joint Chiefs of Staff, commented that:

> If used in numbers, atomic bombs not only can nullify any nation's military effort, but can demolish its social and economic structure and prevent their re-establishment for long periods of time. With such weapons, especially if employed in conjunction with other weapons of mass destruction such as pathogenic bacteria, it is quite possible to depopulate vast areas of the earth's surface, leaving only vestigial remnants of man's material works.[4]

The vestigial remnants of the dawn of the atomic age, especially Bikini, are instructive reminders of the largely unrealized, but still present perils of the age.

NOTES AND SOURCES

The bibliography provides a detailed list of sources consulted as well as those cited. The notes that follow provide attribution for all direct quotes.

CHAPTER ONE

1. A 4th-century BC quotation of Democritus by Epicurus, Harrison, *Cosmology*, p.150.

2. Newton's *Opticks: Or, A Treatise of the Reflections, Refractions, Inflections and Colours of Light*, p.375.

3. Dalton, *A New System of Chemical Philosophy*, p.212.

4. H. T. E., "Science and Esoteric Philosophy: Lord Salisbury's Warning," pp.31–33.

5. Marie Curie "Radium and Radioactivity," pp.461–466.

6. Thomson, "On the Structure of the Atom," p.237.

7. Rhodes, *The Making of the Atomic Bomb*, p.40 and p.42.

8. Rutherford, "The Scattering of α and β Particles by Matter," p.687.

9. Wells, *The World Set Free*, pp.24–25.

10. Wells, p.89 and pp.100–02.

11. Rhodes, *The Making of the Atomic Bomb*, p.44.

12. Ibid., p.44.

13. "the dream of charlatans and scientists for nearly a thousand years," and "But this is only part of the story" are from "Way To Transmute Elements Is Found," *New York Times* of January 8, 1922.

14. From "Breaking Down the Atom" in the London *Times* (January 12, 1933).

15. Szilárd, *The Collected Works: Scientific Papers*, p.183.

16. Rhodes, p.202.

17. From the Nobel Foundation's Nobel Prize biography of Fermi, which is available online at: http://nobelprize.org/nobel_prizes/physics/laureates/1938/fermi-bio.html

CHAPTER TWO

1. From Einstein's letter to Roosevelt of August 2, 1939. This document is available online at: http://hypertextbook.com/eworld/einstein.shtml#first

2. Frisch-Peierls memorandum of March 1940. Available online at: http://www.atomicarchive.com/Docs/Begin/FrischPeierls.shtml

3. Rhodes, *The Making of the Atomic Bomb*, p.356.

4. Oliphant, "The Beginning," p.17.

5. Roosevelt's approval of the project is noted in numerous sources. The President simply initialed the report he received, "OK, FDR." See Rhodes, p.412

6. From the Army Corps of Engineers website: http://www.usace.army.mil/missions/

7. Groves, *Now It Can be Told*, p.4.

8. Rhodes, p.427.

9. Compton, *Atomic Quest*, pp.136–37.

10. Letter from Vannevar Bush to Oppenheimer, February 25, 1943. Rhodes.

11. From the Quebec Agreement of August 19, 1943. Available online at: http://www.atomicarchive.com/Docs/ManhattanProject/Quebec.shtml

12. See Bothwell, *Eldorado*, pp.108, 109–12.

CHAPTER THREE

1. Laurence, *Dawn Over Zero*, p.184.

2. Bainbridge, *Trinity*, p.1.

3. Groves, *Now It Can Be Told*, p.289.

4. From a memo from Parsons to Oppenheimer dated February 19, 1945. Christman, *Target Hiroshima*, p.161.

5. Hawkins, *Manhattan District History*, p.271.

6. Wyden, *Day One*, p.204.

7. Rhodes, *The Making of the Atomic Bomb*, p.658.

8. Available at: http://www.atomicarchive.com/History/trinity/assembly.shtml

9. Rhodes, p.666, from the journal of the weather forecaster, Jack Hubbard.

10. Laurence, p.10.

11. Rhodes, p.673.

12. From Fermi's post-Trinity memorandum on the test, available online at: http://www.lanl.gov/history/atomicbomb/pdf/Enrico%20Fermis%20Observations%20at%20Trinity,%20July%2016,%201945.pdf

13. Wilson, *All in Our Time*, p.230.

14. From a 1964 interview with Oppenheimer, Giovannitti and Freed, *The Decision to Drop the Bomb*, p.197.

15. Laurence, p.187.

CHAPTER FOUR

1. LeMay and Yenne, *Superfortress*, pp.65–66.
2. Bomb characteristics, dimensions, and weights: Campbell, *The Silverplate Bombers*, pp.72, 81, 88. The best source for the technology, characteristics, and the development of the bombs is Coster-Mullen, *Atom Bombs*.
3. Tibbets, *Mission: Hiroshima*, p.140.
4. Ibid., p.151.
5. Ibid., p.154.
6. Ibid., p.157.
7. Ibid., p.170 for more on Tibbet's drop, dive, and turn strategy.
8. Ibid., p.172 for more on the over-water, over-land transition training.
9. LeMay and Yenne, *Superfortress*, p.123 for Tokyo fire-bombing statistics.
10. From a Fifth Air Force Intelligence Report of July 21, 1945, Rhodes, *The Making of the Atomic Bomb*, p.596.
11. LeMay and Yenne, pp.184–85, 191–93.
12. Truman, *Year of Decision*, pp.10–11.
13. Groves, *Now It Can Be Told*, p.267.
14. Rhodes, p.627.
15. Ibid., p.650.
16. Ibid., pp.650–51.
17. Churchill, *Triumph and Tragedy*, p.553.
18. Truman, p.416.
19. Truman's private diary, Rhodes, pp. 690–91.
20. From the Potsdam Declaration. The copy Japan received is available online at: http://www.ndl.go.jp/constitution/e/etc/c06.html

CHAPTER FIVE

1. Tibbets, *Mission: Hiroshima,* p.180.
2. Admiral Ashworth comments at a Los Alamos conference before his death in 2005. Available online at the Los Alamos National Laboratory website at: http://www.lanl.gov/news/index.php/fuseaction/home.story/story_id/7619
3. Thomas and Witts, *Ruin From the Air*, p.xxx.
4. Memorandum dated February 7, 194,5 from Norman Ramsay to Ashworth, in the Frederick L. Ashworth Collection, Manhattan Project Heritage Preservation Association. Available online at: http://www.mphpa.org/classic/COLLECTIONS/CG-FASH/Pages/CGP-FASH-05.htm
5. LeMay and Yenne, *Superfortress*, p.151.
6. The poem "Nobody Knows" Laurence, *Dawn Over Zero*, p.201.
7. Russ, *Project Alberta*, p.33.

8. Memorandum dated August 17, 1945, from Major J. A. Derry to Admiral W. S. De Lany, Campbell, *The Silverplate Bombers*, p.40.

9. Ibid., p.41.

10. Laurence, p.205.

11. Russ, p.60.

12. Laurence, pp.207–208.

13. Tibbets, p.210. Parsons' log of the Hiroshima mission was reproduced in Groves, *Now It Can Be Told*, p.318.

14. Tibbets, p.221.

15. "little pin-point of light, purplish-red" and "everything just turned white in front of me," from Laurence, pp.217–18.

16. Tibbets, p.227.

17. Father Siemes' account, an appendix to the Manhattan Engineer District report on Hiroshima and Nagasaki dated June 29, 1946. Available online at: http://www.yale.edu/lawweb/avalon/abomb/mp25.htm

18. United States Strategic Bombing Survey (USSBS), *The Effects of Atomic Bombs*, p.5. Available online at: http://ibiblio.org/hyperwar/AAF/USSBS/AtomicEffects/AtomicEffects-2.html

19. Laurence, *Dawn Over Zero*, p.219.

20. Tibbets, p.227.

21. USSBS, p.20.

22. Siemes, appendix to the Manhattan Engineer District report.

23. Truman, *Year of Decision*, p.421.

24. Siemes, appendix to the Manhattan Engineer District report.

25. Translated text of the airdropped leaflets. Available online at: http://www.nuclearfiles.org/menu/key-issues/nuclear-weapons/history/pre-cold-war/hiroshima-nagasaki/leaflets-dropped_1945-08-06.htm

26. Tibbets, p.236.

CHAPTER SIX

1. August 6, 1945, White House Statement on the atomic bombing of Hiroshima. Geddes, *The Atomic Age Opens*, pp.11–13.

2. LeMay and Yenne, *Superfortress*, p.153.

3. Fussell, *Thank God for the Atomic Bomb and other Essays*, pp.14–15.

4. Russ, *Project Alberta*, p.65.

5. O'Keefe, *Nuclear Hostages*, p.98.

6. Laurence, *Dawn Over Zero*, p.229.

7. Ibid.

8. Albury, "Bockscar's Bash."

9. Laurence, pp.231–32.

10. Albury, "Bockscar's Bash."

11. Serber, *Peace and War*, p.113.

12. Available online at the Department of Energy's Manhattan Project website at: http://www.cfo.doe.gov/me70/manhattan/nagasaki.htm

13. Laurence, p.234.

14. Figures are from the 1950 City of Nagasaki report on the atomic attack, available online at: http://www1.city.nagasaki.nagasaki.jp/abm/abm_e/qa/heiwa_e/record_e.html

15. Laurence, p.236.

16. Albury, "Bockscar's Bash."

17. Russ, p.71.

18. From Michie Hattori's account, Leary, "Eyewitness to the Nagasaki Atomic Bomb," Available online at http://www.historynet.com/michie-hattori-eyewitness-to-the-nagasaki-atomic-bomb-blast.htm

19. Quotations from Sakue, Burke-Gaffney, "In the Words of an Atomic Bomb Survivor." Available online at: http://www.uwosh.edu/faculty_staff/earns/number3.html

20. Soviet Declaration of War against Japan. Available online at: http://www.yale.edu/lawweb/avalon/wwii/s4.htm

21. From Marshall's handwritten note on Groves' memo of August 10. Burr, "The Atomic Bomb and the End of World War II," document No. 67. Available at: http://www.gwu.edu/~nsarchiv/NSAEBB/NSAEBB162/67.pdf

22. Wallace's diary entry of August 10, Blum, *The Price of Vision*, pp.473–74.

23. War Department transcript of August 13, 1945. Burr, "The Atomic Bomb and the End of World War I," document No. 162, available at: http://www.gwu.edu/~nsarchiv/NSAEBB/NSAEBB162/72.pdf

24. Imperial Rescript of Surrender, Jansen, *The Making of Modern Japan*, p.660.

25. Transcript of Hirohito's speech of August 14, 1945, accepting the terms of the Potsdam Declaration, as transmitted by Domei and recorded by the Federal Communications Commission. Available online at: http://shs.westport.k12.ct.us/jwb/Collab/hiroshima.htm

CHAPTER SEVEN

1. *Time* magazine, August 20, 1945.

2. *New York Times*, August 6, 1945.

3. Geddes, *The Atomic Age Opens*, pp.19–20.

4 *The Times* of London, August 7, 1945.

5. September 1945 Gallup poll, Boyer, *By The Bomb's Early Light*, p.22.

6. Churchill's speech on the "Tragedy of Europe," reported in *The Times* of London, September 20, 1946.

7. The history of the Campaign for Nuclear Disarmament is found on the CND website: http://www.cnduk.org/index.php/information/info-sheets/the-history-of-cnd.html

8. The song titles come from Boyer, *By the Bomb's Early Light*, p.11, and Scheibach, *Atomic Narratives and American Youth*, p.173.

9. *The Beginning or the End* official promotional book, available online at: http://www.atomicbombcinema.com/english/image_gallery/beginning/begin_end_intro.htm

10. Boyer, pp.10–11.

11. From the Kix cereal advertisement. A number of rings, boxes, and ads survive, and some have been sold recently on eBay.

12. Geddes, p.41.

13. Ibid., p.48.

14. Ibid., pp.54–55.

15. Ibid., p.56

16. Ibid., p.217.

17. This passage is found online, both on film and in transcribed form, at the Churchill Centre's website at: http://www.winstonchurchill.org/i4a/pages/index.cfm?pageid=429

18. Boyer, p.54.

19. Herken, *The Winning Weapon*, p.15.

20. Ibid., p.43.

21. Russ, *Project Alberta*, appendix E-29.

22. Ibid., appendix E-33.

23. The Soviet archives summarized in Andrew and Mitrokhin, *The Sword and the Shield*. The US government's intercepts are documented in Haynes and Klehr, *Venona*.

24. Rosenberg et al. v. United States, Supreme Court of the United States, 346 US 273, 1953.

25. Ginés, *The Meaning of Technology*, p.88.

26. "Hold That Monster," *Time*, November 19, 1945.

27. *New York Times*, August 30, 1946.

28. Weller's dispatches were published in 2006 by his son as *First Into Nagasaki*.

CHAPTER EIGHT

1. Geddes, *The Atomic Age Opens*, p.43.

2. Ibid., pp.162–63.

3. *New York Times*, August 12, 1945.

4. LeMay and Yenne, *Superfortress*, p.161.

5. Murrow, *In Search of Light*, p.102.

6. Shurcliff, *Bombs at Bikini*, p.10.

7.   Ibid., pp.10–11.

8.   Davis, *Postwar Defense Policy and the U.S. Navy 1943–45*, p.243.

9.   *New York Times*, August 24, 1945.

10.   *New York Times*, August 25, 1945.

11.   Shurcliff, p.11.

12.   Graybar, *Dictionary of American Biography: Supplement Five, 1951–1955*, pp.65–67.

13.   *New York Times*, January 10, 1946.

14.   Delgado, *Ghost Fleet*, p.21, and Weisgall, *Operation Crossroads*, p.32.

15.   "the effects of atomic explosions against naval vessels in order to appraise the strategic implications of the application of atomic bombs," "military, lesser military and principal scientific and technical objects," and "sufficient data … to permit naval architects and engineers to design more resistant ships," are from the declassified Technical Report on Operation *Crossroads*, Delgado, p.21.

16.   From Blandy's CBS radio broadcast of April 13, 1946, Delgado, p.22.

17.   Boyer, *By the Bomb's Early Light*, p.83.

18.   From the official Navy certificate issued to the sailors and officers who took possession of *Nagato* in Tokyo Bay at the time of the Japanese surrender.

19.   Shurcliff, p.52.

20.   Ibid., p.36.

21.   Ibid., p.ix.

22.   Daly, 'Crossroads at Bikini," p.68.

23.   The Bikini test statistics are from Shurcliff, pp.84, 94–96.

24.   Markwith, "Farewell to Bikini," p.97.

25.   Shurcliff's declassified Technical Report, Delgado, p.55.

26.   "Crossroads Crosstalk" newsletter, July 2, 1946, Delgado, p.56.

27.   Shurcliff's declassified Technical Report, Delgado, p.61.

28.   Bradley, *No Place to Hide*, pp.58 and 64.

29.   The Baker detonation characteristics and effects are discussed by Glasstone, *The Effects of Nuclear Weapons*, pp.45–46, 52.

30.   *New York Times*, August 4, 1946.

31.   Bradley, *No Place to Hide*, pp. 109–10.

32.   From pp.60 and 73 of a declassified report, "The Evaluation of the Atomic Bomb as a Military Weapon," in the US National Archives, as quoted in Delgado, *Ghost Fleet*, pp.95–96.

33.   Bradley, pp. 165–66.

34.   *Washington Post*, February 18, 1949.

35.   Davis, p.246.

36.   *New York Times*, August 1, 1946.

CHAPTER NINE

1. Available online at a site created for the PBS film *Race for the Superbomb* (1999):
    http://www.pbs.org/wgbh/amex/bomb/filmmore/reference/primary/
    trumanstatement.html
    or the Atomic Archive at:
    http://www.atomicarchive.com/Docs/Hydrogen/SovietAB.shtml

2. Available online at:
    http://www.pbs.org/wgbh/amex/bomb/filmmore/reference/primary/
    extractsofgeneral.html

3. Available online at:
    http://www.pbs.org/wgbh/amex/bomb/filmmore/reference/primary/
    extractsofgeneral.html

4. An excellent summary of the history of the British atomic program can be found in
    Arnold, *Britain and the H-Bomb*. Another source worth consulting is Barnaby and
    Holdstock, *The British Nuclear Weapons Programme, 1952–2002*.

5. From the 1953 film *Operation Hurricane*. Available online at the National Archives
    website at:
    http://www.nationalarchives.gov.uk/films/1951to1964/filmpage_oper_hurr.htm
    A transcript of the film's narration is online at:
    http://www.nationalarchives.gov.uk/films/1951to1964/popup/transcript/
    trans_oper_hurr.htm

6. Lapp, *Must We Hide?*, pp.11, 49.

7. Gerstell, *How to Survive an Atomic Bomb*, p.5, 15, 17.

8. The author remembers this film and the drill very well. The film, prepared in 1951
    and released in 1952, is available online at:
    http://cinemaniacal.com/video/view/duck-and-cover.

CHAPTER TEN

1. From the Lawrence Hall of Science website, online at:
    http://lawrencehallofscience.org/lawrence/

2. From the City of Hiroshima's English-language webpage, online at:
    http://www.city.hiroshima.jp/shimin/shimin/shikiten/shikiten-e.html

3. Noted in a number tourist guides, and is available online at:
    http://peace.maripo.com/p_fountains.htm

4. "The Evaluation of the Atomic Bomb as a Military Weapon," US National Archives,
    pp. 60 and 73, Delgado, *Ghost Fleet*, pp.95–96.

BIBLIOGRAPHY

While this is not intended to be an exhaustive bibliography of the origins of the atomic age and the early development and use of atomic weapons, it does include the sources used and cited in the preparation of this book, as well as a number of other useful and noteworthy books, articles, and resources.

BOOKS

Albright, Joseph and Maria Kunstel, *Bombshell: The Secret Story of America's Unknown Atomic Spy Conspiracy* (New York: Times Books, 1997)

Alperovitz, Gar, *Atomic Diplomacy: Hiroshima and Potsdam: The Use of the Atomic Bomb and the American Confrontation with Soviet Power* (New York: Simon & Schuster, 1965)

Alvarez, Luis W., *Adventures of a Physicist* (New York: Basic Books, Inc. Publishers, 1987)

Andrew, Christopher, and Vasili Mitrokhin, *The Sword and the Shield: The Mitrokhin Archive and the Secret History of the KGB* (New York: Basic Books, 1999)

Arnold, Lorna, and Katherine Pyne, *Britain and the H-Bomb: The Official History* (Basingstoke, Hampshire: Palgrave Macmillan, 2001)

Arnold, Lorna, and Mark Smith, *Britain, Australia and the Bomb: The Nuclear Tests and Their Aftermath (International Papers in Political Economy)* (Basingstoke, Hampshire: Palgrave Macmillan, 2006)

Badash, Lawrence, *Scientists and the Development of Nuclear Weapons: From Fission to the Limited Test Ban Treaty, 1939–1963* (Atlantic Highlands, New Jersey: Humanities Press International, Inc., 1995)

Badash, Lawrence, Joseph O. Hirschfelder, and Herbert P. Broida (eds), *Reminiscences of Los Alamos, 1943–1945* (Dordrecht, Boston: D. Reidel, 1980)

Bainbridge, Kenneth, *Trinity* (Los Alamos: Los Alamos National Laboratory, 1976)

Barnaby, Frank and Douglas Holdstock (eds), *The British Nuclear Weapons Programme, 1952–2002* (New York and Milton Park: Routledge, 2003)

Batchelder, Robert C., *The Irreversible Decision, 1939–1950* (Boston: Houghton Mifflin, 1962)

Bernstein, Barton J. (ed.), *Politics and Policies of the Truman Administration* (New York: HarperCollins, 1970)

Bernstein, Barton J. (ed.), *The Atomic Bomb: Critical Issues* (Boston: Little, Brown and Company, 1976)

Bernstein, Barton J. and Allen Matusow (eds), *The Truman Administration: A Documentary History* (New York: 1966)

Bernstein, Jeremy, *Oppenheimer: Portrait of an Enigma* (Chicago: Ivan R. Dee, 2004)

Bethe, Hans, *The Road from Los Alamos* (New York: American Institute of Physics, 1991)

Bickel, Lennard, *The Deadly Element: The Story of Uranium* (New York: Stein and Day Publishers, 1979)

Bird, Kai and Martin J. Sherwin, *American Prometheus: The Triumph and Tragedy of J. Robert Oppenheimer* (New York: Knopf, 2005)

Bird, Peter, *Operation Hurricane* (Worcester: Square One Publications, 1989)

Birdsall, Steve, *B-29 Superfortress in Action (Aircraft in Action 31)* (Carrolton, Texas: Squadron/Signal Publications, Inc., 1977)

Birdsall, Steve, *Saga of the Superfortress: The Dramatic Story of the B-29 and the Twentieth Air Force* (London: Sidgwick & Jackson Ltd, 1991)

Blackett, P. M. S., *Atomic Weapons and East-West Relations* (Cambridge: Cambridge University Press, 1956)

Blackett, P. M. S., *Fear, War, and the Bomb.* (New York: Whittlesey House, 1949)

Blum, John Morton (ed.), *The Price of Vision: The Diary of Henry A. Wallace, 1942–1946* (Boston: Houghton Mifflin, 1973)

Bono, Sam, *The National Atomic Museum: America's Museum Resource for Nuclear Science & History* (Virginia Beach, Virginia: The Donning Company Publishers, 2002)

Bothwell, Robert, *Eldorado: Canada's National Uranium Company* (Toronto: University of Toronto Press, 1984)

Boyer, Paul, *By the Bomb's Early Light: American Thought and Culture at the Dawn of the Atomic Age* (New York: Pantheon Books, 1985)

Boyer, Paul, *Fallout: A Historian Reflects on America's Half-Century Encounter with Nuclear Weapons* (Columbus: Ohio State University Press, 1998)

Bradley, David C., *No Place To Hide* (Boston: Little, Brown and Company, 1948)

Brown, Anthony Cave, and Charles B. MacDonald (eds), *The Secret History of the Atomic Bomb* (New York: A Delta Book, 1977)

Bush, Vannevar, *Modern Arms and Free Men: A Discussion of the Role of Science in Preserving Democracy* (New York: Simon and Schuster, 1949)

Campbell, Richard H., *The Silverplate Bombers: A History and Registry of the Enola Gay and Other B-29s Configured to Carry Atomic Bombs* (Jefferson, North Carolina: McFarland & Co., Inc., 2005)

Carmichael, Virginia, *Framing History: The Rosenberg Story and the Cold War* (Minneapolis: University of Minnesota Press, 1993)

Childs, Herbert, *An American Genius: The Life of Ernest Orlando Lawrence, Father of the Cyclotron* (New York: E. P. Dutton and Company, Inc., 1968)

Christman, Al, *Target Hiroshima: Deak Parsons and the Creation of the Atomic Bomb* (Annapolis, Maryland: Naval Institute Press, 1998)

Churchill, Winston, *Triumph and Tragedy* (Boston: Houghton Mifflin, 1986)

Compton, Arthur Holly, *Atomic Quest: A Personal Narrative* (New York: Oxford University Press, 1956)

Coster-Mullen, John, *Atom Bombs: The Top Secret Inside Story of Little Boy and Fat Man* (Waukesha, Wisconsin: John-Coster Mullen, 2006)

Curie, Eva and Vincent Sheean (translator), *Madame Curie: A Biography* (New York: Da Capo Press, 2001)

Dalton, John, *A New System Of Chemical Philosophy, Part I* (London: S. Russell, 1808)

Davis, Nuel Pharr, *Lawrence & Oppenheimer* (New York: Simon and Schuster, 1968)

Davis, Vincent, *Postwar Defense Policy and the U.S. Navy, 1943–1946* (Chapel Hill: The University of North Carolina Press, 1962)

Dean, Gordon, *Report on the Atom: What You Should Know About the Atomic Energy Program of the United States* (New York: Alfred A. Knopf, 1953)

Delgado, James P., *Ghost Fleet: The Sunken Ships of Bikini Atoll* (Honolulu: University of Hawaii Press, 1996)

Delgado, James P., Daniel J. Lenihan, and Larry E. Murphy, *The Archaeology of the Atomic Bomb: A Submerged Cultural Resources Assessment of the Sunken Fleet of Operation Crossroads at Bikini and Kwajalein Lagoons* (Santa Fe, New Mexico: National Park Service, 1991)

Dorr, Robert F., *B-29 Superfortress Units in World War Two (Combat Aircraft 33)* (Oxford, UK: Osprey Publishing, 2002)

Feis, Herbert, *Japan Subdued: The Atomic Bomb and the End of the War in the Pacific* (Princeton: Princeton University Press, 1961)

Fermi, Laura, *Atoms in the Family: My Life with Enrico Fermi* (Chicago: University of Chicago Press, 1954)

Fermi, Rachel and Esther Samra, *Picturing the Bomb: Photographs from the Secret World of the Manhattan Project* (New York: Harry N. Abrams, Inc., 1995)

Feynman, Richard P., *Surely You're Joking, Mr. Feynman* (New York: W. W. Norton & Company, 1997)

Fussell, Paul, *Thank God for the Atomic Bomb and Other Essays* (New York: Summit, 1988)

Geddes, Donald Porter (ed.), *The Atomic Age Opens* (New York: Pocket Books, 1945)

Gerber, M. S., *The Hanford Site: An Anthology of Early Histories* (Richland, Washington: US Department of Energy, 1993)

Gerstell, Richard H., *How to Survive an Atomic Bomb* (Washington, DC: Combat Forces Press, 1950)

Ginés, Montserrat (ed.), *The Meaning of Technology: Selected Readings from American Sources* (Barcelona: Ediciones UPC, 2003)

Giovannitti, Len, and Fred Freed, *The Decision to Drop the Bomb* (London: Methuen, 1967)

Glasstone, Samuel (ed.), *The Effects of Nuclear Weapons* (Washington, DC: US Atomic Energy Commission, 1957)

Goldschmidt, Bertrand, *The Atomic Adventure: The Political And Technical Aspects* (New York: The Pergamon Press, 1964)

Goldsmith, Barbara, *Obsessive Genius: The Inner World of Marie Curie* (New York: W. W. Norton, 2005)

Goldstein, Donald M., Katherine V. Dillon, and Michael J. Wenger, *Rain of Ruin: A Photographic History of Hiroshima and Nagasaki* (Washington & London: Brassey's, 1999)

Goodchild, Peter, *J. Robert Oppenheimer: Shatterer of Worlds* (New York: Fromm International Publishing Corporation, 1985)

Gowing, Margaret, *Britain and Atomic Energy, 1939–1945* (New York: St. Martin's Press, 1964)

Grant, John L., *Bernard M. Baruch: The Adventures of a Wall Street Legend* (New York: John Wiley and Sons, 1997)

Gray, L. W., *From Separations to Reconstitution – A Short History of Plutonium in the U.S. and Russia* (Livermore, California: Lawrence Livermore National Laboratory, 1999)

Greenaway, Frank, *John Dalton and the Atom* (Ithaca, New York: Cornell University Press, 1966)

Groueff, Stephane, *Manhattan Project: The Untold Story of the Making of the Atomic Bomb* (Boston: Little, Brown & Company, 1967)

Groves, Leslie R., *Now It Can Be Told: The Story of the Manhattan Project* (New York: Harper & Brothers, 1962)

Hachiya, Michihiko, *Hiroshima Diary: The Journal of a Japanese Physician, August 6– September 30, 1945* (Chapel Hill: University of North Carolina Press, 1955)

Hacker, Barton C., *The Dragon's Tail: Radiation Safety in the Manhattan Project* (Berkeley: University of California Press, 1987)

Hansen, Chuck, *U.S. Nuclear Weapons: The Secret History* (Arlington, Virginia: Orion Books, 1988)

Hansen, Chuck (ed.), *The Swords of Armageddon: U.S. Nuclear Weapons Development Since 1945* (Sunnyvale, California: Chukelea Publications, 1995)

Harrison, Edward Robert, *Cosmology: The Science of the Universe* (Cambridge: Cambridge University Press, 2000)

Hawkins, David, *Manhattan District History, Project Y The Los Alamos Project Vol. I. Inception Until August 1945*, LAMS-2532 (Vol. I), (Los Alamos: Los Alamos Scientific Laboratory, 1947)

Haynes, John Earl and Harvey Klehr, *Venona: Decoding Soviet Espionage in America* (New Haven and London: Yale University Press, 1999)

Herken, Gregg, *Brotherhood of the Bomb: The Tangled Lives and Loyalties of Robert Oppenheimer, Ernest Lawrence, and Edward Teller* (New York: Henry Holt, 2002)

Herken, Gregg, *The Winning Weapon: The Atomic Bomb in the Cold War, 1945–1950* (Princeton, New Jersey: Princeton University Press, 1981)

Hersey, John, *Hiroshima* (New York: Knopf, 1946)

Hershberg, James, *James B. Conant: Harvard to Hiroshima and the Making of the Nuclear Age* (New York: Knopf, 1993)

Hewlett, Richard G., and Oscar E. Anderson, Jr., *The New World: A History of the United States Atomic Energy Commission, Volume I 1939–1946* (Berkeley and Los Angeles: University of California Press, 1962)

Hewlett, Richard G., and Francis Duncan, *Atomic Shield: A History of the United States Atomic Energy Commission, Volume II 1947–1952* (Berkeley and Los Angeles: University of California Press, 1962)

Hewlett, Richard G., and Francis Duncan, *Nuclear Navy, 1946–1962* (Chicago: University of Chicago Press, 1974)

Hines, Neal O., *Proving Ground: An Account of Radiobiological Studies in the Pacific, 1946–1961* (Seattle: The University of Washington Press, 1962)

Hoddeson, Lillian, et al. (eds), *Critical Assembly: A Technical History of Los Alamos During the Oppenheimer Years, 1943–1945* (Cambridge, Cambridge University Press, 2004)

Holloway, David, *Stalin and the Bomb: The Soviet Union and Atomic Energy, 1939–1956* (New Haven, Connecticut: Yale University Press, 1994)

Howes, Ruth H., and Caroline L. Herzenberg, *Their Day in the Sun: Women in the Manhattan Project* (Philadelphia: Temple University Press, 1999)

Ishikawa, Eisei, and David L. Swain, *Hiroshima and Nagasaki: The Physical, Medical, and Social Effects of the Atomic Bombings* (New York: Basic Books, 1981)

Jansen, Marius B., *The Making of Modern Japan* (Cambridge: Harvard University Press, 2000)

Johnson, Charles W., and Charles O. Jackson, *City Behind a Fence: Oak Ridge, Tennessee 1942–1946* (Knoxville: University of Tennessee Press, 1981)

Johnson, Leland, *Sandia National Laboratories: A History of Exceptional Service in the National Interest* (Albuquerque: Sandia National Laboratories, 1997)

Johnson, Leland, and Daniel Schaffer, *Oak Ridge National Laboratory: The First Fifty Years* (Knoxville: The University of Tennessee Press, 1994)

Jones, Vincent C., *Manhattan, the Army, and the Atomic Bomb* (Washington, DC: Government Printing Office, 1985)

Jungk, Robert, *Brighter Than a Thousand Suns: A Personal History of the Atomic Scientists* (New York: Penguin, 1964)

Kathren, Ronald L., et al. (eds), *The Plutonium Story: The Journals of Professor Glenn T. Seaborg 1939–1946* (Columbus: Battelle Press, 1994)

Kelly, Cynthia C. (ed.), *The Manhattan Project: The Birth of the Atomic Bomb in the Words of Its Creators, Eyewitnesses and Historians* (New York: Black Dog & Leventhal Publishers, 2007)

Kennett, Lee, *A History of Strategic Bombing* (New York: Charles Scribner's Sons, 1982)

Kesaris, Paul, *A Guide to the Manhattan Project: Official History and Documents* (Washington, DC: University Press of America, 1977)

Kramish, Arnold, and Eugene M. Zuckert, *Atomic Energy for Your Business: Today's Key to Tomorrow's Profits* (New York: David McKay Company, Inc., 1956)

Kunetka, James W., *City of Fire: Los Alamos and the Atomic Age, 1943–1945.* (Albuquerque: University of New Mexico Press, 1979)

Kurzman, Dan, *Blood and Water: Sabotaging Hitler's Bomb* (New York: Henry Holt, 1997)

Kurzman, Dan, *Day of the Bomb: Countdown to Hiroshima* (New York: McGraw-Hill, 1986)

Lamont, Lansing, *Day of Trinity* (New York: Atheneum, 1965)

Lanouette, William, *Genius in the Shadows: A Biography of Leó Szilárd, The Man Behind the Bomb* (New York: Scribners, 1992)

Lapp, Ralph, *Must We Hide?* (Cambridge, Massachusetts: Addison-Wesley, 1949)

Laurence, William L., *Dawn Over Zero: The Story of the Atomic Bomb* (New York: Alfred Knopf, 1946)

LeMay, Curtis and Bill Yenne, *Superfortress* (London: Berkley Books, 1988)

Loeber, Charles, *Building the Bombs: A History of the Nuclear Weapons Complex* (Darby, Pennsylvania: Diane Publishing Company, 2004)

Maddox, Robert James, *Weapons for Victory: The Hiroshima Decision Fifty Years Later* (Columbia: University of Missouri Press, 1995)

Mason, Katrina R., *Children of Los Alamos: An Oral History of the Town Where the Atomic Age Began* (New York: Twayne Publishers, 1995)

McMillan, Priscilla J., *The Ruin of J. Robert Oppenheimer and the Birth of the Modern Arms Race* (New York: Viking, 2005)

Murrow, Edward R., *In Search of Light: The Broadcasts of Edward R. Murrow, 1938–1961* (New York: Alfred A. Knopf, 1967)

Newton, Isaac, *Opticks: Or, A Treatise of the Reflections, Refractions, Inflections and Colours of Light*, fourth edition (London: Printed for William Innys, 1730)

Nichols, Kenneth D., *The Road to Trinity* (New York: Morrow, 1987)

Norris, Robert S., *Racing for the bomb; General Leslie R. Groves, the Manhattan Project's Indispensable Man* (South Royalton, Vermont: Steerforth Press, 2002)

O'Keefe, Bernard J., *Nuclear Hostages* (Boston: Houghton Mifflin, 1972)

Overholt, James (ed.), *These Are Our Voices: The Story of Oak Ridge 1942–1970* (Oak Ridge: Children's Museum of Oak Ridge, 1987)

Pacific War Research Society, *The Day Man Lost: Hiroshima, August 6, 1945* (Tokyo and New York: Kodansha International, Ltd, 1982)

Pasachoff, Naomi, *Marie Curie and the Science of Radioactivity* (New York, Oxford University Press, 1996)

Pash, Boris T., *The Alsos Mission* (New York: Award House, 1969)

Paul, Septimus H., *Nuclear Rivals: Anglo-American Atomic Relations, 1941–1952* (Columbus: Ohio State University Press, 2000)

Peierls, Rudolph, *Bird of Passage: Recollections of a Physicist* (Princeton: Princeton University Press, 1985)

Polmar, Norman, *The American Submarine* (Annapolis: The Nautical and Aviation Publishing Company of America, 1981)

Polmar, Norman, *The Enola Gay: The B-29 That Dropped the First Atomic Bomb* (Brassey's, 2004)

Powers, Thomas, *Heisenberg's War: The Secret History of the German Bomb* (New York: Alfred A. Knopf, 1993)

Preston, Diana, *Before the Fallout: From Marie Curie to Hiroshima* (New York: Walker, 2005)

Quinn, Susan, *Marie Curie: A Life* (New York: Da Capo Press, 1996)

Rhodes, Richard, *Dark Sun: The Making of the Hydrogen Bomb* (New York: Simon & Schuster, 1995)

Rhodes, Richard, *The Making of the Atomic Bomb* (New York: Simon & Schuster, 1986)

Robinson, George O., *The Oak Ridge Story: The Saga of a People Who Share in History* (Kingsport: Southern Publishers, 1950)

Russ, Harlow W., *Project Alberta: The Preparation of Atomic Bombs for use in World War II* (Los Alamos, New Mexico: Exceptional Books, 1990)

Sale, Sara L., *The Shaping of Containment: Harry S. Truman, The National Security Council, and The Cold War* (Saint James, New York: Brandywine Press, 1998)

Sanger, S. L. and Robert W. Mull, *Hanford and the Bomb: An Oral History of World War II* (Seattle, Washington: Living History Press, 1989)

Schaffer, Ronald, *Wings of Judgment: American Bombing in World War II* (New York: Oxford University Press US, 1985)

Scheibach, Michael, *Atomic Narratives and American Youth: Coming of Age with the Atom, 1945–1955* (Jefferson, North Carolina: McFarland, 2003)

Schweber, S. S., *In The Shadow of the Bomb: Bethe, Oppenheimer, and the Moral Responsibility of the Scientist* (Princeton: Princeton University Press, 2000)

Seaborg, Glenn T., *A Chemist in the White House: From the Manhattan Project to the End of the Cold War* (Washington, DC: American Chemical Society, 1998)

Seaborg, Glenn T., *The Transuranium Elements* (New Haven: Yale University Press, 1958)

Segré, Emilio, *A Mind Always in Motion: The Autobiography of Emilio Segré* (Berkeley: University of California Press, 1993)

Segré, Emilio, *Enrico Fermi: Physicist* (Chicago: University of Chicago Press, 1970)

Serber, Robert and Robert P. Crease, *Peace & War: Reminiscences of a Life on the Frontiers of Science* (New York: Columbia University Press, 1998)

Sherwin, Martin J., *A World Destroyed: Hiroshima and the Origins of the Arms Race* (New York: Vintage Books, 1987)

Shurcliff, William A., *Bombs at Bikini: The Official Report of Operation Crossroads.* (New York: Wm. H. Wise & Company, Inc., 1947)

Shurcliff, William A., *Operation Crossroads: The Official Pictorial Record* (New York: Wm. H. Wise & Company, Inc., 1946)

Smith, Alice Kimball, and Charles Weiner, *Robert Oppenheimer: Letters and Recollections* (Stanford: Stanford University Press, 1980)

Smith, Ralph Carlisle, David Hawkins, and Edith C. Truslow, *Manhattan District History: Project Y, the Los Alamos Story* (Los Angeles: Tomash, 1983)

Smyth, Henry DeWolf, *Atomic Energy for Military Purposes: The Official Report on the Development of the Atomic Bomb Under the Auspices of the United States Government, 1940–1945* (Princeton: Princeton University Press, 1945)

Stout, Wesley W., *Secret* (Detroit: Chrysler Corporation, 1947)

Strickland, Donald A., *Scientists in Politics: The Atomic Scientists Movement, 1945–46* (Lafayette: Purdue University Press, 1968)

Sweeney, Charles, et al., *War's End: An Eyewitness Account of America's Last Atomic Mission* (New York: Avon Books, 1997)

Sylves, Richard T., *The Nuclear Oracles: A Political History of the General Advisory Committee of the Atomic Energy Commission, 1947–1977* (Ames: Iowa State University Press, 1987)

Szasz, Ferenc Morton, *British Scientists and the Manhattan Project: The Los Alamos Years* (New York: St. Martin's Press, 1992)

Szasz, Ferenc Morton, *The Day the Sun Rose Twice: The Story of the Trinity Site Nuclear Explosion, July 16, 1945* (Albuquerque: University of New Mexico Press, 1984)

Szilárd, Leó, Barnard T. Feld and Gertrud Weiss Szilard (eds), *The Collected Works of Leó Szilárd. Volume I: Scientific Papers* (London and Cambridge, Massachusetts: M.I.T. Press, 1972)

Teller, Edward, *The Legacy of Hiroshima* (New York: Doubleday, 1962)

Thomas, Gordon, and Max Morgan Witts, *Enola Gay: Mission to Hiroshima.* (New York: Stein and Day, 1977)

Thomas, Gordon, and Max Morgan Witts, *Ruin From the Air,* (Scarborough House, 1990)

Tibbets, Paul W., Jr., *Mission: Hiroshima* (New York: Stein and Day, 1985)

Titus, A. Costandina, *Bombs in the Backyard: Atomic Testing and American Politics* (Reno: University of Nevada Press, 1986)

Truman, Harry S., *Year of Decision* (New York: Doubleday, 1955)

Ulam, Stanisław, *Adventures of a Mathematician* (New York: Charles Scribner's Sons, 1983)

United States Atomic Energy Commission, *Uranium, Plutonium, and Industry: A Summary of the U.S. Atomic Energy Program* (Washington, DC: US Atomic Energy Commission, 1953)

United States Congress, Special Committee on Atomic Energy, *Atomic Energy Act of 1946. Hearings before the Special Committee on Atomic Energy, United States Senate, Seventy-Ninth Congress, second session, on S. 1717, a Bill for the Development and Control of Atomic Energy* (Washington, DC: Government Printing Office, 1946)

United States Strategic Bombing Survey, *The Effects of Atomic Bombs on Hiroshima and Nagasaki* (Washington, DC: Government Printing Office, 1946)

Walker, J. Samuel, *Prompt and Utter Destruction: Truman and the Use of Atomic Bombs Against Japan* (Chapel Hill: University of North Carolina Press, 1997)

Walker, Stephen, *Shockwave: Countdown to Hiroshima* (New York: HarperCollins, 2005)

Weart, Spencer R., *Nuclear Fear: A History of Images* (Cambridge: Harvard University Press, Massachusetts, 1988)

Weisgall, Jonathan M., *Operation Crossroads: The Atomic Tests at Bikini Atoll* (Naval Institute Press, Annapolis, 1994)

Weller, George and Anthony Weller (ed.), *First Into Nagasaki: The Censored Eyewitness Dispatches on Post-Atomic Japan and Its Prisoners of War* (New York: Three Rivers Press, 2006)

Wells, H. G., *The World Set Free: A Story of Mankind* (London: MacMillan and Co., Ltd, 1914)

Williams, Robert C., and Philip L. Cantelon (eds), *The American Atom: A Documentary History of Nuclear Policies from the Discovery of Fission to the Present, 1939–1984* (Philadelphia: University of Pennsylvania Press, 1984)

Williams, Robert C., *Klaus Fuchs, Atom Spy* (Cambridge: Harvard University Press, 1987)

Wilson, Jane (ed.), *All In Our Time: The Reminiscences Of Twelve Nuclear Pioneers* (Chicago: The Bulletin of the Atomic Scientists, 1975)

Winkler, Allan M., *Life Under A Cloud: American Anxiety About the Atom* (New York: Oxford University Press, 1993)

Wyden, Peter, *Day One: Before Hiroshima and After* (New York: Simon and Schuster, 1984)

Yamahata, Yosuke, *Nagasaki Journey: The Photographs of Yosuke Yamahata, August 10, 1945* (San Francisco: Pomegranate Artbooks, 1995)

Ziegler, Charles A. and David Jacobson, *Spying Without Spies: Origins of America's Secret Nuclear Surveillance System* (Westort Connecticut: Greenwood Publishing Group, 1995)

ARTICLES

Albury, Charles Don, "Bockscar's Bash" *Flight Journal* (August 2005). Available online at
http://findarticles.com/p/articles/mi_qa3897/is_200508/ai_n14825582

Burke-Gaffney, Brian (ed.), "In The Words Of An Atomic Bomb Survivor," *Crossroads: A Journal Of Nagasaki History And Culture*, No. 3 (Summer 1995), available online at
http://www.uwosh.edu/faculty_staff/earns/number3.html

Chadwick, J., "The Existence of a Neutron," *Proceedings of the Royal Society*, A, 136,

Curie, Marie Sklodowska, "Radium and Radioactivity," *The Century Magazine* (January 1904)

Daly, Thomas N., "Crossroads at Bikini," *United States Naval Institute Proceedings*, Vol. 122, No. 7 (July 1986)

Delgado, James P., "Documenting the Sunken Remains of USS *Saratoga*," United States Naval Institute *Proceedings*, Vol. CXVI, No. 10 (October 1990)

Delgado, James P., "Operation Crossroads," *American History Illustrated*, Vol. XXVIII, No. 3 (May/June 1993)

Graybar, Lloyd, "William Henry Purnell Blandy," in John A. Garraty (ed.), *Dictionary of American Biography: Supplement Five, 1951–1955* (New York: Charles Scribner's Sons, 1977)

"Hold That Monster," *Time* (November 19, 1945)

H. T. E., "Science and Esoteric Philosophy: Lord Salisbury's Warning," *Lucifer*, Vol. 5, No. 85 (September 15, 1894)

Leary, William L. and Michie Hattori Hattori, "Eyewitness to the Nagasaki Atomic Bomb," *World War II* (July/August 2005), available online at:
http://www.historynet.com/michie-hattori-eyewitness-to-the-nagasaki-atomic-bomb-blast.htm

Markwith, Carl, "Farewell to Bikini," *National Geographic*, Vol. 90, No. 1 (July 1946)

Oliphant, Mark, "The Beginning: Chadwick and the Neutron," *Bulletin of the Atomic Scientists*, Vol. 38, No. 10 (December 1982)

Partington, J. R., "The Origins of the Atomic Theory," *Annals of Science*, Vol. 4, No. 3 (July 1939)

Rutherford, Ernest, "The Scattering of α and β Particles by Matter and the Structure of the Atom," *Philosophical Magazine*, Series 6, Vol. 21 (May 1911)

Rutherford, Ernest, "Collisions of Alpha Particles with Light Atoms. IV. An Anomalous Effect in Nitrogen," *The London, Edinburgh and Dublin Philosophical Magazine and Journal of Science*, 6th series, No. 37, 581ff (1919)

Stones, G. B., "The Atomic View of Matter in the XVth, XVIth, and XVIIth Centuries," *Isis*, Vol. 10, Part 2, No. 34 (January 1928)

Thomson, J. J., "On the Structure of the Atom: an Investigation of the Stability and Periods of Oscillation of a number of Corpuscles arranged at equal intervals around the Circumference of a Circle; with Application of the Results to the Theory of Atomic Structure," *Philosophical Magazine*, Series 6, Vol. 7, No. 39 (March 1904)

Wheeler, N. J., "British Nuclear Weapons and Anglo-American Relations 1945–54," *International Affairs*, Vol. 62, No. 1 (Winter 1985–86).

MANUSCRIPTS, EPHEMERA, AND INTERNET RESOURCES

Atomic Archive, an excellent site that "explores the complex history surrounding the invention of the atomic bomb – a crucial turning point for all mankind": http://www.atomicarchive.com/

The Atomic Heritage Foundation, formerly the Manhattan Project Heritage Preservation Foundation, established "to preserve the historical importance of the Manhattan Project, to recognize and memorialize the efforts of the Manhattan Project veterans, and to promote the safe and beneficial use of atomic energy": http://www.mphpa.org/classic/

"Atomic Platters: Cold War Music from the Golden Age of Homeland Security." Released in August 2006 by Bear Family Records, BCD 16065 FL. The issue includes five CDs and one DVD with an accompanying book. Information available online at: http://www.conelrad.com/media/atomicmusic/

Bikini Atoll: http://www.bikiniatoll.com/

Brians, Paul, "Nuclear Holocausts: Atomic War in Fiction," is a comprehensive survey of fictional depictions in English of nuclear war and its aftermath by Brians, Professor of English at Washington State University, Pullman, Washington: http://www.wsu.edu/~brians/nuclear/

The Bureau of Atomic Tourism, "dedicated to the promotion of tourist locations around the world that have either been the site of atomic explosions, display exhibits on the development of atomic devices, or contain vehicles that were designed to deliver atomic weapons": http://www.atomictourist.com/?NF=1

Burr, William (ed.), "The Atomic Bomb and the End of World War II: A Collection of Primary Sources. National Security Archive Electronic Briefing Book No. 162," Posted – August 5, 2005. Updated – April 27, 2007. Online as part of the National Security Archive: http://www.gwu.edu/~nsarchiv/NSAEBB/NSAEBB162/index.htm

"The Decision to Drop the Atomic Bomb," webpage of the Harry S. Truman Library and Museum: http://www.trumanlibrary.org/whistlestop/study_collections/bomb/large/index.php

"Documentation and Diagrams of the Atomic Bomb," a website of the University of California, Berkeley: http://www.nuc.berkeley.edu/neutronics/todd/nuc.bomb.html

"Enola Gay," the official website of General Paul W. Tibbets, Jr.: http://www.enolagay.org/

"The Enola Gay and the Smithsonian Chronology of the Controversy Including Key Documents 1993–1995," a website of the Air Force Association:

http://www.afa.org/media/enolagay/chrono.asp

Hiroshima Peace Memorial Museum: http://www.pcf.city.hiroshima.jp/top_e.html

Los Alamos Historical Society, http://www.losalamoshistory.org/

Los Alamos National Laboratory History, "this website traces the history of Los Alamos from the days of Little Boy and Fat Man, to the development of the hydrogen bomb, to the stockpile stewardship program of today": http://www.lanl.gov/history/

"The Manhattan Project, An Interactive History," developed by the United States Department of Energy Office of History and Heritage Resources, is an internet resource that "will total some 120,000 words and over 200 pages and 500 images, including photographs, maps, and drawings": http://www.cfo.doe.gov/me70/manhattan/index.htm

Manhattan Engineering District, *The Atomic Bombings of Hiroshima and Nagasaki,*

the 1946 report by the MED, is available online at: http://www.atomicarchive.com/Docs/MED/index.shtml

Nagasaki Atomic Bomb Museum: http://www1.city.nagasaki.nagasaki.jp/na-bomb/museum/museume01.html

National Museum of Nuclear Science and History: http://www.atomicmuseum.org/

Oak Ridge National Laboratory History: http://www.ornl.gov/ornlhome/history.shtml

"Race for the Superbomb," a website from PBS' "American Experience": http://www.pbs.org/wgbh/amex/bomb/

Rosenberg et al. v. United States, Supreme Court of the United States, 346 US 273 is accessible online at: http://www.law.umkc.edu/faculty/projects/ftrials/rosenb/ROS_CT4.HTM

"The Beginning or the End," Movie Press Package, available online at: http://www.atomicbombcinema.com/english/image_gallery/beginning/begin_end_intro.htm

Trinity Site, a website of the White Sands Missile Range, is a website with "links that will provide you with information on the history of the site, how to get there and some of the historic images": http://www.wsmr.army.mil/pao/TrinitySite/trinst.htm

INDEX